CW01022716

SKY WARS

CONTEMPORARY WORLDS explores the present and recent past. Books in the series take a distinctive theme, geo-political entity or cultural group and explore their developments over a period ranging usually over the last fifty years. The impact of current events and developments are accounted for by rapid but clear interpretation in order to unveil the cultural, political, religious and technological forces that are reshaping today's worlds.

SERIES EDITOR
Jeremy Black

In the same series

Britain since the Seventies
Jeremy Black

SKY WARS

A History of Military Aerospace Power

DAVID GATES

REAKTION BOOKS

Published by Reaktion Books Ltd
79 Farringdon Road
London EC1M 3JU, UK

www.reaktionbooks.co.uk

First published 2003

Copyright © David Gates 2003

All rights reserved
No part of this publication may be reproduced, stored in a retrieval
system, or transmitted, in any form or by any means, electronic,
mechanical, photocopying, recording or otherwise, without the
prior permission of the publishers.

Printed and bound in Great Britain
by Biddles Ltd, Guildford and King's Lynn

British Library Cataloguing in Publication Data
Gates, David, 1955–
    Sky wars : a history of military aerospace power. –
    (Contemporary worlds)
    1. Air power – History 2. Air warfare – History
    I. Title
    358.4′009

ISBN 1 86189 189 X

Contents

Preface

This book's publication coincides with the centenary of the first controlled, powered flight. Barely 66 years after the Wright brothers' remarkable, pioneering feat, a still more astonishing one occurred when Neil Armstrong descended from the lunar-module of *Apollo* 11 to become the first man to walk on the Moon. Yet the year of this book's appearance also witnessed what has widely been described as the first 'space-age war', which only serves to underscore the mixed blessings that have flowed from our quest to slip 'the surly bonds of Earth', as John Gillespie Magee so eloquently phrased it in his poem *High Flight*.

Since it would be impossible – certainly in a work of this size – to begin to chart the full extent of the ramifications within human civilization of momentous events such as these, I have confined myself to an examination of the impact that air and aerospace power have had on one of history's great catalysts, warfare. Even within this field I have been obliged to be selective, not least because the parameters of 'military' history remain elusive. I have, however, sought to provide a fairly detailed analysis of the evolution of air power through the most important aerial campaigns of the past 65 years especially, and to explore some of the major issues that surround the possession and use of aerospace power – one of the cardinal symbols and instruments of modernity.

I am grateful to all those – both in Britain and abroad – who helped me in the production of this book and to the publishers who made it possible. Any errors are mine alone.

Part One

History

Chapter 1

War in and from the Skies, 1903–1943

When compared with the evolution of land and maritime warfare over thousands of years of history, the development of war in the air appears as rapid as it does spectacular. Just one hundred years have now elapsed since the Wright brothers' crude aeroplane, propelled by a 12-horsepower petrol engine, performed the astonishing feat of staying aloft for some 40 metres. Through this achievement, one of the greatest and most persistent dreams of humankind – that of emulating the powered, sustained and directed flight of birds with a craft that was heavier than air – was finally fulfilled.

That such a capability would have military applications had long been recognized. Lighter-than-air balloons, which were at the mercy of the prevailing wind, had been intermittently employed in warfare since the 1790s, usually as moored observation platforms. The first attempts to add some form of steering system and propulsion unit were made as early as the mid-1800s, but without much success.[1] By 1900, however, Count Ferdinand von Zeppelin had refined this concept, producing the rigid, navigable airships that bore his name. Inflated with hydrogen, a highly inflammable gas, these were typically 450 feet (150 m) long and, driven by several small engines, could achieve speeds of up to 47 mph (75 kmh) and altitudes of up to 6,000 feet (1,828 m). Initially used for travel and transportation, they were to be adapted for military purposes during the First World War, notably the dropping of high-explosive and incendiary bombs on various towns in Britain and France. By that time, however, the aeroplane's superiority was already becoming clear, and the future of the ponderous and very vulnerable airship was commensurably doubtful.

Indeed, the advent of the plane promised the conquest of time and space, the furtherance of humankind's growing mastery of nature and the extension of the white man's domination of the globe. For those living at the beginning of the twentieth century, the very idea of air travel was as intriguing and exciting as subsequent generations were to find that of space exploration. This was at least in part because of the growth of science fiction. Long before the time of his death in 1905, Jules Verne, the great pioneer of that genre, had produced several works that, coincident with and influenced by the technological and scientific discoveries of the second industrial revolution, envisioned not just air and space craft, submarines and cars, but also the rise of enlightened, international brotherhoods and idyllic societies. Similarly, H. G. Wells, who was a scientist by education, strove to predict the nature and effects of the civilization that emerged during his lifetime (1866–1946) – an era that was characterized by ever-more urbanization, industrialization and 'globalization', all of which was underpinned by scientific and technological advances. Although a Darwinist, Wells sensed that humankind's biological evolution had peaked, and that future development would essentially be shaped by cultural and historical processes. His book of 1902, *Anticipation of the Reaction of Mechanical and Scientific Progress upon Human Life and Thought*, highlighted the incipient revolutions in the fields of aeronautics and information transfer. We have already noted the rise of the Zeppelin and other dirigibles with regard to the first of these, while, as far as the second is concerned, Guglielmo Marconi had been refining the use of electro-magnetic waves of radio frequency to transmit and receive messages since 1892. By the turn of the century, his wireless telegraphy system was being used to send signals in Morse code to ships at sea and in transoceanic communications. For decades thereafter, this medium was to remain useful in all situations where background noise or interference might render speech unintelligible. However, the development of radio telephony was also underway as early as 1904 and, within two decades, as the bulk and weight of sets were reduced and short-wave transmitters were introduced, it had established itself as the most flexible method of communication, not least from one plane to another and between aircraft and their bases and command centres.

Wells surmised that such innovations, together with steadily growing economic interdependence, would lead to a world state that would be dominated, not by democratic institutions and principles, but by a meritocracy comprising elite scientists, technocrats and managers. In this regard, his outlook differed from that of Verne. Their visions overlapped in other respects, however. By the end of the latter's life, urbanization, industrialization, consumerism and commercialization were already having a detrimental impact on both the Earth and its inhabitants. Verne's liberal, utopian dreams were being dashed, not least by the very scientific progress that he celebrated. Indeed, to many, the coming of the aeroplane seemed a mixed blessing and imparted new life to that ancient metaphor for technological hubris, the mighty sun's melting of the wax that held together the wings fashioned by Icarus. The tendency to scrutinize every scientific breakthrough for possible martial applications alarmed both Verne and Wells. If clashes within living memory, notably that between France and Prussia in 1870–71, were disturbing enough, then the Russo-Japanese War of 1904–5 provided telling insights into what violent confrontations between increasingly industrialized and sophisticated powers were likely to entail. In fact, apart from the tank, aircraft, flame-thrower and toxic chemical weapons, this war saw the use of every basic type of military technology that was to be exploited in that of 1914–18. It was a strikingly atypical and commensurably shocking armed conflict in another sense, too: for once, battle casualties actually exceeded those losses among military personnel that were caused by malnutrition, disease and accidental injury.

Wells's War of the Worlds (1898) had been a work of science fiction, but in Anticipation he echoed the contents of Ivan Bloch's recent thesis, La Guerre future, which had been published in English in 1899 as Is War Now Impossible? This prophesied that, alongside entrenchment tactics and barbed wire, technical enhancements – notably those that further increased the rate, accuracy and lethality of fire from artillery, machine guns and shoulder arms – would render successful offensive operations all but impracticable. With their armies mired in gory, interminable trench warfare, strategic stalemate would set in and states would face defeat on the home front through economic and societal disintegration – the very fate that was destined to befall Russia, Turkey and the Central Powers in 1917–18. Wells, however, rightly anticipated that any such strategic deadlock would spawn a quest for countermeasures to restore the potency of offensive operations. This, he feared, would lead to the development of warfare in ways that might have truly ruinous consequences for civilization. Predicting that the existing generation of mass armies would be supplanted by one of much smaller but far more professional and technologically advanced units of troops, he also foresaw the exploitation of air power on a grand scale. By the second half of the twentieth century, he suggested, huge aerial armadas would be the mainstay of armed forces and would assail one another and surface targets.

He was to elaborate on this theme in his predictive novel of 1908, *The War in the Air*. This envisaged planes and airships conducting operations on a global basis, striking at shipping and industrial and population centres, none of which would be able to offer much resistance to attacks from the skies. The outcome, Wells reasoned, would be economic and social collapse. Indeed, in his view, the potential destructiveness of future conflicts was such that they would inevitably prove counterproductive; the human race should – and eventually would, he opined – unite under the banner of a single, worldwide republic, if only to avoid internecine confrontations. (The possibility of a civil war, such as the one that had engulfed the American Republic in the 1860s, was one he overlooked.) In the light of the pioneering research in the sphere of atomic physics undertaken by Henri Becquerel, Ernest Rutherford, Fredrick Soddy and Sir William Ramsay, Wells's inferences turned that much more baleful and his calls for unification commensurably more urgent. In 1903 Ramsay established that helium was a by-product of the radioactive decay of radium, thereby making a discovery that was central to the understanding of nuclear reactions. That same year, Rutherford and Soddy concluded that atoms contained immense reserves of energy and, within a few months, the latter was speculating to Britain's Corps of Royal Engineers that, one day, it might be possible to liberate this power through nuclear fission, thereby creating a weapon of unprecedented potency. Certainly, in his book *The World Set Free* (1914), which was released as the Great War dawned, Wells predicted that there would be atomic armaments by 1933. Nuclear war would eventually ensue, which, again, he expected, would bring about societal and economic prostration, followed by redemption in the guise of the global republic.

Prophetic though at least some of Wells's musings turned out to be, the precise way in which air power was actually incorporated into warfare owed rather less to visionaries and theorists than it did to the deeds of practitioners, to the realities of combat, to the limitations of technology and to the varying institutional dynamics and often shifting strategic priorities of individual countries. For all its significance, Orville Wright's cursory flight of December 1903 did not attract very much attention, and two years were to pass before he and his brother, Wilbur, had refined their primitive plane sufficiently for it to be able to stay aloft for distances of up to 24 miles (38 km). In fact, it was only in 1908, when they brought their aircraft to Europe and Wilbur performed several flights for all to see, that public enthusiasm and interest were kindled.

The following year witnessed not only Louis Blériot's flight over the Channel, which was accomplished at an average speed of 40 mph (64.36 kmh), but also a spate of air meetings, including those at Doncaster in England and at Brescia in Italy. As well as large crowds of onlookers, these shows attracted a clutch of celebrities who, although being predominantly young men, had already acquired reputations as daredevils; predictably, they seized on the aircraft as the pinnacle of fun and fashion and the very exemplification of modernism. It was at Doncaster, in a competition in which several 'magnificent men in their flying machines' participated – among them Samuel Franklin Cody, a builder of kites that were big enough to support a man – that a French pilot achieved a speed of 50 mph (80.45 kmh) and thus set a new world record. The importance of a seemingly trivial event at Brescia, however, was to prove less ephemeral, as we shall see. Here, the renowned Italian writer Gabriele d'Annunzio persuaded the American pilot and aeronautical engineer Glenn Curtiss to take him up for a ride. This experience profoundly affected d'Annunzio, who came away convinced that powered flight would transfigure civilization and warfare and spawn a new ruling elite.[2]

D'Annunzio was by no means the only person to hold such opinions at this juncture, especially in Italy, where the nostrum of proto-Fascism struck a chord with many people.[3] In 1910 Curtiss began a sequence of trials in which he sought to hit targets from the air, including ships, with either dummy or live bombs. Dependable bomb-sights were a prerequisite for success, and his experiments marked the start of what was to prove a lengthy quest for such devices. Nevertheless, bombs were first to be dropped in anger as early as 1911. During that year, the Tripolitan War between Italy and the Ottoman Empire broke out when the former sought to wrest control of Libya from the Porte. This confrontation saw the very first use of aeroplanes in combat, the Italians employing a handful of them to observe and attack their Turkish adversaries.

D'Annunzio travelled to the war zone, reporting on events for European newspapers and eulogizing the Italian pilots and their machines until the fighting fizzled out. This occurred in October 1912, when the Porte, confronted with a still greater threat in the form of the Balkan League and anticipating hostilities in this quarter, hastily made peace with Rome by ceding Cyrenaica and Tripolitania. Sure enough, the first of a succession of ethnic, religious and territorial disputes that was to drag on until the end of the 1900s was soon underway, as the Turks turned to defending their European provinces against the invading Greeks, Montenegrins, Serbians and Bulgarians, the last of whom used aircraft to attack Adrianople (now Edirne) in what they erroneously believed to be the first bombing raid in history. By jeopardizing the wider balance of power, the struggle in the Balkans was to make a pivotal contribution to the outbreak of the First World War in August 1914. To the frustration of d'Annunzio and his ilk, however, Italy remained aloof from the fighting until May 1915. As French military fortunes waned and waxed, as the Japanese sided with the Allies and the Turks with the Central Powers, as the Germans gained impressive victories in Lorraine and at Tannenberg, as British Imperial forces fought in Flanders, off the Falklands and in the Gallipoli Peninsula, and, not least, as the Austrians faltered in Serbia and Galicia, d'Annunzio busied himself with a new role, that of espousing Italy's active participation in the conflict.

He was aided in this cause by, among others, some of the Futurists, notably his fellow writer Filippo Marinetti. His foremost contribution in this regard was the publication of a collection of his essays under the telling rubric *Guerra sola igiene del mondo* (1911–15; *War: The World's Only Hygiene*). This promulgated one of proto-Fascism's core tenets: war could serve as a cathartic.[4] In the eyes of d'Annunzio and others, not least Benito Mussolini – the future founder of the Fascist Party, Fasci di Combattimento, and subsequently *il Duce* – Italy was in need of, not just aggrandizement, but also purging and revitalization.[5] War would be instrumental in the accomplishment of these broader social, cultural and political objectives, while air power in particular was increasingly looked upon as both the hallmark of a modern, advanced state, the key to a vibrant future, and as the offensive weapon par excellence. Indeed, it is noteworthy that Mussolini – who served in the infantry in the First World War and thus witnessed the stalemate and anonymous carnage of ground operations – was a great admirer of Blériot, wrote extensively on aeronautical matters, learnt to fly in 1919 and was thereafter always keen to be associated with aviators and flight, a relationship for which he was to be acclaimed by, among others, Guido Mattioli in his book *Mussolini, Aviator, and his Work for Aviation* (1939), which appeared in three languages.

Although perhaps unpalatable in some senses, one should not dismiss the notion of war as a vehicle for transformation. Essentially a revolutionary activity that alters relationships both within and between states, it tends to bring out the best as well as the worst in people and has proved one of history's greatest agents for change, much of it for the better. For, ironic though it might be, the exigencies of armed conflict have often led to, for example, discoveries and innovations of great benefit to humankind. Neither, whether one concludes with hindsight that proto-Fascism and Fascism were visionary or reactionary movements, should one underestimate the appeal that they held for the many Europeans who were seeking an alternative to liberalism, socialism and, later, Bolshevism. There were, after all, several nuances within the broader fascist 'mood', and it was to take on various hues from one country to another; what, for instance, eventually emerged as National Socialism in inter-war Germany differed in several respects from the fascist creeds contemporaneously encountered in Italy, Spain, or among Oswald Mosley's few followers in Britain. Similarly, whereas Hitler's attitude towards, among other things, Jews and political change through violence were made clear for all to see in his book *Mein Kampf,* which he began as early as 1924, Italo Balbo, the celebrated Italian aviator, although a prominent member of Fasci di Combattimento, disliked racism and was to regard his country's entry into the Second World War as a catastrophe. Yet amidst all this diversity were some common characteristics, notably proto-Fascism's tremendous interest – particularly on the part of the numerous luminaries who were among its most prominent disciples – in new and emerging technology, above all the aircraft and the other elements of machine warfare: the armoured train and car, improved propellants and explosives, radio, rapidly firing small arms and artillery, dreadnoughts and, as time went by, the tank and toxic chemical weapons, among which were chlorine, phosgene, hydrogen cyanide and mustard gases, the products of chemical research laboratories and industries that had had their inventiveness stimulated by war.

For the Italian Fascists more than any others, air power had a totemic significance. Symbolic of modernity, it heralded a new epoch that should, they believed, be shaped by an elite comprising technocrats and scientists, not the plebeian, moribund, decadent institutions of liberal democracy. As the first practitioners of aerial warfare, the pilots of the Tripolitan campaign became celebrities in Italy, as here and elsewhere aviators and their machines were aestheticized and acclaimed. Just as the armoured knights of the medieval age had represented the dominant strata of society and had been widely regarded as not only the supreme form of martial strength, but also as the very embodiment of romantic heroism, chivalry and panache, so too were military flyers now seen as men of action, boldness, skill and fortitude who, mounted on high-technology steeds, promised to be as potent a force for moral regeneration as in battle. Lauded in art, prose and verse, many – particularly fighter pilots, who liked to clad themselves in stylish leather jackets and silk scarves – were to become popular heroes of almost mythical proportions, not least because they appeared to have restored a degree of individualism and dynamism to combat at a time when the anonymous, squalid slaughter of the trenches threatened to prevail, and thereby bring about strategic deadlock.

When Britain's Royal Air Force (RAF) – the world's first independent air force – was established in 1918, its trappings and equipment comprised a telling blend of cutting-edge technology and venerable martial customs. Modern, metallic-blue uniforms were adorned with accoutrements – notably sashes, aiguillettes and swords – that were traditionally associated with mounted regiments. Similarly, alongside rather futuristic laboratories, workshops and aircraft hangars were educational and administrative buildings that were often constructed in elegant, Neo-classical styles, such as those at Cranwell in Lincolnshire. The Germans, too, enjoyed drawing analogies between the fighter 'ace' and the knights of old. Especially within the so-called Flying Circus – the flights of elite pilots led by the likes of Manfred von Richthofen and Oswald Boelcke – the terminology of the jousting tournament was in daily use, while planes were frequently decorated with ancient heraldic devices and distinctive colours. Actually, although the public's impression that they enjoyed an enviable autonomy was to persist for many years thereafter, before the end of the First World War most fighter pilots – grouped into squadrons and 'wings' that flew in prescribed formations – were also to find themselves waging mass, anonymous warfare more often than not. Among others, Eddie Rickenbacker, the celebrated American 'ace', who had once anticipated that 'The excitement of automobile racing . . . [could] not compare with what I knew must come with airplane fighting in France', was quickly disillusioned, concluding that aerial warfare was 'nothing more than scientific murder'.[6]

The RAF pilots who were to participate in the Battle of Britain in 1940 – Winston Churchill's 'Few' – would have doubtless concurred. Contrary to many visionaries' expectations, within a few years of being adapted for military purposes air power had become an instrument of attritional combat, not an alternative to it. In fact, during the Second World War, losses among RAF personnel were to exceed 99,000 in killed, wounded and missing alone. Revealingly, this is half as many again as the Royal Navy's 66,000 and almost a quarter of the British Army's total of around 417,000.[7]

Whether engaged in war, sport or spectacle, all flyers face a common foe: the skies themselves, which are, as the recent loss of the space shuttle Columbia underscored, as unforgiving as they are beautiful. Unless the Earth's gravitational pull can be thwarted, what goes up must come down. While aloft, significant repairs are very seldom practicable; and although many military aircraft can be refuelled on the wing, this is a dangerous, skilful undertaking with certain technological prerequisites: in addition to the recipient machine having been suitably modified through the fitting of an ingestion valve to its nose, both the nozzle on the hose trailed by the tanker and the pressure level within it must be compatible.

An aircraft's ability not merely to stay in the air but also to maintain controlled flight depends upon several factors.[8] Whereas some of these might be considered intrinsic and technical – such as the aircraft's aerodynamic properties, and the amount of fuel for, and the energy generated by, its engines – many are environmental. Leaving aside atmospheric quirks – notably the phenomena known as temperature inversion, wind chill and thermals (which are the rising currents of warm air exploited by gliders and soaring birds such as condors and albatrosses) – altitude and temperature vary inversely within the troposphere. This inevitably culminates in sub-zero conditions above a certain height, even when much milder circumstances prevail at sea level. Extreme temperatures can have detrimental effects on people and machinery, both of which can overheat or be frozen stiff, although cold more commonly afflicts aviators. For instance, bomber crews in the Second World War were frequently exposed to temperatures of minus 18–30° Celsius, and their oxygen masks tended to start freezing up at a height of 20,000 feet (6,100 m). The resulting oxygen deprivation intensified their susceptibility to the cold, and often led to hypothermia and frostbite, with the attendant loss of digits, limbs and even life itself. Under certain conditions, ice can begin to form on the aircraft, adding substantially to its weight and degrading its manoeuvrability. Similarly, the engines and rotor blades of helicopters can be damaged by the dust that they throw up when landing and taking off in arid conditions, while, because of the salt found in seawater, the metallic parts of all aircraft operating in maritime situations can prove particularly susceptible to corrosion. In any case, since air pressure diminishes with altitude and the atmosphere becomes more rarefied, lethal conditions will eventually be encountered as an aircraft gains height. At around 63,000 feet (19,000 m), decompression will, for instance, cause the human bloodstream to boil. If life is to be sustained, such environmental threats have to be artificially neutralized, notably through the use of pressurized fuselages or special flying suits, helmets and breathing apparatus.

Besides oxygen deprivation, low atmospheric pressure and extreme temperatures, other perils and irritants can be present. Among these are: hazardous weather conditions, notably air turbulence and buffeting winds (which can reach speeds of several hundred mph a few miles above the Earth's surface), and hail or electrical storms; or poor visibility caused by dazzling sunshine, darkness, thick cloud, precipitation, fog and atmospheric pollution, including dust, smoke and the haze generated by certain industrial emissions and exhaust fumes. Whenever the ground cannot be seen clearly enough to discern landmarks, or when passing over essentially featureless terrain, notably large plains or stretches of water, navigating an aircraft becomes appreciably harder; the pilot's senses and reasoning have to be supplemented with the use of instruments that can vary in their finesse and sophistication. Flying in formation, which is frequently required of military aviators, can also pose certain difficulties and dangers, not least the risk of collision. Noise, vibration and radiation can be troublesome, too, as can motion sickness, including, at worst, 'greying out', which is unconsciousness or death as a result of the adverse physiological effects of high-speed aerobatics and very rapid acceleration or deceleration. Air-crew can also fall victim to such everyday bodily experiences as illness and, on longer flights especially, cramp, hunger, dehydration, sleeplessness and mental or physical fatigue.

To such corporal discomforts can also be added boredom and a sense of isolation, if not loneliness. Even the ultimate command of an air battle has tended to prove an unusually distant, solitary and all-absorbing affair.[9] Aerial combat itself directly involves relatively tiny numbers of personnel, and the operation of an aircraft and its weapon systems, which is frequently performed by just one or two people, can be as demanding as it is hazardous. One side-effect of weariness is a condition known as 'coning', whereby the sufferer exhibits an inability to concentrate on anything other than the immediate preoccupation. For aviators, this is ineluctably the goal of flying to a given destination, to which air-crew debilitated by coning tend to subordinate all other considerations. In any case, a cockpit, with its dials, levers and switches, forms a technological interface with the outside world and is a somewhat surreal environment, especially when the plane is flying in darkness or at high altitudes and speeds. Indeed, last, but by no means least, are the problems posed for aviators by fear.[10] While many people find flying a nerve-racking experience in itself, aerial warfare inevitably subjects its participants to additional ordeals. In the final analysis, any equipment is only as good as the human beings using it, and the fundamental purpose of military discipline is to try to enable personnel to overcome the trepidation that, pardonably enough, they can experience in combat. Nevertheless, it is common for performance to be adversely affected by the psychological and physical strains of battle.

One of the earliest prominent victims of flight was Samuel Franklin Cody, who perished in an accident in 1913. A distant relation of 'Buffalo Bill', he had helped design and build the UK's first dirigible and, in October 1908, had made the first officially recognized aeroplane flight in Britain, using a canvas and bamboo biplane that was dubbed 'British Army Aeroplane Number One'.[11] That same year, the USA also ordered its first aircraft – from the Wright brothers – for military use. However, in the UK at least, recognition of the potential contribution that air-craft could make to all basic areas of military operations – combat, reconnaissance, command and logistics – was slow in coming. The government was reluctant to provide any funding, and the development of British aviation consequently depended on the efforts of a few enterprising enthusiasts such as Edwin Roe, Thomas Sopwith and Frederick Handley-Page.[12] Similarly, the first military pilots learnt to fly essentially as if it were a hobby; they were instructed in their own time and at their own expense.

In view of the dramatic growth of German air power especially, this approach was soon discarded as inadequate. In 1912 a 'Royal Flying Corps' was established in the UK but, divided into separate Naval and Military (Army) Wings, it was essentially regarded as a support unit for the existing services. (The creation of an autonomous air force, as opposed to subordinate, adjunct units with aerial capabilities, did not occur until as late as April 1918. Nevertheless, the RAF was the first force of its kind in the world and was underpinned by an equally unique air ministry that was set up in December 1917.) The division of Britain's available air power into distinct Wings reflected the lingering uncertainty that surrounded the aviator's precise role in warfare. Just as, in the past, there had been competing visions of how other, once novel military innovations – such as machine guns and submarines – might best be organized and used, the emergence of airships and planes provoked a widespread and often divisive doctrinal debate. On the one hand, there were those enthusiasts who argued that armed conflict could be transformed through air power's perceived capability to avoid sequential operations: whereas surface forces have to achieve tactical breakthroughs in order to fulfil operational objectives, which in turn lead to strategic progress, in theory at least aerial attacks could be undertaken on all three levels from the outset of any war and thus might secure politically exploitable results swiftly and comparatively cheaply. Winston Churchill, for instance, an advocate of both an independent air force and the establishment of a fully fledged air ministry, observed at the height of the First World War that:

> At sea, the increased power of the defensive in mines and submarines has robbed the stronger Navy of its rights. On land . . . the modern defensive . . . has been elevated into a fine art. But the air is free and open. There are no entrenchments there. It is equal for the attack and for the defence.[13]

Although nobody could dispute the underlying truth of these remarks, there were those who, on the other hand, regarded aircraft much as most of their contemporaries were to see tanks, which for many years after their initial development were primarily designed and employed as infantry-support weapons. According to this school of thought, air power's ability to exploit the third dimension and gain the ultimate 'high ground' was clearly very useful, but it was essentially just another new component that needed to be successfully subsumed into the existing combined-arms war machine to magnify its strength and flexibility.

The experience of the First World War necessitated and facilitated both organizational and technological innovation. In the design of military aircraft, not only have several attributes to be considered – primarily the operating range and ceiling, speed, manoeuvrability, including the pace of acceleration, climbs and turns, vulnerability and armament – but also reconciled with one another, since they tend to be mutually competitive; any improvement in one of these qualities is likely to be at the expense of another. At the outset of conflict, planes were still constructed overwhelmingly from wood, had undercarriages that could not be retracted and cockpits that were open to the elements. As well as bombs, which might in practice be nothing more than grenades, any armament took the form of other hand-held weapons wielded by the crew, or coaxial machine guns that were bolted to the fuselage. Alongside better, more powerful engines, which improved the speed, range, ceiling and load-bearing capacity of these machines appreciably, one other technical refinement deserves special mention since it greatly enhanced the scope for using the aircraft's limited firepower effectively. This was the synchronization gear that, first installed in German Fokker monoplanes, allowed machine guns to be discharged safely between the propeller blades at targets lying ahead; in a dogfight, the pilot had the comparatively simple task of aligning his plane with its quarry and, once in range, pulling the trigger. Certainly, the Fokker inflicted heavy losses on its Allied counterparts during the winter of 1915–16. This provoked a British response, not least in the form of new fighters, among them the Sopwith Camel, which had a ceiling of 22,000 feet (6,700 m) and could achieve speeds of up to 120 mph (194 kmh), and squadrons devoted exclusively to attaining air superiority.

Important doctrinal and organizational changes were also taken in hand. German bombing raids on towns in the UK killed some 1,400 people and seemed the harbinger of things to come, not least when a week of attacks in September 1917 sent 300,000 Londoners in search of sanctuary in the city's Underground stations. Not only was air power rendering conventional distinctions between non-combatants and combatants anachronistic, but also, and for the first time in armed conflict, people who were far removed from what was regarded as the seat of the fighting were being made to feel vulnerable. Certainly, the psychological and material blows inflicted by German Zeppelins and Gotha and Riesenflugzeug bombers spawned a review of air defence measures by General Jan Smuts and Sir David Henderson. This not only recommended the establishment of the RAF but also prophesied the awesome potential that ever-improving aircraft would have for changing the face of warfare: '[T]he day may not be far off when aerial operations, with their devastation of enemy lands and destruction of populous centres on a vast scale, may become the principal operations of war, to which the older forms of [army] . . . and naval operations may become secondary and subordinate.'[14] Indeed, in October 1917 the British founded a Wing of planes that was devoted to 'strategic' bombing missions. Equipped with such aircraft as the Handley-Page O/100 and O/400, it steadily intensified its attacks on Germany over the next twelve months.

Whereas the disappointing results of a strategic aerial campaign begun in 1914 quickly stifled enthusiasm for such projects in France, elsewhere interest in both the concept and the capability persisted. Large aircraft were seen as the key to success and, although they were the most technologically backward of the Entente powers, Russia and Italy, somewhat ironically, pioneered the design and construction of heavy bombers. Igor Sikorsky, the celebrated Russian aeronautical engineer, had a four-engined machine ready for active service as early as the winter of 1914, while, during the following summer, the tri-motor devised by Giovanni Caproni first went into action with the Italian armed forces. Concomitant doctrinal thinking was also taking place. In

May 1917 d'Annunzio, who had in the interim acquired a distin-guished war record, including notable service in the skies, drew up a memorandum for the Chief of the Italian General Staff, Luigi Cadorna. He suggested that, while air power should continue to give close support to surface units through bombing and strafing raids and reconnaissance operations, its real forte should be strategic attacks on the enemy's industrial heartland so as to disrupt the production of armaments and other vital *matériel*. If flotillas of large, powerful planes were used, notably Caproni's, up to 100 tonnes of bombs at a time might be dropped on selected targets.[15]

Caproni had been encouraged to design and build his bomber by Colonel Giulio Douhet (1869–1930), who also happened to be a friend of d'Annunzio. A professional soldier with a substantial reputation as a military theorist, Douhet had long since been fascinated by the indus-trialization of warfare and had written various pamphlets on electrification and on the substitution of mechanical for muscular power. 'War follows the evolution of industry in the application of the machine', he was soon to conclude. 'In the same way that the machine multiplies production, its introduction into the modern army multi-plies destruction.'[16] By 1909 he had realized that controlled flight could open up new horizons, both literally and figuratively speaking. The following year he published *I problemi dell'aeronavigazione*, which, rather bewilderingly, scarcely touched on the problems of aerial navigation. Instead, it was a visionary sketch of how war might be waged in and from the skies. Destined to become the pre-eminent theorist on this subject, Douhet was not yet persuaded that air power was the supreme form of martial strength, but he was especially struck by the potential of the plane, dismissing airships as too unwieldy and vulnerable. He also realized that the successful exploitation of aircraft in war would call for timely and substantial preparation and invest-ment during peace. As was the case with navies, which required a large amount of infrastructure for their construction, maintenance, repair and utilization, creating an effective air force had certain prerequisites, including a developed aeronautical industry. Still, at a time when many states were lavishing money and other resources on their battle fleets, Douhet believed that spending on air power would prove far more cost-effective, not least because of the greater flexibility offered by planes. For, whereas there are certain parallels that one could draw between maritime and aerial warfare, naval units are ineluctably that much more constrained than aircraft by geography. Two-thirds of our planet's surface are covered by the seas, but all of it is cloaked in the atmosphere. In theory at least, there is no point on the globe that cannot be reached by aircraft.

This fact alone convinced Douhet that the plane had tremendous potential as a reconnaissance platform and in the provision of close support to surface forces. Indeed, in *I problemi* he envisaged great fleets of aircraft carrying out such missions, if not strategic bombing operations. In 1912 he joined the leadership of the army's aerial battalion and was tasked with the preparation of a report for the war ministry on the structure and organization of air units. Still uncertain as to how aerial warfare might actually evolve, he did not yet press for the establishment of a discrete air force and favoured the acquisition of planes that might be used for a variety of roles. Stressing the need for intimate collaboration with industry, he befriended Caproni at this juncture, encouraging him to develop his plans for a heavy bomber. Indeed, in 1914 Douhet, allowing his enthusiasm to get the better of his judgement, placed an order for the plane without first obtaining permission from either his military or political masters. He was promptly banished to the infantry.

This was not the last occasion on which Douhet's zeal was to get him into trouble. He made enemies within Italy's military and political hierarchy, first as an advocate of her entry into the Great War and, thereafter, as a vociferous critic of the way in which the conflict was prosecuted. Rapidly disillusioned and embittered by the unavailing offensives and sanguinary positional warfare, it was only a matter of weeks before he was calling for the imaginative use of air power to break the deadlock. The army, he opined in a succession of memoranda to its top brass, should confine itself to the defensive while, in the interim, resources were channelled into expanding Italy's capacity for aerial operations. Industrial production should be adjusted so as to enable planes to be turned out in the way that Fiat manufactured motor vehicles, and more air-crew should be trained.[17] An armada of

1,000 heavy bombers, he reasoned, could simply fly over or round any defences and, venturing up to 300 miles (480 km) beyond the front line, directly assail the very kernel of the Central Powers. Dropping up to 500 tonnes of bombs per raid, it should strike at industrial centres, ports, lines of communication and supply, arsenals, governmental departments, banks and other nodes for lack of which the wider war effort would collapse. Once the enemy's means of production and morale had been severely weakened, the emphasis should be switched to an interdiction campaign that would deprive his front-line forces of reinforcements, supplies, information and political guidance. Finally, the enemy's army itself should be assailed, initially from the rear.[18] 'The powerful aeroplane', Douhet insisted, ' . . . is the best weapon to strike a fatal blow . . . [for it] attacks not only the fist but the heart, and cuts the nerves and veins of the arm.'[19]

Part of Douhet's crusade on behalf of air power included the lobbying of members of parliament, to some of whom he disclosed classified information. This illicit behaviour came to light after he inadvertently left a confidential document on a train and it was handed in to the authorities. Despite being court-martialled and sentenced to a year in prison, his enthusiasm remained undimmed. Indeed, he was now persuaded that the aircraft possessed the potential to become the ultimate military instrument. Writing to General Cadorna yet again, he amended his earlier campaign plan, arranging the sets of targets into a pattern that, from the Battle of Britain onwards, would come to dominate aerial strategy. Securing control of the skies over the enemy's territory was now to be the initial priority. This was to be achieved through attacks not just on hostile aircraft, but also against aerodromes and aeronautical engineering and production plants, all of which would pave the way for unfettered operations against other targets by vast fleets of Allied bombers.[20] Finally, in July 1917, Douhet joined d'Annunzio and Caproni in submitting a memorandum to Carlo Porro, Chief of the General Staff, advocating the foundation of an independent air force.

By this time, the USA had entered the war. Among the first American soldiers to arrive in Europe was William Mitchell (1879–1936), who initially acted as an observer attached to the Allied air forces. As a staff officer in 1912, he had composed a report on the US Army's need for an air corps, and he became its assistant head in June 1917. In this capacity, he worked closely with the Bolling Aeronautical Commission that had been despatched to Europe to ascertain what types of aircraft the US Army Air Service would need and for what roles. Envisaging an air arm that would, like that of the British, have some capacity for strategic as well as tactical operations,[21] the commission was interested in procuring bombers designed by Handley-Page. Britain's aviation industry was expanding rapidly at this point and was soon to employ 350,000 workers. Indeed, her output proved sufficient to satisfy a large part of America's demand for planes as well as her own, with much of the balance being provided by Caproni. As part of this acquisition process, both the Commission and Mitchell had dealings with Hugh Trenchard, who was then in command of the British air corps in France, Caproni and, if only indirectly, with Douhet, his friend.

These last two men drew up a document for the Americans on the subject of aerial warfare in which they advocated the en masse bombing, by night, of Germany's industrial centres. Nothing much came of this ambitious plan, not least because locating and hitting even quite large targets in daylight, let alone darkness, was difficult enough with the navigational aids and bomb-sights then available. Billy Mitchell, who was keen to see aerial warfare tested to the limit, was to lament the coming of the end of the First World War because it left so many possibilities unexplored in this and other regards. He anticipated a time when strategic bombing on a grand scale, including nocturnal attacks, would be feasible and would leave entire cities in ruins. Yet, for all his passionate belief in the potential of air power, he remained convinced that any changes it wrought would not make fleets and armies per se redundant, as Douhet was soon to come close to arguing. If, as some experiments that Mitchell himself conducted in 1921 were to underscore, capital ships seemed increasingly susceptible to aerial attacks from carrier- or land-based planes, submarines, which could exploit the third dimension, appeared far less vulnerable. Likewise, on land, the sheer diversity and numbers of combat units, together with their capacity for entrenchment, dispersal and concealment, suggested the need for combined arms operations, not just blows delivered from the air. In fact, Mitchell, always more of an advocate of air power than a theorist, later confessed that he hatched only one scheme to end the attritional carnage of the Great War. Revealingly, this comprised a thrust that, spearheaded by large formations of tanks, would link up with numerous parachutists dropped behind the defensive German lines.[22]

The view that air power was an auxiliary arm was a widespread one at this juncture. Although more than 100,000 combat aircraft were constructed in the course of the conflict, the role played by aviators in the First World War was an important but essentially subordinate one; the deeds of the 'aces' – such as Manfred von Richthofen, Albert Ball, Edward Mannock, René Fonck and Charles Nungesser – might well be legendary, but decision was secured through surface combat involving, above all, troops, artillery, gas, machine guns and tanks. Indeed, in the UK, while the air force emerged from the war as the largest in existence, no sooner was the fighting over than a cost-conscious government, pressed by its admirals and generals, scrutinized the possibility of dissolving the RAF and returning its units to the control of the other two services. Initially championed by Air Marshal Trenchard, the Chief of the Air Staff (CAS) from 1919 until 1930, and Winston Churchill, in his capacity as Minister for War and Air, the RAF ultimately survived the quest for peacetime economies and, allotted a central role in home and imperial defence, secured its future as an independent service. The Women's Royal Air Force and the Fleet Air Arm, by contrast, were less successful in this regard; the former was disbanded and the latter managed to delay its transfer to the command of the Royal Navy only until 1937. Similarly, so severe were the post-war cutbacks in the US Army Air Service that Mitchell, fearing its annihilation, began a desperate campaign to shield it. This included calling, in 1919, for the force to be given both institutional and operational independence, a proposal that the Bolling Commission had made two years earlier but which Mitchell had not embraced.

If only because there was comparatively little recent combat experience from which lessons might be drawn, at this juncture most soldiers and sailors somewhat pardonably underestimated the potential of air power. During the First World War, a number of important tasks had been identified as suitable roles for aviators, including tactical and strategic bombing, countering hostile airships and planes, and strafing enemy troops, supply columns and guns. Airborne platforms also had much to recommend them as spotters for friendly artillery batteries and for scouting assignments in general. The development of aerial photography – made feasible by Kodak's perfection of film in place of the cumbersome plate – greatly facilitated timely intelligence-gathering from the air, not least with regard to the assessment of damage inflicted by gunfire and bombing raids on targets deep in enemy territory. If reels that were ready for processing and examination could not be flown directly to the relevant headquarters, they could usually be dropped, in protective canisters, by parachute to await collection.

Flying boats, together with planes that could be launched from ship-mounted catapults or which, fitted with floats, could be brought back on board by cranes, had also proved their worth in maritime reconnaissance and air–sea rescue operations. The Americans had pioneered the use of vessels as take-off and retrieval platforms for aircraft. In 1910 one was launched from a specially constructed stage on USS *Birmingham* and, the following year, one successfully took off from and then alighted on the quarterdeck of USS *Pennsylvania*; again, a stage was utilized, with wires attached to sandbags serving as arresting gear. The first dedicated aircraft carrier, however, was Britain's HMS *Argus*, a converted merchantman fitted with an unobstructed flight deck. Although completed before the war ended, she never saw action. Nevertheless, the UK and some other states had evidently grasped the potential of such vessels: in 1918 the Royal Navy purchased a partially complete Chilean battleship for conversion into the carrier HMS *Eagle*; in 1922 the US Navy followed suit by modifying a collier hull to make the USS *Langley*; while the Japanese quickly introduced the *Hosho*. The last of these seems to have been laid down as an oiler and then fashioned, apparently with British help, into something akin to HMS *Hermes*, the Royal Navy's first custom-built carrier, which was ordered in 1917.[23]

That the carrier would come to supplant the battleship as the capital ship of leading navies was not yet foreseeable. Nor, in the 1920s and the early 1930s, was it easy to reconcile many of the claims that some theorists made on behalf of air power with actual combat experience. After the Great War, one of the principal preoccupations of, for instance, the RAF, the world's leading air force, was the policing of the globe's trouble spots. In the aftermath of the Versailles Treaty, the League of Nations had entrusted the administration of Germany's former colonies and the non-Turkish regions of the defunct Ottoman Empire to the victorious powers. The mandates allocated to Britain as part of this process included those of Mesopotamia (Iraq) and Palestine, part of which became Transjordan. These territories were in violent turmoil, as was Somaliland in the Horn of Africa, where the so-called Mad Mullah and his followers were on the rampage. Bringing so much as a semblance of law and order to such vast, largely inhospitable tracts of land would have strained the capabilities of even a substantial army. Aircraft, however, co-operating with 'flying' columns of soldiers, were ideal for monitoring the situation on the ground and reacting almost instantaneously to any threatening developments. This was, moreover, a far cheaper solution, in both lives and money, than committing dozens of battalions to laborious, and potentially inter-minable, counter-insurgency operations. Indeed, the policy of 'air control' proved a great success. Across Somaliland and the Middle East, rebellious tribesmen were harried into submission by attacks from prowling DH.9A planes, while, at Kirkuk in Iraq at the start of the Kurdish insurrection of 1922–4, the first ever airlift of troops was accomplished with the aid of Vickers Vernon transporters. A similar operation occurred during the troubles in Afghanistan in 1928–9, when, in the midst of winter, the RAF executed an unprecedented evac-uation of civilians from the beleaguered city of Kabul.[24]

Impressive though they were, such humanitarian and 'constabulary' operations furnished few clues as to what the aviator's role in any new, set-piece confrontation between the great powers' fleets and armies might be. Douhet, however, believed that he knew. In 1921 he encap-sulated his reasoning about aerial operations in *Il dominio dell'ario*, a second, expanded edition of which was published in 1926. According to *Command of the Air*, aircraft now constituted the dominant form of military power. Italy's surface units should be scaled down accordingly, while the air force should be given both more resources and independent status, together with an air ministry to help foster its development and coordinate its links with industry.

While Mussolini, himself an air-power enthusiast, was to endorse the last three of these four suggestions, there were bound to be those who disagreed with Douhet's strategic analysis, if only because of inter-service rivalry. However, there were doubters even within and on the fringes of the Italian air corps, including several senior officers and Italo Balbo, who became the under-secretary at the air ministry in 1926 and secretary three years later. In particular, they found Douhet's conviction that aircraft would always be able to attack at times and places of their choosing too abstract. He scarcely entertained the possibility of an effective air defence, and his emphasis on strategic bombers and targets to the detriment of fighter aircraft and tactical support missions would, they feared, leave dangerous gaps in the armed services' capabilities.

The 1926 version of *Il dominio dell'ario* extended the debate further afield, securing its author an international reputation and casting the spell of 'Douhetism' over, among others, Mitchell, whose perpetual agitation for improvements to the USA's readiness for aerial warfare was proving as tireless as it was irritating to some of his superiors. Between 1919 and 1921 he produced numerous journalistic articles and memoranda and appeared before Congressional committees to mount a steadfast defence of the US Army Air Service in particular and the 'ability to do something in the air' in general. *Our Air Force*, the book he published in 1921, summarized his thinking at this point: he favoured the creation of a balanced air corps much like those he had seen in Europe, and reasoned that command of the skies would prove a prerequisite for future operations by surface forces. Within four years, however, following a trip to Europe during which he met Douhet and became more familiar with his writings, Mitchell's own views, encapsulated in his *Winged Defense* of 1925,[25] had become that much more extreme, as had his ongoing attacks on some members of America's military hierarchy and their attitudes to air power. Not least because of its use of such language as 'criminal negligence' and 'almost treasonable' maladministration, the report he released that same year concerning the USA's lack of preparedness for aerial warfare led to his being court-martialled.[26] He left the army in 1926, but continued to campaign on air power's behalf until his death ten years later.

In *Winged Defense* and his long-awaited recollections of the Great War, which finally appeared in 1926, Mitchell echoed Douhet's radical thesis that air power would reign supreme in any future conflict. It would hasten the end of fighting by demolishing the foundations of the antagonists' strength through bombing that would yield not just tactical but also strategic and thus political results. This would, at the very least, diminish the significance and duration of operations mounted by surface forces in general, while other, particular missions would become more difficult if not impracticable. Indeed, some platforms and practices would be rendered obsolete. Mitchell prophesied that aircraft carriers would, as the Italians had already concluded, prove inordinately vulnerable to attacks by land-based planes and that the maritime transportation of armies would be supplanted by airlifts of the kind pioneered by the British in Iraq.[27]

All of ten years later, much of Douhet's and Mitchell's reasoning had still to be validated or invalidated, while those who drew any conclusions at all from the fighting in Ethiopia and from the incipient Spanish Civil and Sino-Japanese Wars reacted to them in differing ways. The prevailing atmospheric and combat conditions encountered in Manchukuo led the Japanese Army's air corps to concentrate on training crews to man aircraft that had been developed and optimized for short-range, cold-weather operations. In the 1940s neither these men nor their machines were found to be particularly adaptable to the climatic and strategic environment of the Pacific war, although they were to prove of appreciable use in China and Burma. The Italians, too, were somewhat misled by their adventures in Ethiopia. After its seemingly successful operations here, where it was pitted against a virtually defenceless opponent, their air force, which regarded itself as the custodian of Douhet's theoretical legacy, was widely overrated by friend and foe alike. It might have learnt much from its experience in Spain, particularly with regard to the evident need for joint command arrangements and operations. Instead, however, it stubbornly remained aloof from the rest of the Italian armed services, thereby dashing any hopes of potentially fruitful collaboration, with the navy especially.

In fact, primarily because of inter-service wrangling, the fleets of Italy and Germany remained the only sizeable ones that did not have control over their own aviation during this period. The Kriegsmarine never set up a discrete fleet air arm, and the Italians did not do so until the middle of 1941. Nor did either of these major maritime powers, in stark contrast to Japan, Britain and the USA, ever possess a serviceable aircraft carrier. While the Italians laboured to convert a passenger liner into one, the work was barely complete at the time of their capitulation in 1943. Seized by the Nazis, who had aided in her construction, the *Aquila* was quickly incapacitated by Allied bombers.[28] Rather more surprising is the Germans' own failure to produce a carrier, for they not only had ambitious plans for such vessels but also learnt much of value from their combat experience in the Iberian Peninsula, not least with regard to the close coordination of air and surface forces. They quickly found, however, that they possessed insufficient resources to realize all of their blueprints for aerial and other military capabilities. On the other hand, they also discovered that, contrary to a widespread belief, dogfights were still practicable, despite the attainment of ever-faster speeds in the air. It was therefore essential that fighter aircraft and their crews be prepared for more than the interception of hostile bombers, a task with which many aviators, in part at least because of Douhet's ubiquitous influence, were fixated.

Although the razing of the Basque town of Guernica by the German Kondor Legion in April 1937 constituted the first saturation bombing of civilians yet seen and helped to strengthen belief in Douhet's conviction that the bomber would always get through and ravage its target, there were those who nonetheless argued that, if confronted with proper defences, the bomber might prove anything but formidable. Indeed, the Russians surmised that strategic bombardment was likely to prove so ineffectual that they cancelled production of their new heavy bomber, the TB-7, broke up the strategic wing of their air force and concentrated their efforts on building planes and organizational structures that could give their army close, tactical support. This particular decision mirrored that of the Germans, who, having been prohibited from having any aircraft under the Versailles settlement, had been mere onlookers during some of air power's most formative years. They, too, were persuaded by their experience in Spain that the new, autonomous Luftwaffe should accentuate tactical, rather than strategic bombing, capabilities. In any case, they were bent on producing large numbers of planes as swiftly as possible, a priority that, combined with a shortage of suitably powerful engines and other essentials, effectively ruled out their creating a fleet of heavy bombers at this juncture. Perennial material constraints and a rather nebulous doctrine eventually helped to turn their air arm into something of a jack of all trades and a master of none.

Any air force's capabilities are at least partly determined by the quality of its equipment. During the inter-war period, the pace of technological refinement was such that aircraft and their potential altered dramatically, the most obvious change occurring in the basic shape of airframes. Indeed, fixed-wing aviation underwent a transformation within the space of a few years, with designs moving in the main away from those of the biplane to those of the streamlined monoplane: flimsy wood, fabric and wire structures gave way to metal fuselages that had enclosed cockpits and which required no internal bracing; variable pitch propellers were introduced; and retractable, rather than fixed, undercarriages became the norm. Other, parallel advances had profound implications for performance. Automatic pilots were among these, as were motors that were not only more powerful but also designed for use in rarefied air. In turn, this new generation of piston engines, together with the development of pressurized clothing, heated by electrical circuitry, permitted vastly higher altitudes to be attained, culminating, in 1937, in a British Bristol setting a new record of 54,000 feet (16,460 m). Indeed, as scientists pondered and developed means of protecting military personnel in general against noise, blast and the vagaries of climate, the research undertaken in the sphere of aviation medicine proved of far-reaching significance.

At the same time, innovations such as the Sperry and Norden xv bomb-sights afforded appreciably greater accuracy in the dropping of bombs than had formerly been the case. For a generation of aviators fascinated by the concept of strategic attacks in particular, breakthroughs such as these seemed auspicious.[29] Certainly, confronted by the twin challenges of their own vulnerability and the aeroplane's ascendancy, the Zeppelins and other airships that had played a prominent role in the First World War gradually lost favour until, in the wake of the R-101 and *Hindenburg* disasters, they were finally abandoned, the last military versions being broken up in 1940. The aeroplane, on the other hand, emerged as the offensive weapon par excellence, and the opinions of many commentators at this time duly reflected those of Douhet: if armed conflict could not be deterred through the mere threat of retaliatory attacks, a new generation of bombers promised, by raining down death, destruction and demoralization from high altitudes, to inflict decisive damage quickly and with virtual impunity.[30]

Mitchell, however, like H. G. Wells before him, had anticipated that aeroplanes would transfigure everyday life as well as warfare, not least in the field of travel. The first commercial flights began in Florida in 1914 and, after the First World War, the number of operating companies and routes began to mushroom. The Italians in particular adored fast planes, much as they loved sports cars. Just as Charles Lindbergh's journey from New York to Paris in 1927 was to turn him into an international superstar, so too did the mass flights of Italian pilots thrill the public. Led by Italo Balbo, they criss-crossed the Mediterranean and the Atlantic between 1928 and 1933, securing Balbo pride of place on the front pages of innumerable magazines and newspapers. In all, he and his countrymen set 110 records for speed and endurance flying between 1927 and 1939.

Indeed, between the two world wars, the performance of aircraft improved significantly in both these respects. If the first non-stop crossing of the Atlantic – which, taking just under sixteen hours, was accomplished by Alcock and Brown in 1919 – seemed astonishing, within twenty years of this another feat occurred that was as remarkable as it was portentous: a Vickers Wellesley bomber flew more than 7,000 miles (11,300 km) without halting from Upper Heyford in England to Darwin, Australia. Indeed, by 1943, British bombers such as the Stirling, Halifax and Lancaster could travel between 1,300 and 2,000 miles (2,100–3,200 km) to deliver payloads of up to 22,000 pounds (10,000 kg), while contemporary fighter aircraft, such as the British Spitfire XII, the German Messerschmitt 109G and the Russian Lavochkin LA-7, all had optimum speeds of some 400 mph (644 kmh) and maximum ranges of at least 250 miles (402 km) if fitted with under-wing fuel tanks (drop tanks). Perhaps most remarkable of all was 'The Cadillac of the Skies', the American Mustang, which, initially ordered by the British as a ground-attack aircraft, was at first powered by an Allison motor. When, in the P-51B version, this was replaced with a Rolls-Royce Merlin engine, the original aircraft's ceiling was doubled and, if equipped with drop tanks (which were made from a laminated paper compound to minimize any loss of speed and manoeuvrability), its range was extended up to as much as 700 miles (1,125 km). (The later P-51D model had a maximum operating radius of some 800 miles / 1,290 km.) More generally speaking, aircraft performance in all these regards was to be further improved by technical refinements that were made as the conflict progressed.

A state's capacity for developing and maintaining air power ineluctably depends to a large extent upon its economic, technical and industrial base. By 1940 the Italian Air Force (the Aeronautica Militare Italiana), for instance, consisted of 1,700 front-line planes, even the best 900 of which were outdated. Two of the three types of bomber at its disposal – the Savoia-Marchetti SM.79 and the CRDA Z.1007 – were constructed mostly from wood in a bid to conserve metal stocks, while the Fiat CR.42 biplane fighter, which had only entered service that year, could achieve a top speed of just 260 mph (418 kmh). Moreover, as radio telephones remained in short supply until as late as mid-1942, sophisticated aerial intercommunication was all but impossible. It is little wonder that, in the early fighting over the Mediterranean and the Middle East, a couple of hundred ageing RAF planes, many of them 1936-vintage Gladiators, proved more than a match for their Italian opponents, despite being outnumbered by more than two to one.

A paucity of radios also hampered the Russians' attempts to imitate the Germans' interlocking of surface and aerial units until the USSR began to take delivery of the American-built P-39 Airacobra in 1942. This plane's two radio transmitters and three receivers greatly eased the problems surrounding the command and control of air power, not least in combined-arms operations. Driven by a v-12 Allison engine and rather awkward to handle at altitude, the P-39 had an effective ceiling of just 15,000 feet (4,572 m), but this usually proved sufficient, particularly since the aircraft's cardinal assignment was the provision of cover for friendly ground forces. Although the need to maintain an adequate and timely flow of replacement components for machines that originated from Buffalo, New York, compounded the logistical difficulties encountered in conducting aerial warfare, the P-39, despite its many shortcomings, bolstered Soviet combat capabilities until more sophisticated machines – notably the Lavochkin LA-7 and Yakolev Yak-9D – became available. The Russians ultimately acquired as many as half of the 9,584 Airacobras that were produced.[31]

The Japanese, by contrast, designed some quite advanced aircraft, yet they struggled to keep up in the race to manufacture planes rapidly and in adequate quantities. The first version of their A6M Zero, which entered service in 1940, was light and, if somewhat lacking in fire-power, endowed with both great agility and reach. But although it proved highly successful in the opening months of the Pacific war, it was not until 1944 that the Japanese developed brand new fighters that were a real match for their Western counterparts, namely the navy's Kawanishi N1K2-J Shiden and the army's Nakajima Ki.84 Hayate. Owing to attacks on the manufacturing plants and a dearth of raw materials and qualified aeronautical engineers, neither of these planes was produced in great numbers. In any case, by this stage of the war Japan had insufficient pilots left who were capable of getting the optimum performance out of these sophisticated machines.

As early as the mid-1930s it had become apparent that the sheer pace of technological innovation could make it difficult for competing states to keep abreast of one another in terms of air power. On the eve of the Second World War, the efforts of Britain and France to rearm in order to meet the resurgent threat from Germany were bedevilled by this complication, among others. If the improvements in land warfare equipment, notably tanks, were substantial, then those affecting aircraft were breathtaking. At the beginning of 1934, for instance, the RAF still resembled the corps of wooden biplanes that had fought in the First World War, while the Armée de l'Air likewise consisted of a mass of obsolete machines accumulated during the 1920s. Not least because perennial inter-service disagreements about the precise combat role of aviation distorted French procurement policies, spawning a wasteful bid to perfect an all-purpose aircraft, it was not until 1936 that the air ministry recognized the importance of specialized interceptors. It promptly ordered a large number of the Dewoitine D.520, the very best of its period. By 1939, however, these were already outclassed by their British and German counterparts, as was the Morane-Saulnier MS.406, France's most numerous fighter, which had a top speed of 300 mph (480 kmh) and a maximum operating radius of just 250 miles (400 kmh).

The French aircraft industry, alas, was poorly placed to rectify either qualitative or quantitative deficiencies in haste. Only one factory was configured with mass-production techniques in mind, most plants being just little workshops, many of them lamentably backward; whereas building each MS.406 required an average of 18,000 man-hours, a Messerschmitt 109 could be turned out in just 5,000. Consequently, when, in 1939, German production was nudging 3,000 planes per year, France was unable to manufacture a fifth of this figure. Nevertheless, French firms predictably objected to their government's endeavours to make up this shortfall by purchasing abroad.[32] For example, although the promising prototype of the American P-38 – which, with machine guns clustered around a cannon in its nose, packed substantial punch and, powered by two turbo-charged engines, could exceed 400 mph (644 kmh) – caught the eye of the air ministry as early as the spring of 1939, the placing of an order was postponed until the end of that fateful year, when French rearmament efforts in general were suddenly but belatedly redoubled.

As a result of such problems, France entered the Second World War with an air force that was fatally weak in size and quality. Germany, meanwhile, had amassed an air arm that was not only much larger than either its British or French counterpart but which also included many more modern machines. Although the outcome for France was a calamity, Britain managed to withstand the German onslaught. This was largely because, in addition to various expansion schemes initiated between 1934 and 1939, in 1937 Sir Thomas Inskip, as Minister for Coordination of Defence, elected to begin switching the emphasis from a doctrine of deterrence and retaliation based on strategic bombing to one that focused more on active defensive measures, notably the use of fighters. These could in any case be manufactured more cheaply and faster than bombers. Indeed, in April 1940, while French production was still languishing at around just 60 planes per month, the UK's finally outstripped that of Germany.[33] Under Lord Beaverbrook, Minister of Aircraft production in Churchill's war cabinet, this trend continued. Fighter output doubled, with 100 new Spitfires and Hurricanes being turned out every week and no fewer than 4,576 aircraft being manufactured between May and August 1940.

Whereas this ensured an adequate supply of planes to the RAF during a critical period, shortages of fully trained air-crew were to prove more worrying. Although the victorious Germans had lost 1,400 planes in the course of their invasion of France, the odds facing the RAF in the subsequent Battle of Britain during the summer of 1940 appeared overwhelming. Not least because it, too, had lost many pilots and machines on the European mainland, its front-line strength was barely a third of that of the Luftwaffe and it still included many obsolete Gladiator, Fury and Defiant fighters. Any numerical inferiority was, on the other hand, partly offset by the calibre of most of its personnel and its Hurricane and Spitfire interceptors, and partly by a generally superior command, control and communications infrastructure that included 'radar' (Radio Detection and Ranging). Guided by this and backed up by an increasingly elaborate, integrated air-defence network, which consisted of anti-aircraft (AA) batteries, observers, searchlights, shelters and barrage balloons, the RAF was ultimately able to thwart the German Luftwaffe.

The Luftflotten suffered from various handicaps, too, although the British could be pardoned for having thought otherwise, initially at least. Having emerged victorious in the fighting for Poland, the Benelux states, Denmark, Norway and France, the three Luftflotten that were to participate in the campaign included many experienced crews and some of the most successful commanders of the air power epoch: Albert Kesselring, Hugo Sperrle, who had led the Kondor Legion in Spain, and Hans-Jürgen Stumpff. However, whereas the Luftwaffe had largely been designed for and had become accustomed to providing close support for German troops, in seeking to clear a way for the invasion of the UK, Operation 'Sea-lion', it was confronted with a new challenge, since the Battle of Britain was a large, self-contained clash between aerial forces. With no German surface units to assist it or poised to take immediate advantage of any breakthrough, the Luftwaffe found itself with an independent role for which it was neither trained nor ideally equipped.

The British aviators, too, encountered some doctrinal shortcomings at the start of the campaign. For many years, Fighter Command had been preoccupied with planning for operations against unescorted bombers and, unlike the Germans, who had benefited from their experience in the Spanish Civil War, had given less thought to the minutia of the dogfight. The RAF's prescribed, basic tactical formation was V-shaped, the 'tight vic' of three aircraft. This soon proved more vulnerable and less flexible than the pairs and fours in which Luftwaffe fighters were habitually deployed. It was not until 1941 that official British doctrine endorsed much the same practice. In the interim, Churchill's 'Few' had to learn through experience and improvise as best they could. In other respects, however, they enjoyed appreciable advantages over their opponents. Although it normally took the RAF at least fifteen minutes to plot the approach of an attacking *Gruppe* and get their fighters into a position to intercept it, radar alerted the British the moment that their adversaries began to assemble a formation for an attack, and thus spared the RAF the need to mount repeated patrols that would have dispersed and wasted its meagre resources. Fighters could be concentrated precisely where they were needed and, when no threat was looming, could remain at their bases undergoing replenishment and repairs while their crews snatched some rest. Indeed, the very proximity of their aerodromes to the battle zone gave the RAF the upper hand in terms of the frequency and duration of their combat sorties. By contrast, while Axis planes could, from their Continental bases, reach southern England in as little as six minutes and London within half an hour, they could not linger over either for long. The mainstay of their fighter squadrons, the Messerschmitt 109, had too little fuel to remain in British airspace for more than a short period –

just ten minutes over London – whereas the larger, twin-engined Me 110, which had somewhat better endurance, was too ponderous to tackle a Spitfire or Hurricane. Too often deprived of adequate escorts, the bombers in the Luftflotten were deficient as well in that they were medium, rather than strategic, machines with commensurably smaller payloads and, because of incompatible radio sets, frequently had difficulty communicating with their escorts. The Germans' priority had always been to provide good air-to-surface links between army units and a Luftwaffe that was primarily geared to their support.

The German commanders were in any event unsure what to bomb and when. 'The selection of objectives . . . and determining the order in which they are to be destroyed', Douhet had observed, 'is the most difficult and delicate task in aerial warfare, constituting what may be defined as aerial strategy.'[34] Not least for lack of an official doctrine with regard to strategic bombing, the Luftwaffe proved fatally inconsistent in its approach, assailing many targets, among them ports, cities and coastal shipping, that, while not unimportant, were hardly the keys to securing victory in a battle for air supremacy. The most promising attacks began on 12 August 1940 and climaxed during the first week of September: the radar at Ventnor was bombed, as were several front-line fighter bases. The RAF was sucked into trying to protect these vital but vulnerable facilities in a spiralling, attritional battle. Numerous planes and pilots were lost, but the Luftwaffe greatly overestimated the damage it was inflicting. On 7 September, erroneously believing the RAF to be all but destroyed and that an assault on London would lure it into a conclusive encounter, the Germans suddenly swung the weight of their attack against Britain's capital, committing 300 bombers escorted by twice as many fighters. The RAF did not take the bait, however, and, while London burned, recuperated. When, on 15 September, the Luftwaffe launched what was evidently intended to be the *coup de grâce*, it hit back en masse. Although the campaign was essentially defensive in nature, British tactics had always contained an offensive element. Now, Wings comprising several squadrons of fighters confronted the hostile bombers while others kept their escorts at bay.

Thereafter, the Luftwaffe, disheartened and badly mauled, confined itself to mounting sporadic and ever-smaller daytime raids on British towns in a desperate bid to demoralize the inhabitants and disrupt manufacturing output, particularly the production of planes and other *matériel*. Meanwhile, Hitler postponed Operation 'Sea-lion' indefinitely and began preparing to invade the Soviet Union. By the autumn, the German attacks on Britain's population and industrial centres – the so-called Blitz – were increasingly taking place under the cover of darkness and were escalating again. By mid-November, almost a million incendiaries and some 13,000 tonnes of high-explosive bombs had been dropped on London alone. The British government had long since taken the unpalatable precaution of separating millions of children from their families and, in the largest organized movement of people in their country's history, evacuating them from this and other urban areas that were likely to be bombed. Particularly vulnerable adults, notably mothers with very young infants, were also removed to safety by the authorities, while a further two million children and grown-ups were evacuated by charities and their own relations. Most civilians, however, had to remain behind and continue working and living as best they could. More than a few perished or were injured, not as a direct result of enemy action, but because of the increased potential for accidents amidst the 'black-out', which, by stifling emissions of artificial light, sought to prevent prowling raiders from spotting their targets. In all, more than 43,000 people were killed and a further 139,000 hurt before the Blitz fizzled out in May 1941. Roughly two million homes were destroyed, mostly in the capital, and tremendous damage done to the infrastructure of the UK's principal ports, railways and cities.

Mounting an effective defence against these nocturnal raids was far from easy, particularly in the campaign's early stages. Searchlights could seldom pick out planes more than 12,000 feet (3,660 m) up, AA guns were in short supply and, like the RAF's night fighters, lacked a dependable means of locating their quarry. The Luftwaffe, by contrast, was guided to its objectives by an electronic navigation system, Knickebein, and its more refined cousins, the X- and Y-Geräte. Basically, these generated Lorenz beams – streams of Morse code divided into either dots or dashes – from transmitters located along the fringe of the Continent. These emissions could be picked up by receiving sets that were fitted to all German multi-engined bombers. To make their way to a given position, aircraft simply followed one beam until it intersected another. Here, the sound of the dots and dashes would interlock into a single tone and thereby indicate the proximity of the selected target, regardless of whether it was visible to the human eye. Two or more such beams could be aligned over any point in the UK and could channel planes to within 1,000 metres of it.

It was thus possible to launch attacks that, by the standards then prevailing, were quite accurate yet did not expose the bombers to much hostile observation and fire. In fact, it was only in the spring of 1941 that the UK's air defences really became sufficiently elaborate and sophisticated to pose a major threat to nocturnal raiders. For most of the Blitz, the latter suffered an average loss-rate of just 1 per cent. As time passed, however, in addition to deploying more AA guns and searchlights, the British began jamming the Germans' navigational transmissions. Still more significant was the harnessing of radar systems to both surface batteries and night fighters, notably the Beaufighter. These measures helped to increase German casualties appreciably, accounting for most of the 600 bombers that were lost in the Blitz as a whole. Indeed, electronic detection capabilities were destined to make a major contribution to the outcome of this campaign and of that against the U-boat wolf packs in the Atlantic, just as they had helped to secure the RAF's victory in the Battle of Britain.

The early 1930s had witnessed attempts to perfect sound 'mirrors' – huge, concave walls that funnelled the audible emissions from distant aircraft into receptors. However, not least because of the ever-increasing speeds of combat planes, which commensurably reduced the amount of warning time such a mechanism might provide, this crude way of detecting aircraft as a prelude to concentrating defences against them was soon rendered all but useless. Still, the underlying principle was not without merit. Certainly, by 1936 all of the major powers were independently experimenting with radar, whereby radio – rather than sound – waves are reflected off a target into a receiving 'dish'. In a monostatic radar, both the receiving and transmitting antennae are located together, whereas bistatic systems can separate the two, often over very considerable distances. Most radars of this period emitted rapid 'pulses' of energy, between which the 'echoes' from targets were received and processed. The information thus gathered still had to be interpreted, filtered and evaluated by human beings, which remains a demanding job, requiring special training, great skill and a lot of experience; genuine, potential targets have to be distinguished from 'clutter' – background radiation – and the strained, raw data, of which there can be a great deal, then has to be appraised and acted upon in a timely and appropriate fashion.

For all its practical complexities, however, radar provided the conceptual basis for not just electronic detection but also warfare and navigation systems that, initially used by aircraft, were soon being exploited by other platforms. The discovery, by the British early in 1940, of the cavity magnetron – an electronic vacuum valve that generated microwaves suitable for high-powered 'tactical' sets – was a momentous refinement, since it was to pave the way for such centimetric radar systems as the AI Mark VII and the ASV (Air-to-Surface) Marks II and III. These last two devices were incorporated into suitably capacious planes for anti-submarine operations in the Atlantic. Here, the Allies' principal difficulties lay in finding ways to keep such a colossal area under surveillance, particularly the very midst of the ocean, to detect U-boats and to destroy them when they were located. Maritime aerial patrols, like nautical blockade duties, are largely tedious, unglamorous missions in which one faces as much of a potential threat from the environment as from enemy action. Nevertheless, closing the gaps in the protection that could be afforded to Allied convoys was a crucial contribution to the overall war effort.

Through the introduction of more escort carriers and long-range planes – notably Sunderland and Catalina flying boats, and B-24J Liberators, which had sufficient endurance to reach 1,000 miles (1,600 km) or more from their bases – by mid-1943 the Allies were sealing the chinks in their armour. As well as helping to find and annihilate the German surface raiders, notably the mighty *Bismarck* and, later, her sister ship *Tirpitz*, aerial platforms also took the lead in carrying the fight to the enemy's submarines. Special low-level sights had been developed for greater accuracy in the making of attacks, which were executed with bombs and depth-charges by numerous, roaming aircraft. The exploitation of radar clinched the victory, however, by effectively solving the problems associated with the detection of U-boats. Sensitive enough to discern one on the surface, the ASV apparatus had a profound impact on the Battle of the Atlantic, for all submarines of this period were incapable of spending much time under water. Here, they had only limited power – provided by rechargeable batteries – for propulsion, air purification and the satisfaction of all their other energy requirements. Above the waves, by contrast, they could freely ingest fresh air and make use of their deck-mounted cannon and their cardinal power plant, diesel engines. These motors permitted much greater cruising speeds and also regenerated the electrical cells that were relied upon when the craft was submerged. In 1942, their heyday, the U-boats' ratio of losses against Allied ships was only one to fourteen. Largely as a result of the proliferation of centimetric radars, during 1943 this sagged beneath affordability to as low as one to two. When linked to powerful searchlights, notably the Leigh Light, these sensors even robbed the submarine of the protection once afforded by darkness. Although the Germans subsequently responded to the threat posed by ASV detection by adding the Schnorkel breathing device to their U-boats, by this juncture Allied air and naval supremacy was such that even this could only slow, not stop, their slide to defeat. The UK, the Americans' gateway to Europe, survived the wolf packs' blockade and, with the Atlantic sea lanes increasingly secure, could host the build-up for the 'D-Day' landings.[35] These, virtually unhindered by the Kriegsmarine, eventually took place in June 1944.

Tactical radar also assisted greatly in nocturnal operations against enemy planes. Indeed, on coming into service in March 1941, Britain's progenitorial airborne set, the AI Mark VII, was first installed in a Blenheim night fighter. Generally, however, the RAF's interceptors were choreographed by ground controllers using a network of static early warning radars, the so-called Chain Home. This was steadily improved and extended to enable it to detect, not just aircraft that were flying at comparatively high altitudes, but also platforms operating much nearer to the surface. Here, it is possible for aircraft to evade detection by exploiting radar 'shadows' and the 'clutter' generated by the landscape; although it calls for tremendous piloting skills, they can duck beneath the radar beams by flying within valleys and generally hugging the Earth's contours.

As the Blitz's first phase was nearing its climax in autumn 1940, HMS *Illustrious*, a carrier in the British Mediterranean fleet, steamed to within striking range of the Italian naval base at Taranto. On 11 November, 21 of her Swordfish planes flew the intervening 180 miles (290 km) to launch a surprise attack on the warships in the anchorage. Thanks to careful photographic reconnaissance, the Royal Navy knew the precise positions of the enemy ships and of the barrage balloons, AA batteries and anti-torpedo nets that had been allotted for their protection. A pair of planes in each of the two waves of Swordfish illuminated the principal targets with flares before seeking to distract the Italian gunners with diversionary attacks. Despite the strength of the port's defences and difficult though it was to assail vessels with torpedoes in shallow waters, three battleships and a cruiser were hit, and the rest of the flotilla was compelled to seek refuge in other harbours – all for a loss of just two aircraft.

The success of this audacious raid, moreover, inspired the Japanese to seek to replicate it with a grand, pre-emptive blow against the base of the US Pacific Fleet at Pearl Harbor, Hawaii, on 7 December 1941. In fact, having travelled, undetected, in excess of 3,000 miles (4,800 km) to get to within 275 miles (440 km) of their prey, their carrier task-force, under Vice-Admiral Chuichi Nagumo, sank or damaged no fewer than sixteen vessels, of which six battleships, three light cruisers and three destroyers were among the former and two battleships among the latter. More than 290 aircraft were also destroyed or damaged, virtually all of them while still on the ground, and some 3,600 military personnel and civilians were killed or injured. Just 29 planes from the attacking squadrons were shot down. American losses would doubtless have been greater still had a third wave of aircraft assailed the dockyard's fuel storage and repair facilities, as had been planned. Nagumo, however, having failed to catch his adversaries' own carriers in port, was fearful of a counterstroke and, content with his tactical triumph, ordered a withdrawal.

In the age of the motorcar, tank, aeroplane and oil-fired ships, of all the natural resources that developed states required to further and maintain their status, none was more vital than petroleum products. The Japanese, lacking their own reserves of oil and of strategically important ores, feared for their future as a major power if they failed to obtain secure supplies of these commodities. This quest had largely precipitated their lengthy conflict with the Chinese; and in 1940, with the demise of French and Dutch rule in Indo-China and the East Indies respectively, the tantalizing possibility of seizing the sizeable deposits in these regions presented itself as well. In the September of that year, the USA had begun seeking to condition Tokyo's behaviour by imposing economic sanctions, to which the Japanese had responded by formally joining the Axis and by redoubling their efforts to find alternative supplies of raw materials. Japan's fate seemed sealed, however. Eventually, heedless of the misgivings of their own emperor, a figurehead with more influence than genuine power, the cabinet, which was dominated by the military, resolved to fight. While the rationale behind assailing Pearl Harbor was to deal the USA a blow that was sufficiently heavy to persuade her to make a compromise peace and pursue a more conciliatory policy with regard to Tokyo's territorial and economic ambitions in South-East Asia, it actually had a very different effect: it dragged the vengeful Americans not just into the struggle for hegemony within the Pacific basin but also the wider war. On 10 December, as Japanese planes sank the formidable British warships *Repulse* and *Prince of Wales* off Malaya, thereby underscoring the vulnerability to aerial attack of the battleship, once the ultimate icon of martial might, America declared war on Japan. The next day, Germany and Italy did the same to the USA.

The UK promptly became a pivotal base of operations for the American armed services, not least the US Eighth Air Force. In fact, between June 1942 and December 1945 here and elsewhere more than 160 sites on what was legally British soil were earmarked for use by combat elements of the US Army Air Force (USAAF). It is little wonder that the UK was widely referred to by American military personnel as 'Airstrip One'. Dominating the air and sea corridors into and from north-western Europe, the British Isles formed an ideal stepping stone to the Eurasian landmass. With the Battle of Britain won, the threat of a German invasion had receded, and the Americans were able to begin amassing troops, planes, ships, supplies and other equipment in the UK in preparation for combined amphibious and aerial assaults on the European and African continents. By mid-1943 the Allies were closing the 'air gap' over the central Atlantic and, greatly aided by accurate, pooled intelligence and the mass production of 'Liberty' freighters and other merchantmen, were beginning to win the battle of attrition against Germany's U-boats, 47 of which were sunk in May alone. This, together with the opening up of the Mediterranean, permitted an increase in the flow of men and *matériel* into the UK, paving the way for, among other operations, the combined bomber offensive against Germany, and the combined landings at Salerno and Anzio, in Normandy and on the French Riviera. Similarly, in the Pacific theatre, the Allies' rapid seizure of crucial strategic outposts enabled them to 'leap-frog' across Japan's defensive perimeter, establishing forward bases from which air forces in particular could molest the very fountain-head of her power.

The Allies' early bids to assail targets in Germany were bedevilled by, among other problems, navigational difficulties. At the start of the Second World War, the British had the most elaborate doctrine for strategic bombing yet devised. They had compiled a lengthy list of suitable targets within Hitler's Reich, including chemical and armaments factories, petroleum refineries, steelworks, coal mines, bridges, road and rail links, marshalling yards and harbours.[36] However, they were initially reluctant to implement their grand plan for fear of provoking massive German reprisals. (It is worth noting here that the bombardment of London on 7 September 1940 might well have been in retaliation for an RAF raid on Berlin that had itself been precipitated by an earlier, unintentional German attack on the UK's capital.) The war's opening campaigns then confirmed what had been widely suspected, namely that, if opposed by sufficient high-performance fighters, diurnal raids by bombers at or beyond the reach of any escort was too hazardous a venture. Accordingly, when, in a desperate reaction to France's incipient fall, the RAF's Bomber Command had finally intensified its operations, it had launched its assaults under the cover of night.

While this made it harder for the German air defences to locate and destroy the attacking squadrons, it made it equally difficult for the latter to descry their objectives. 'Black-out' measures, designed to prevent even the tiniest shaft of artificial light being glimpsed from above, compounded this problem. Even when the raiders could find the target, flak and fighter attacks often drove them off it, vitiating any attempt at accurate bombing. A survey undertaken in the summer of 1941 by D. M. Butt, a member of the British Cabinet's secretariat, highlighted the consequences. Having scrutinized 633 damage-assessment photographs, he concluded that only 4,065 of the 6,103 sorties mounted against 28 selected targets actually bombed them. Furthermore, just one in every three of the aircraft that did reach their proper destinations and attacked them managed to drop their payloads within 5 miles (8 km) of the designated aiming point. So far as targets within the Ruhr area were concerned, moreover, this figure slumped to only one bomber in ten, for here the effects of darkness were frequently compounded by industrial haze.[37]

All of this meant that the precision bombing originally envisaged by the RAF was not practicable with the available technology. Striking relatively small, discrete targets was a matter more of luck than design, leaving the area bombing of comparatively large ones, notably urban centres, as the only feasible tactic. Charles Portal, who became CAS in October 1940, sensed this long before the Butt Report was compiled. He began overhauling the RAF's strategic thinking while simultaneously initiating improvements to its operational capabilities. Bigger and better bombs and aircraft were devised, and the development of new navigational aids and specialist 'pathfinder' units to locate and illuminate targets began in earnest. These various projects came to fruition under Arthur Harris, whom Portal appointed as the head of Bomber Command early in 1942. During that year, more trained crews and some 2,000 heavy bombers, among them 178 Lancasters, were added to the RAF's order of battle, enabling far greater tonnages of high explosive and incendiaries to be carried further afield and disgorged on a selected target. The B-17G Flying Fortresses of the USAAF's Eighth Air

Force, under Carl Spaatz and Ira Eaker, also began to arrive in the UK that summer. Particularly if deployed in large, tight formations, these sturdy, high-flying bombers, which bristled with machine guns, would fend off all but the heaviest of fighter attacks, Spaatz and Eaker reasoned. The B-17 was thus ideal for daytime operations against discrete targets, during which, it was believed, it would be able to make optimum use of the Norden bomb-sight, an instrument that the Americans were reluctant to share with the RAF.

Whereas Mitchell had envisaged the obliteration of an adversary's population and industrial centres through indiscriminate area bombing, the official doctrine evolved by the US Air Corps Tactical School during the inter-war period favoured thoughtful, pinpoint targeting as a relatively painless way of inducing economic and societal collapse.[38] In fact, Eaker himself, together with his commanding general Henry Arnold, had just completed writing a book on this theme and related matters.[39] As late as the summer of 1943, this approach was still being presented to wider American society as the key to success, notably in an animated film produced by Walt Disney. The cartoon was based on, and named after, a recent theoretical work by Alexander de Seversky, *Victory through Air Power*. It encapsulated the author's basic contention, that the morale of the enemy's population could be undermined

> by destroying effectively the essentials of their lives – the supply of food, shelter, light, water, sanitation, and the rest. . . . Bombardment from on high must fit strictly to the pattern of aerial blockade, systematically wrecking the implements and channels of normal life until a complete breakdown of the will . . . and the ability to fight is accomplished.[40]

Cinema audiences were evidently delighted by the spectacle of swarms of bombers methodically crippling the German, Italian and Japanese economies, particularly since all this mayhem was inflicted without any casualties being incurred on either side. Indubitably, popular acclaim secured Seversky a place in the pantheon of military theorists, allowing him to enjoy appreciable influence until his death in 1974. Yet this was rather undeserved. His underlying thesis – that air power now constituted the dominant form of military might – was hardly original, while his vision of 'aerial blockade' bore little resemblance to the realities of strategic bombing, as so many American aviators were finding to their cost.

Indeed, the Eighth Air Force's confidence in its own technological and doctrinal superiority was to be badly shaken within a few months of its first being ordered into action, particularly when the B-17s ventured far beyond the reach of UK-based escorts to assail targets deep in Germany, most notably Schweinfurt. Of the 291 planes that set out for that town on 14 October 1943, 60 were shot down and 142 damaged. Losses like these were unsustainable, and the Americans had to suspend their plans for further deep-penetration, daytime assaults.[41] In the interim, having exponentially increased its capacity for concentrating firepower, the RAF had been able to start a sequence of strategic attacks that grew in scale and intensity. Lübeck and Rostock – coastal towns that were relatively close at hand and easy to find – were Harris's first victims. However, as the British developed electronic navigational devices to rival Knickebein, the mounting of nocturnal raids well inside Germany became a more viable proposition.

The first such apparatus, which came into service early in 1942, was Gee. This enabled an aircraft to calculate its bearings with the aid of a matrix of emissions generated by three transmitters in England. Since dependability varied inversely with distance, the British, obliged to venture further from home, enjoyed less success with this method than the Luftwaffe had achieved with Knickebein when attacking the UK; the propinquity of their facilities in occupied Europe bestowed a significant advantage on the Germans in this regard. Still, there was an appreciable improvement in bombing accuracy until they resorted to jamming Gee's transmissions. By early 1943 the RAF, however, had acquired a new navigational system that was far harder to interfere with. Known as 'Oboe' because its sound was redolent of that of the musical instrument, this used two overlapping radar arcs that, emitted by ground stations in the UK, could reach as far as the 'horizon' formed by the curvature of the Earth, a maximum distance of some 280 miles (450 km). The first arc dissected the target, enabling the intervening range to be calculated with a high degree of accuracy. Constantly vectored by means of compact, on-board sensors that received, amplified and returned the pulses to the transmitters, a Wellington, Stirling or Mosquito 'pathfinder' could be guided along this arc, the bombers following in its wake. Meanwhile, the second radar beam monitored the leading plane's progress along the arc until the objective was reached. A signal to release the bombs was then sent. The later American Shoran and the British Gee-H systems worked on the same principle, but with the transmissions originating from the aircraft, each of which also made its own flight-control computations. Having only to echo their respective pulses, the surface stations could thus simultaneously interact with numerous planes.

In 1943 the Germans established Sonne, a powerful transmitter network sited along the littoral promontories of occupied Europe. This generated an elaborate web of low-frequency emissions that extended up to 1,000 miles (1,600 km) and could be detected by standard communication receivers. When used in conjunction with special maps, the pulses from the ground stations confirmed the current position of ships or aircraft with a high degree of accuracy. The envious Allies copied this simple but ingenious methodology, the RAF replicating the German maps from captured specimens. The Consol system, as it was known, proved invaluable to the planes of Coastal Command in particular.

However, as the radar 'horizon' ineluctably constrained the utility of devices that were at all reliant upon ground hubs, interest in developing self-contained, airborne systems steadily increased. By 1943 RAF Bomber Command was using a ground-scanning, centimetric set, the H2S, the quality of which was incrementally refined as the war progressed. The echoes from this apparatus were displayed on a cathode-ray screen and could be viewed alongside printed maps. The clarity of the signals varied with the topography, the faintest echoes being generated by stretches of water and open countryside, while the strongest came from built-up areas. The British shared this new technology with their American allies, who went on to develop both their own version of the H2S, the H2X, and the APS-20, the most sophisticated terrain-mapping radar of this era, with which the USAAF equipped its B-29 Superfortress bomber. Likewise, airborne jamming devices were developed to neutralize the Axis powers' electronic detection and targeting systems. As well as installing one by the name of 'Mandrel' in its bombers, in 1944 the RAF established 100 Group, a unit equipped with a variety of aircraft that were specially adapted for electronic warfare assignments. Some of its Mosquito fighters, for instance, were fitted with an apparatus known as 'Serrate', which could lock on to the emissions from the radars aboard enemy night fighters. Others were furnished with 'Perfectos'. This devious machine got a 'fix' on German interceptors by tapping into the pulses from the transponders that they relied on to distinguish friendly from hostile planes. Similarly, the USAAF's attacks on Japanese targets were increasingly screened by 'Porcupines', B-29s that were packed with assorted jamming devices.

One of the simplest but most effective of these was metallic chaff, which, when released into the atmosphere, gently drifted earthwards, generating thousands of false echoes on any snooping radar. The British, who dubbed these bits of metallic foil 'Window', first used them during the massive, nocturnal attacks launched against Hamburg at the end of July 1943. In addition to two daylight raids mounted by American aircraft, RAF bombers made more than 3,000 sorties against this great port and industrial centre, with many of the planes discharging large quantities of chaff as well as their payloads of incendiaries and high-explosive bombs. Although the city had seemed well protected by artillery batteries and fighters, largely because of 'Window' its defences were overwhelmed. Casualties among the attacking RAF squadrons were some 75 per cent below average; only a dozen of the 746 planes committed on 25 July, for example, were lost. By contrast, Hamburg and its inhabitants suffered immensely. The incendiaries kindled countless separate blazes that, sucking in air at ever-greater speeds and spreading sparks in all directions, rapidly coalesced into a single inferno. Around 8 square miles (20 sq. km) – roughly half – of the city were eventually engulfed by a *Feuersturm*. Its hurricane-force winds and temperatures of several hundred degrees centigrade devoured everything in their path. With the fire brigade left virtually powerless, nearly 600 industrial, petroleum and armaments plants were destroyed or damaged, while 45,000 people perished in the conflagration. Most of the survivors had to be evacuated.[42]

Harris – less so Spaatz, oddly enough – has since been subjected to much bitter criticism for ordering such indiscriminate, area-bombing raids, but it was a policy that he inherited and to which there was no operationally viable alternative. While, unlike some of his political masters and military colleagues, he doubted that the Germans' morale would collapse under aerial bombardment, he realized that their industrial base and communications network would have to be destroyed if the war were to be won. Although this ineluctably demanded the infliction of death, injury and terror on civilians, including those under Nazi occupation and the 150,000 Germans who suffered imprisonment – or worse – for political dissension,[43] it also called for immense courage and sacrifices on the part of the aviators involved. In their celebrated foray against the Ruhr's Sorpe, Eder and Möhne dams in May 1943, for example, perhaps the most demanding precision attack of the entire war, Guy Gibson's elite 617 Squadron lost eight out of the nineteen Lancasters that were committed to the raid.[44] In all, nearly 56,000 men in the RAF's Bomber Command were killed, while their valiant comrades in the USAAF's Eighth Air Force sustained more than 45,000 casualties. In any case, historical events have to be viewed in context, including the *mentalité* that prevailed at the time. To apply the liberal values to which some people in 2003 subscribe to events that occurred in the midst of a 'total' conflict in 1943 is questionable, intellectually and otherwise.

Above all, aerial bombardment was a military and political imperative. Imperfect and unpalatable though the policy might have been, for much of the war's opening phase the British and Americans had little else with which to strike and distract Hitler's Reich and, thereby, do something to assist the USSR to evade subjugation. For all their efforts, the brave members of the various Continental resistance movements – many of whom were as dependent on the RAF's drops of weapons and other basic equipment as the secret agents of the Special Operations Executive (SOE) were reliant on it for their insertion and retrieval – could do little more than irritate the occupying powers. Bombing alone offered some hope of inflicting real harm, even if the prospects of doing so were not all that good.[45]

This was partly because Germany's war machine was, to begin with, capable of absorbing quite a lot of damage. With most of occupied

Europe's resources at her disposal, including seven million slave labourers, the strain on her economy did not come to rival that on the UK's until as late as 1942. Consequently, her industry was, initially at least, less susceptible to disruption than some disciples of Douhet were tempted to believe. Nevertheless, the strategic bombing offensive eventually did immense damage, slashing her productivity. Moreover, it compelled Germany, the linchpin of the Axis, to divert an ever-greater proportion of her available *matériel* and some two million people into either passive or active air defence and, to keep her industries and transport web functioning, clean-up and repair assignments.

For instance, during the period 1942–4 Germany had to accentuate the manufacturing of fighters rather than bombers, with the latter declining from over half of all the aircraft produced to less than one in five. This severely truncated the close support that the air force could furnish the German armies, not least in offensive operations on the Russian front.[46] Furthermore, by the end of 1943, no fewer than 70 per cent of the Luftwaffe's fighter squadrons were tied up in air-defence operations in the Western theatre, as were more than 55,000 guns and their crews. Among the latter were 75 per cent of the disposable Krupps 88-millimetre artillery pieces that were also the deadliest anti-tank cannons that the Germans possessed.[47] By 1944 a third of all gun and a fifth of all ammunition production was being devoured by air defence, as was a third of the total output of optics and perhaps two-thirds of all the radar and other electrical equipment that was being manufactured.[48]

Indeed, the Germans made considerable use of electronic detection and warfare devices in their endeavours to thwart the Allied bombing raids, particularly the nocturnal attacks of the RAF. After having tried, albeit with negligible success, to jam the Chain Home during the Battle of Britain, they established their own early warning system, the so-called Kammhuber Line, the sophistication and extent of which were gradually increased. This divided the skies over the northern reaches of 'Fortress Europe' into sectors, each of which was patrolled by interceptors that were guided by ground-based radars and controllers. Blinded by 'Window', it failed disastrously during the Hamburg raid, prompting the adoption of new procedures. *Wilde Sau*, as the latest tactics were known, gave night fighters the liberty to roam at will over a town that was under attack. Keeping above a stipulated altitude to avoid their own AA batteries' salvoes, they engaged bombers that were revealed by searchlights or flares, or that were silhouetted against the glow of blazing buildings.

This approach was superseded by *Zahme Sau*, a tactical methodology that was introduced in the winter of 1943. At its heart was a new airborne radar, the SN-2, a device that could be fitted into two-engined fighters and was not duped by ordinary chaff. Again, ground monitors provided the interceptors with a running commentary on the bombers' broad movements, but now they were assailed on their way to and from the target, the fighters using the radar to close in on their quarry. Casualties began to mount. Out of the 795 aircraft that raided Nuremberg on the night of 30 March 1944, for example, 94 were lost.[49] It was only with the fortuitous capture of an intact SN-2 that the Allies uncovered its inability to cope with the 'clutter' caused by 'Rope' – long coils of metallic foil that unravelled as they descended – and thereby found a way of countering the Luftwaffe's latest stratagem. Indeed, it was not until this stage that they finally secured enduring advantages in the wider electronic war.

But defeating the resilient Germans was seldom easy, not least because of the ingenuity of their scientists, engineers and technicians. By mid-1944 they were ready to unleash some revolutionary armaments that they had been perfecting and stockpiling for some time. With the unveiling of this technology, a new era would be ushered in: the space age.

Chapter 2

The Aerospace Era, 1943–2003

On 18 June 1940 Winston Churchill told the House of Commons:

> The Battle of France is over. I expect that . . . [for] Britain is about
> to begin. Upon this . . . depends the survival of Christian
> civilization. . . . The whole . . . might of the enemy must very
> soon be turned on us. Hitler knows that he will have to break us
> in this island or lose the war. If we can stand up to him all
> Europe may be free, and the life of the world will move forward
> into broad, sunlit uplands; but if we fail, then the whole world,
> including the United States and all that we have known and
> cared for, will sink into the abyss of a new dark age made more
> sinister, and perhaps more prolonged, by . . . a perverted
> science.[1]

These words proved remarkably prophetic. By thwarting the
Luftwaffe in the Battle of Britain, the RAF saved the UK from immediate
invasion. Although this was an essential precondition for the general
victory that Churchill, in his very first parliamentary statement as
Prime Minister, had specified was Britain's ultimate war aim,[2] it
was not a sufficient one. Without control of the Atlantic and
Mediterranean sea lanes, even her continued independence remained
in doubt, while, for all his bravura, Churchill himself acknowledged
that she needed new allies. As early as 4 June he was anticipating
that:

We shall defend our island, whatever the cost may be. We shall . . . never surrender, and even if this island or a large part of it were subjugated and starving, then our Empire beyond the seas, armed and guarded by the British Fleet, would carry on the struggle, until . . . the new world, with all its power and might, steps forth to the liberation of the old.[3]

With most of the Continent either overrun by German and Italian forces or facing imminent conquest, Britain and her Commonwealth partners were simply not strong enough to challenge the hold that the Axis powers had acquired over so much of mainland Europe and North Africa. Indeed, fearful that the strong French flotillas based at Mers-el-Kébir, Oran and Dakar might fall into hostile hands, during July 1940 Churchill ruthlessly authorized British warships and planes from the carrier *Ark Royal* to destroy them. Disarming such potential enemies was no less essential than the securing of new allies. Yet where were the latter to be found? At this juncture, the USSR was still colluding with the Nazis, while Japan was preparing to join the Axis. Above all, the USA, the world's most powerful liberal democracy, was not destined to enter the war formally for another eighteen months. She was, however, gradually being embroiled in active efforts to preserve the principle of free navigation across the Atlantic. This was to ease the burden on the British, whose homeland would have to host any American forces committed to operations in Europe and whose global network of outposts would be invaluable for supporting military ventures elsewhere.

Despatched on 15 May 1940, as the British Expeditionary Force (BEF) was being pushed into retreat for Dunkirk, the first telegram sent to President Roosevelt by Churchill on becoming premier had included a plea for 40 or 50 old destroyers to enable the UK to ward off the threat of invasion from mainland Europe and to prosecute the Battle of the Atlantic. Ten days later, as the evacuation of the BEF began, Britain's chiefs of staff concluded that any future hopes of victory rested on the UK enjoying 'the full economic and financial support of the United States, . . . possibly extending to active participation on our side'.[4] However, gripped by isolationist sentiments and officially neutral until after the Japanese attacked Pearl Harbor and Italy and Germany declared war upon her in December 1941, the USA was initially constrained in the development of her partnership with Britain. Still, eager to aid a fellow democracy to which America had very strong historical and cultural ties and with which she had overlapping strategic interests, Roosevelt sought to bolster the UK's resistance to the Axis powers by all means short of going to war. From 1940 onwards he expanded America's own defensive capabilities in a radical fashion, but still hoped to leave any actual fighting to the British. Endeavouring to make the USA into 'the great arsenal of democracy', he strove to mitigate the impact of the Neutrality Acts of 1935–7 with new legislation in 1939 and 1941, including the Lend-Lease Act that he was to endorse in March 1941. Nominated for a third term of office in July 1940 and convinced of the UK's determination to fight on, first by the Royal Navy's pitiless destruction of the wavering French fleet at Mers-el-Kébir and then by the Battle of Britain, Roosevelt was politically stronger and more determined than ever. Nevertheless, because of legal constraints and Congressional sensitivities, he was not at liberty simply to transfer even ageing warships to the UK. Rather, an exchange took place, whereby the latter began receiving the destroyers while the US secured 99-year leases for air and naval bases in the British West Indies, Newfoundland and Bermuda.

Concluded on 2 September 1940, this deal was an implicit acknowledgement by the Americans that the Royal Navy in particular and Britain's armed forces in general formed the USA's first line of defence, certainly on her eastern flank. Conversely, the allocation to the US of military outposts on the British territories bordering the western Atlantic constituted recognition by London that these facilities comprised 'the inner circle of American defence'.[5] It was not, as we shall see, the last time that the UK was to use bases over which she enjoyed sovereignty as an important bargaining chip in her wider dealings with the USA. As Washington came to appreciate in the course of both the Second World War and the subsequent Cold War, in the age of the aircraft even more than that of the ship, Britain's own geographical position was an immensely advantageous one when it came to dealing with opponents on the Eurasian landmass in particular. If, so far as this region was concerned, the UK was 'Airstrip One' – as so many American servicemen and women dubbed her – then some of her overseas possessions were scarcely of less importance for the domination of other parts of the globe. Indeed, her empire had been founded on an enormous network of choke points, islands and other strategically important outposts, from which both access to the various continents and their surrounding seas could be controlled and potential or actual adversaries confronted. Hitler, who was never much of a strategist, blundered badly when he failed to subordinate all else to the subjugation of Britain. He too readily accepted the outcome of the Battle of Britain and then allowed that campaign to degenerate into the Blitz, which was never likely to cow such resolute opponents. Indeed, he regarded its last raids as little more than a diversion for his impending invasion of the USSR. This assault was to compound his earlier error, exposing Germany to a struggle on two fronts and to a string of catastrophic defeats that, beginning with Stalingrad, helped to turn Churchill's triumphal vision of June 1940 into reality.

During 1942, just as her quest for more mineral wealth began to draw Japan's armies from Malaya into Burma, so too a large part of the German forces within the USSR started gravitating towards the Caucasian oilfields. Accounting as they did for two-thirds of Soviet output, control of these was as much an imperative for the Russians as it was a tantalizing prospect for the invaders. Indeed, the debacle of Stalingrad had its origins in the latter's broader attempts to seize them.

Having captured Rostov, gateway to the Caucasus, by the end of July 1942, Axis units were thrusting both southwards towards Chechnya and eastwards towards the Volga. Stretching for some 25 miles (40 km) along the bluffs on the left bank of that mighty river, Stalingrad – now Volgograd – soon came under attack from elements of the battle-hardened German Sixth Army and Fourth Panzer Army commanded by Friedrich Paulus. On 23 August the Luftwaffe also joined in the assault, committing every plane available on the Russian front to bombing raids that went on for three days. A second spate of intensive, aerial bombardment followed in mid-October, reducing much of what remained of the city to rubble. However, as was to prove the case with the vast Benedictine abbey overlooking Cassino during the fighting in

Italy in early 1944, it was found that the ruins, debris and numerous bomb craters lent themselves to defence in a battle that was in any case very different from the mercurial *Blitzkrieg* to which the German forces were both accustomed and geared. Try as it might, Paulus's army group, which lacked sufficient armoured and artillery units, could not overwhelm the resolute garrison, who, disputing every inch of the rambling town, were increasingly aided by the vanquisher of Napoleon's Grande Armée, 'General Winter'. Worse still, on 19 November the besiegers fell victim to a Russian pincer manoeuvre that was as massive as it was unforeseen. Crushing the poorly armed and weakly motivated Hungarian, Italian and Romanian forces that guarded Paulus's flanks, its jaws closed around him three days later, trapping some 240,000 Axis troops with as few as 100 serviceable tanks and 1,800 guns among them.

Until other ground forces could break through to assist the belea-guered army, Hermann Goering, the Luftwaffe's Commander-in-Chief, thought he could sustain it by means of an air-bridge. He calculated that, weather permitting, and providing that bombers were used to supplement the available transporters, 300 tonnes of food, ammu-nition, medical supplies, petroleum products, clothing and other necessities might be ferried in each day. Hitler thought that this would suffice, although the encircled twenty divisions actually needed at least 800 tonnes. In practice, a combination of atrocious weather conditions, including surface temperatures of minus 30° Celsius and lower, feeble escorts, long distances – which grew as the Red Army continued to push westwards while simultaneously squeezing the perimeter held by the trapped soldiers – and numerous enemy fighters and AA batteries meant that an average of just 80 tonnes per day got through. By this stage in the war, the Luftwaffe's units in the Eastern theatre were down to a quarter of their official strength, with many aircraft grounded through shortages of fuel, lubricants, spares, technicians and experienced pilots. There were, for instance, fewer than 400 fighters on the entire Russian front, and many of these were inoperable. Their adversaries, by contrast, had amassed 1,400 planes around Stalingrad alone, among them squadrons of new Lavochkin La-7s and Yakolev Yak-9DS, with which they could counter the fearsome Messerschmitts.

Belated though their introduction was, wider and better use of radio links also enabled the Russians to concentrate and direct their air power rather more effectively than in past campaigns.[6] Certainly, the transporters trying to breach the Stalingrad blockade suffered heavily as a result of inadequate protection and the hostile elements, 488 planes and twice as many crewmen being lost in seven weeks. Whereas some 30,000 wounded and sick Axis soldiers were evacuated before the last airstrip was overrun by Soviet troops in mid-January, thereafter such supplies as did arrive had to be dropped by parachute, a somewhat unpredictable process. Many cargoes inevitably fell into Russian hands. The plans to relieve Paulus by land also proved impracticable and, on 31 January 1943, he formally surrendered all those men in his immediate vicinity who had not yet perished from cold, hunger or wounds. The one remaining sizeable pocket of Germans – some six divisions – clung on for another day.

Axis losses at Stalingrad were immense. The prisoners alone included a field marshal, 24 generals, 2,000 officers and 110,000 other ranks. Enough *matériel* to equip a quarter of Germany's entire army was also destroyed or captured, while the Italian, Romanian and Hungarian contingents in Paulus's force were virtually annihilated.[7] Moreover, the defeat's psychological, moral and political ramifications were every bit as serious as its strategic consequences. The Red Army's burgeoning physical strength and fighting spirit had been amply demonstrated, as had its growing operational effectiveness. Containing, never mind defeating, it threatened to prove ever more difficult. Indeed, most of Hitler's Eastern front was now in jeopardy, not least because, having lost 155,000 troops at Stalingrad, a quarter of all their men in the USSR, the Romanians had concluded that the Axis could not win the war. In August 1943 they turned on their erstwhile partners, exposing the whole of south-eastern Europe to Russian invasion and endangering Germany's only source of natural oil.

The catastrophe at Stalingrad also came hard on the heels of another grave setback for the Axis powers. In September 1942 Field Marshal Erwin Rommel had been thwarted in his latest bid to penetrate into Egypt at Alam Halfa, not least because of the skilful coordination of the opposing British land and air units, the latter of which now contained numerous Spitfires and other fighters capable of outmanoeuvring and outgunning the Messerschmitt 109F. The 'Desert Fox' had then been assailed by General Montgomery's forces at El Alamein and thrust back through Libya. By the time of Paulus's surrender at Stalingrad, the Afrika Korps was withdrawing into Tunisia. Rommel himself returned home on sick leave early in March 1943. His soldiers, however, hemmed in by advancing armies along a coastline that was blockaded by enemy ships, submarines and planes, could no more escape entrapment than they could the searing heat and countless flies. Nor had they any hope of reinforcements or supplies. By mid-May it was all over. The 238,000 men that had survived the hammering administered by the Allies' guns and aircraft capitulated.

It was a victory that bore comparison with Stalingrad and which left the Western Allies in uncontested possession of numerous ports and airfields along the African littoral. Malta, too, was still in their hands. Only 60 miles (97 km) from Sicily, the island had endured repeated bombing raids since it was first assailed by Italian planes in June 1940. Bolstered by Luftwaffe units, the attacks had escalated in the opening months of 1941 before the demands imposed by Hitler's invasion of Russia reduced their scale. In December, however, the raids resumed with increased ferocity. Indeed, between 1 January and 24 July 1942, only one period of 24 hours passed without an attack occurring, while the tonnage of bombs dropped on Malta was more than double that which had ravaged London during the Blitz. The maritime convoys on which Malta's survival depended were severely mauled as well, with U-boats, minefields and planes taking a heavy toll of Allied merchantmen and their escorts. Among the latter were carriers, fighters from which sought to reinforce the handful of aircraft and AA guns at the garrison's disposal. Many of these new machines were destroyed on the ground as soon as they landed, but the safe arrival of 61 Spitfires redressed the balance somewhat. Simultaneously, the Luftwaffe's mounting commitments elsewhere granted the defenders some respite. When in October 1942 the mass attacks began afresh, they were able to withstand them.[8]

Following the annihilation of the Afrika Korps in May 1943, the Allies began to stage sorties from their Mediterranean airstrips against

Italy. Somewhat ironically, Douhet's homeland was poorly prepared to impede them. With neither active nor passive defences worth mentioning, the peninsula's industrial and population centres fell victim to both diurnal and nocturnal raids by RAF bombers. As the inhabitants took refuge in the surrounding countryside, output plummeted by 60 per cent. This, together with major strikes in Milan and Turin, crippled both the war effort and the wider economy, which helped to bring about Mussolini's fall in July 1943 and his country's descent into civil war a few weeks later.[9] Although the Nazis subsequently proclaimed the ailing Duce head of the Italian Social Republic (ISR) – a puppet polity that was intended to underscore the Axis's continuity and legitimize the German occupation of the peninsula, which culminated in parts of it being annexed by the Reich – he never enjoyed real influence again. Neither could Hitler protect him when both his own regime and the ISR collapsed. Along with other prominent Fascists, Mussolini was condemned by the government that eventually arose from the Committees for National Liberation. Accordingly, he was shot by the partisans who captured him in April 1945.

Part of the crisis that first toppled him was the invasion of Sicily by British and American forces in July 1943. This included the first of several grand airborne operations that the Western Allies were to undertake over the next two years. Whether dropped by parachute from suitable aircraft or landed in gliders that were towed to within reach of their objective by sufficiently powerful planes, airborne units could be inserted silently behind enemy lines. Whereas parachutists were likely to be scattered by the prevailing wind but could land almost anywhere, gliders could, at worst, belly-flop on to any sufficiently uncluttered terrain, facilitating the concentration of a body of men at a given point. Most models were spacious enough to accommodate at least 25 soldiers with all their kit, or a light vehicle or two. Equipped with the usual shoulder arms and, perhaps, a few heavier but nonetheless man-portable weapons – such as mortars and heavy machine guns – and small vehicles, notably jeeps, airborne troops were essentially infantry. Although ideal for administering cursory, surprise attacks, they lacked the means to wage pitched battles, not merely because of their meagre firepower but also owing to their limited logistical sustainability. The Germans used gliders extensively and imaginatively in the war's early stages, their Fallschirmjäger being employed for dramatic coups against vulnerable targets in Norway, Denmark and, above all, Belgium, where, as well as crucial bridges over the Meuse, they captured the seemingly impregnable fortress of Eben Emael by alighting on its roof. Had Hitler ever implemented Operation 'Sea-lion' in 1940, this would also have included landings around London and behind Dover Castle.

His invasion of Crete in May 1941, however, proved a turning-point. Here, as an opening move, the Fliegerkorps were called upon to assault and capture the airstrips at Heraklion, Réthimnon and Máleme so that reinforcements could be rushed in. Although these were not as heavily protected as they might have been, the lightly equipped Fallschirmjäger were aghast to find them held in some strength. They suffered very heavy casualties, 25 per cent in all, mostly at the first two aerodromes, which they assailed to no avail. Máleme's relatively few defenders, by contrast, were overwhelmed, enabling the Germans to bring in fresh troops. They eventually dislodged the remaining Allied garrisons, the remnants of which were evacuated by the Royal Navy. Subjected to escalating aerial bombardment, three cruisers and six destroyers were sunk and seventeen other vessels were damaged.[10]

In addition to underscoring the vulnerability of maritime forces to attack by land-based aviation, the battle for Crete also highlighted the inherent limitations of airborne troops. Horrified by their losses, never again would the Germans risk their Fallschirmjäger in a major contested landing. During the invasion of Sicily, on the other hand, their Allied counterparts sustained comparatively few casualties as a result of enemy action. Thanks to a combination of good intelligence and successful deception schemes, their drop zones were mostly free of hostile units that might have challenged their insertion; the enemy's air power was effectively neutralized; the two airborne divisions that began the assault were numerically strong enough to overcome any immediate resistance; and the main invasion force, covered by naval gunfire, disembarked promptly and smoothly enough to give them timely support. Indeed, opposition to the airborne units came principally from the vile weather. Adverse winds led to just 54 out of one British brigade's 144 gliders actually landing on terra firma. The rest ditched in the Mediterranean, drowning many of their occupants.[11]

From Sicily, the Americans and British moved against the Italian mainland, landing on its 'toe'. The caretaker administration that was formally recognized by the Allies was eager to join them and promptly negotiated Italy's surrender. In the interim, however, the Germans deployed sixteen divisions to disarm their erstwhile partners and parry the Allies' anticipated thrust up the peninsula, the spine of which comprised easily defensible countryside. This was a very different environment from the sprawling, mostly uninhabited deserts of North Africa, where armies seldom found naturally strong positions that could not be turned by armoured and mechanized units, and where fighter-bombers might pound anything that they caught out in the open. The rocky uplands not only provided the Germans with cover and good fields of fire and observation, but also funnelled their opponents' advance into the narrow valleys and coastal plains where it was easily checked. In this war of positions rather than manoeuvre, progress was painfully slow. Although the Allies secured air supremacy within a month, amidst the dreadful weather and mountainous terrain, with its soaring peaks and low cloud, they were unable to make it tell. Coordinating surface and aerial attacks proved particularly difficult, not least at Cassino. In fact, it was not until June 1944 that the German lines were breached and Rome taken.

Eight months before these events, the Fifteenth USAAF was established in Italy. Aided by 205 Group, RAF, it carried out Operation 'Strangle' – a series of raids against the German lines of supply and communication – as well as the razing of the great monastery at Cassino and other 'tactical' assignments. However, it mostly inflicted blows on strategic targets in the ISR and the Balkans, notably the Ploesti oilfields in Romania, which were well protected, not least by mountain chains and their remoteness. The Americans lost 350 heavy bombers here alone. There were forays into France, too, the northern and western reaches of which had long since been subject to Allied aerial attacks. In late 1942 and early 1943 the U-boats' pens at Brest, Lorient,

Saint-Nazaire and La Pallice had, for instance, been bombed heavily and repeatedly, but to little avail. Mostly housed in deep, virtually impenetrable bunkers, the submarines and their repair and replenishment complexes remained largely unscathed, whereas the surrounding towns were ravaged by explosions and fires. Indeed, these raids highlighted a moral dilemma that confronted the strategic planners. If causing deaths and injuries among civilians of the Axis states was disagreeable, killing those in occupied countries was as repugnant as it was politically counterproductive. Bombing seemingly discrete military targets was entirely justifiable and conformed with well-intentioned directives to avoid – or at worst minimize – what nowadays is often termed 'collateral damage'.[12] Yet, even if technological constraints and the laws of physics had not made the fulfilment of such expectations impracticable, the inability to discriminate between belligerents and non-belligerents in a 'total' war would have done so. Disentangling the military and civil sectors of a developed economic and social system was no more feasible in the 1940s than it is today. These particular raids were, after all, mounted in a bid to help stop the pitiless sinking of the merchantmen on which the survival of not just Britain's war effort but also so much of her population depended.

The activation of the Fifteenth USAAF and the growth of the Eighth and Ninth in the UK testified to the burgeoning strength of America's air power under Henry 'Hap[py]' Arnold. With him as commanding general, her air force expanded in a few years from 20,000 personnel with a few hundred planes to 2,400,000 with 80,000 modern machines. On New Year's Day 1944 he told his principal subordinates in Europe: 'My personal message to you – this is a MUST – is to, "*Destroy the enemy Air Force wherever you find them in the air, on the ground and in the factories.*"'[13] By this juncture, the Russians had gained air superiority on the Eastern front, and Carl Spaatz had already identified control of the skies as the key to winning the war in the West. During a period when the Luftwaffe's receipt of new and replacement fighters was slackening, the numbers attached to the Eighth USAAF quadrupled. Fitted with drop tanks to extend their reach, P-47D Thunderbolts, Lightnings and, as they came into service, P-51B Mustangs – the most formidable of all – were dispatched en masse to embroil the Germans' interceptors in an attritional battle they could scarcely hope to sustain. In November and December 1943 it claimed, respectively, 21 and 23 per cent of the Luftwaffe's pilots. By the spring, half of its remaining fighters and a quarter of its pilots were being lost each month.[14] As its ability to counter diurnal raids steadily diminished and the winter weather began to abate, the Allies' bombers joined the fray. Constantly protected by squadrons of Mustangs, the B-17s of the 'Mighty Eighth' resumed their campaign against targets deep in Germany. Their gambit was the so-called Big Week in February 1944, when, in round-the-clock forays, more than 6,000 British and US bombers deluged fighter production lines and related industrial plants with some 20,300 tonnes of bombs. Although the Americans lost 254 planes in this operation, among them 28 escorts, and Bomber Command – still molested by German night fighters that were guided by SN-2 airborne radars – lost 157 aircraft, the tactics were working: Luftwaffe casualties in the dogfights were crippling, and the bombing set back Germany's output of interceptors by two months.

The British had often been anxious to threaten a variety of targets if only to stop the Luftwaffe concentrating its defensive resources. From mid-November 1943 until the end of the following March, however, 9,000 of the RAF's 20,000 strategic sorties were executed against Berlin. Tremendous destruction was wrought, but at a cost of 1,047 planes lost and 1,682 damaged, many irreparably, the victims of long, perilous flights and the Germans' *Zahme Sau* tactics. Since Bomber Command's front-line strength averaged 900 planes, such casualties were prohibitive; just as the Mustang was turning the tide of the daytime battle in the Americans' favour, the campaign against the capital of the Reich had to be suspended.[15] For all the physical damage that they inflicted, the costly raids did not demoralize the Berliners any more than they had the inhabitants of other towns. On the contrary, the common threat they posed drove classes and communities together. Bombs could and did not distinguish between Nazis and non-Nazis; between rich and poor; between those who persecuted and those who aided Jews; and between those who wanted the war to end and those who, if only because they were more fearful of the Allies' demand for their unconditional surrender, did not. The banners that festooned

Germany's ruined cities on Hitler's birthday spoke volumes: *Unsere Mauern brechen – aber unsere Herzen nicht* ('Our walls are breaking, but not our hearts').

At this juncture, there was in any case some disagreement within the Allied high command as to what targets the strategic air offensive should focus on. Harris persisted in arguing for more area bombing, whereas Portal favoured the obliteration of Germany's petrochemical industry through 'pinpoint' attacks. By contrast, Air Chief Marshal Sir Arthur Tedder – deputy to the Supreme Commander, General Eisenhower – wanted the demolition of crucial transport links in France to be given precedence in preparation for the impending 'D-Day' invasion, Operation 'Overlord'.

Their quest for a compromise that adequately satisfied these competing demands was eased by the remorseless annihilation of the German aeroplane industry and of the Luftwaffe's material assets and air-crews. Confronted by diminishing numbers of night fighters and having identified countermeasures to the SN-2 radar, on which *Zahme Sau* relied, Bomber Command gradually built up its squadrons, refining their tactics and increasing the sophistication of their equipment. By September 1944 its front line comprised more than 1,000 machines, predominantly Lancasters, which were backed up by increasingly dependable navigational and targeting aids. All of this endowed the British with an unprecedented capacity for inflicting destruction through both precision and area bombing at a time when, with resistance and loss rates declining, raids were already becoming appreciably more cost-effective. The RAF's continuing partnership with the Eighth USAAF not only caused serious fuel shortages that hamstrung, among many other things, the Germans' armoured and mechanized units as well as their military aviation, but was also to leave yet more of their cities in ashes, notably Dresden, the heart of which was incinerated in February 1945.[16]

In addition, heavy bombers made a substantial contribution to the preparations for 'Overlord', as did the Allies' tactical air forces, which also lightened the workload of the B-17s and Lancasters by eliminating numerous 'strategic' targets with precision – rather than saturation – bombing. Between 1 April 1944 and 'D-Day', 6 June, 11,000 planes flew more than 200,000 sorties in support of the impending invasion, dropping 195,000 tonnes of bombs on coastal fortifications, gun batteries, radars, aerodromes, supply dumps, road and rail bottlenecks and industrial targets. Although these raids cost 2,000 aircraft and killed or injured 10,000 French civilians, the Germans' forward defences, as Tedder had hoped, were further weakened and their ability to reinforce and re-supply them was significantly degraded. Railway traffic, for instance, slumped by two-thirds overall, while the destruction of 75 bridges and tunnels through pinpoint attacks by fighter-bombers effectively severed the immediate invasion zone and much of northwestern France from the transport network. Air power also made possible one of the cleverest of several deception schemes that misled the defenders as to the landings' true location. Flying in circuits that edged towards the French shore, two small flotillas of planes released clouds of 'Window' in meticulously devised patterns that eventually extended over 224 square miles (580 sq. km) of the English Channel. Picked up by the Germans' Seetakt coastal radars, the chaff appeared to be invasion fleets making for Boulogne and Le Havre.[17]

Whereas some of the soldiers that landed on 'D-Day' met stiff resistance – among them the American airborne divisions that were inserted overnight to cover the invasion's western flank – the Allied air forces encountered few adversaries to deal with. They disposed of 12,000 planes, 5,600 of which were fighters, whereas the opposing Third Luftflotten had just 466 serviceable combat aircraft at hand and could mount only 189 sorties. Moreover, most of its reinforcements were destroyed, either while en route or as they were sucked piecemeal into the unequal contest. By the end of June, its fighters were outnumbered by eleven to one. With the skies above it utterly dominated by the enemy, the German army, too, found movement a perilous undertaking, certainly in daylight. Even Rommel, its commander, who had grown accustomed to operating with inadequate air cover in Africa, found this exasperating.[18] He could neither regroup, nor reinforce, nor re-supply his units, which, once located by their adversaries, were in danger of being attacked both from the air and on the ground. This placed them in a terrible dilemma. Although troops might seek to avoid detection and mitigate the impact of aerial bombardment through concealment and dispersal, they had to concentrate if they were to resist hostile surface forces successfully. Once so deployed, however, they were that much more vulnerable to the firepower at the Allied air forces' disposal.[19] Indeed, Rommel's existing appreciation of this predicament can only have been intensified by injuries he received when, early in July, a prowling Spitfire strafed his car.

With the Allies gaining the upper hand, Hitler looked to exotic technologies to tilt the scales in his favour. German scientists had a good knowledge of nuclear matters and, for a while, explored the possibility of producing an atomic weapon. That nothing came of this was partly because of active and passive resistance to it. Werner Heisenberg, a Nobel laureate and Germany's pre-eminent physicist, seems to have overstated the difficulties involved in a bid to prevent the Nazis from realizing this goal.[20] The Allies, too, endeavoured to retard the development process, most notably through attacks on the Norwegian hydro-electric plant that was used to manufacture 'heavy water' (deuterium), a crucial ingredient. After a foray by British glider-borne engineers had ended in disaster, early in 1943 Norwegian SOE agents parachuted in to damage the apparatus. Their success, combined with air raids, led to the Germans' seeking to transfer both the deuterium and the equipment elsewhere. It was finally lost in the depths of Lake Tinnsjø, when Allied saboteurs sank the vessel that was transporting it. However, important though all of this was, by this stage the Nazis had recognized that they possessed neither sufficient time nor material and human resources to bring this project and all the others that were in hand to fruition. Priorities had to be established and choices made. Among the new armaments and equipment that were brought into service were jet aircraft and long-range rockets.

The Germans, using a Heinkel He 178, had first begun experimenting with jet propulsion in 1939. Their efforts led to the production, in 1944, of the Arado AR 234 medium bomber and the Messerschmitt 262A. Capable of attaining 540 mph (869 kmh), the latter was far faster than any fighter powered by a piston engine, whereas the former, able to carry a payload of 3,300 pounds (1,500 kg) at up to 450 mph (724 kmh), could also outrun most. Fortunately for the Allies, dwindling resources and the methodical destruction of her aircraft industry kept these impressive planes a novelty, but Germany had stolen a march on her competitors, notably Britain's Frank Whittle. This engineer and aviator had patented a turbojet as early as 1930, but it was not until 1939 that his company was awarded contracts for its w1 engine and the E-28/39 airframe. First tested in 1941, production of the Meteor proceeded slowly, with the first planes entering service late in 1944.

By this time, Messerschmitt had also perfected the Me163. This light, tail-less interceptor had a liquid-fuelled rocket motor that, although it could burn for no more than fifteen minutes, could propel it to speeds nearing 600 mph (965 kmh) in horizontal flight. Using the engine intermittently to gain and regain altitude, the pilot flew the aircraft like a glider, usually attacking bombers from above. Still more significant, however, was the Germans' application of such ideas to uninhabited devices. Rockets had been exploited for military purposes for centuries, but, because of the difficulties involved in guiding them to a target, had yet to fulfil their potential. Several leading states had tactical weaponry of this genre by, or shortly after, the onset of the Second World War. Most – like the Russian Katyusha, nicknamed 'Stalin's Organ' – were inexpensive substitutes for artillery pieces and were used to plaster parts of battlefields with volleys of fire. Others were more sophisticated. Britain, for instance, had a system that, employed in positional air defence, hurled a barrage of projectiles high into the sky. Their warheads were furnished with either time fuses or an electro-optical sensor that, light permitting, detected the shadows of aircraft. Several close-range anti-armour weapons were also rocket-propelled, notably the American Bazooka, which inspired the German Panzerfaust and Panzerschreck.

During the Anglo-American conflict of 1812–15, the British had bombarded some coastal settlements in the USA with Congreve tactical rockets launched from ships. In 1944, however, the UK herself came under missile attacks that were a good deal more destructive. First tested in December 1942, and in development and production ever since, jet-propelled German v-1s began falling on London in mid-June 1944. Simply aligned with the target before ignition, after which it climbed to around 4,000 feet (1,200 m), the v-1 initially carried a warhead containing 1,875 pounds (850 kg) of high explosive, had a range of 125 miles (200 km) and a maximum velocity of about 400 mph (644 kmh), though subsequent refinements increased its reach and payload somewhat. It was launched from a ramp, kept level by a gyroscope and, once its fuel supply was exhausted or automatically disconnected at a predetermined point, it plunged to the ground, detonating its warhead. The sound of the motor faltering tended to alert anyone below to the imminence of the explosion. In all, about 10,000 V-IS were unleashed against Britain. Most were surface-launched, though a few were released from specially adapted aircraft, an innovation in itself. Altogether, 7,488 reached the UK, of which 3,531 breached her defences.[21]

Although Britain already possessed an integrated network of these, comprising fighters, radar, observers, AA guns, barrage balloons and air-raid shelters, tactics had to be extemporized to cope with the novel threat posed by the fast, low-flying 'Doodle-bugs', which were quite vulnerable to fire but hard to espy. Once detected, many fell victim to either radar-guided Tempest interceptors, or to belts of AA cannon that, having got an electronic or visual 'fix' on the target, discharged shells fitted with proximity fuses. The relatively short range of the V-1s also meant that their launch ramps lay within comfortable striking distance of Allied planes in particular. Several were spotted and bombed, while others were overrun by troops advancing from the Normandy bridgeheads. There were, by contrast, almost no active countermeasures that one could instigate against the larger, super-sonic V-2, which became operational in September 1944. Propelled by a liquid-fuelled rocket motor, it could deliver a 2,150-pound (975 kg) warhead up to 200 miles (322 km). Burning for no more than 65 seconds, the powerful engine overcame the Earth's gravitational pull, thrusting the V-2 along a parabolic trajectory that might soar as high as 60 miles (96 km) into space. As the missile coasted silently downwards, its speed could reach 3,600 mph (5,792 kmh), until, slowed by the friction generated by the atmosphere, it thudded into the ground at 2,500 mph (4,022 kmh).

In all, 1,054 of these early space-age weapons were fired against Britain from sites along the European littoral.[22] They required only a suitable patch of concrete as a launch pad and, as both they and their paraphernalia were mobile, could move about while remaining in reach of their targets. Finding and then either driving them out of range or destroying them on the ground – counterforce operations – constituted the only defence against them. (Indeed, first conceived in 1942, the missile had a lengthy, complex gestation that was prolonged by heavy aerial attacks on the research and testing facility at Peenemünde.) Once launched, they struck with impunity. As with the v-1, however, aiming them was largely guesswork; out of the 1,359 unleashed against London in a bombardment that lasted until late March 1945, just 518 hit the target.[23] Still, together with the v-1, they caused appreciable disquiet among the communities they overshadowed. At a time when the Allies were in the ascendancy, these *Vergeltungswaffen* – 'retaliation weapons' – gave Germany the capability to mount random, insidious attacks by day or night.

Nevertheless, such armaments were never likely to prove much more than a localized nuisance. This was partly because of the missiles' primitive design – which made their attacks too imprecise and indiscriminate – but predominantly because of the Nazis' inability to harness them to a viable political and military strategy. The shifting focus of the bombing raids during the Battle of Britain; the Blitz, with its attacks on population centres; the firing of v-weapons against London and other cities, notably Antwerp: all these events highlight the core problem in aerial strategy, that of identifying an opponent's Achilles heel, something against which a knock-out blow might be delivered. To this day, it is questionable whether this has ever been accomplished by conventionally armed air power alone. Only the use of weapons of mass destruction (WMD) would appear to have achieved this. Yet, decisive though the nuclear attacks on Japanese cities in 1945 turned out to be, nobody at the time could be certain that they would prove so. They should in any case be viewed in context. They inflicted not just mass casualties, as so many conventional raids had done – and, indeed, as had the use of biological agents, notably anthrax, by the Japanese in eastern China in 1942 – but also the instantaneous destruction of infrastructure on a grand scale. Moreover, they constituted the *coup de grâce* against an opponent who had no comparable armaments with which to retaliate and who had been ground down beforehand by years of conventional warfare.

Had the Nazis succeeded in building atomic weapons, it is likely that they would have been tempted to try to use them, probably against London and Soviet cities, employing the v-2 as the most dependable delivery system. Yet, utterly unscrupulous though he was, Hitler was deterred from incorporating the mass-casualty weaponry he did possess – notably sarin gas – into rockets or any other projectiles lest the Allies stage reprisals with their own chemical or biological agents. Poisonous gases had been used extensively in the war of 1914–18 and, as we have seen, Douhet for one anticipated that this would recur in any future conflict. As it was, the v-weapons inflicted more psycholog-ical than physical harm, killing less than 8,900 people between them – about a fifth of the deaths caused by manned bombers in the Blitz as a whole.[24] It would have been astonishing if this essentially aimless and comparatively insignificant destruction had cowed the hitherto indomitable British. Indeed, the very name *Vergeltungswaffen* is reveal-ing. It suggests that the Germans themselves regarded them more as instruments of denial than of coercion. Certainly, they did not spawn demoralization to the extent that Hitler had hoped they would. If only by means of the simple expedient of suppressing reports on the scale of the bombardment and the casualties it inflicted, the British authorities averted any widespread panic.[25]

After London, the v-weapons' cardinal target was to be the great Belgian port of Antwerp, which, unlike the harbours along the Channel, had survived 'D-Day' and its immediate aftermath unscathed. As they swept eastwards, the British and American armies hoped to seize the city's dockyard intact and make it the anchor of their supply chain. It finally fell and opened to traffic in late November 1944. By this time, however, the Allies' advance was stalling, largely because of their logistical difficulties but also because of the partial failure of Operation 'Market Garden'.

Launched on 17 September, this was an impetuous bid to turn the Germans' northern flank by thrusting an armoured column more than 60 miles (96 km) across the Rhine delta to Arnhem. Since eight water-courses – including the broad Maas and Waal Rivers as well as the

Neder Rijn itself – lay between the British tanks and their destination, the operation's outcome largely turned on the capture – intact – and retention of a chain of bridges, a task that was allotted to 20,000 parachutists and glider-borne troops.[26] The American 101st and 82nd Airborne Divisions managed to fulfil their objectives with a blend of dash, sacrifice, heroism and skill, but a crossing at Zon was demolished by its defenders before it could be seized. A replacement had to be improvised, which further delayed the advance of the armoured and mechanized units; their movements confined to narrow causeways that were easily obstructed and defended, they were already running behind schedule. German resistance was, moreover, intensifying, not least because a complete copy of the Allies' plans had fallen into their hands, revealing every detail of what was afoot. Two SS Panzer divisions, which just happened to be refitting in the area, were being flung into the fray, and the British First Airborne Division especially soon found itself confronted by overwhelming firepower.

It had alighted near Arnhem on a drop zone that was all of 7 miles (11 km) from the objective. Its radios had failed, making it difficult to assemble its scattered units and coordinate their actions, and its jeeps had been lost in the landing. After four hours, only a solitary battalion of paratroops had gained the objective, while their colleagues were struggling to evade encirclement by German tanks. As depicted in the film of 1974, *A Bridge Too Far*, this handful of brave men clung to the crossing's northern end for some days. Changeable weather, the breakdown in communications and their opponents' remorseless advance left them with little hope of being reinforced or re-supplied by air, but Polish parachutists did land on the southern bank and strove, in vain, to relieve them. Neither could the approaching British armour get through. On the night of 25 September, those Allied soldiers who could, perhaps 2,500 men, withdrew to the far shore. They were unable to extricate nearly 8,000 of their comrades.[27]

This setback, combined with the ongoing struggle for Antwerp, temporarily robbed the Allies of the initiative. The Germans started bombarding that port with v-weapons in October and also made it the ultimate objective of their massive counter-offensive through the Ardennes in December 1944. Air power's strengths and limitations shaped much of the so-called Battle of the Bulge. More accustomed than the British and American armies to fighting in winter conditions, German tanks, screened from observation and bombardment by snow, fog and low cloud, surprised the few American troops in their path and headed for the Meuse. On 22 December, however, the skies began to clear and the Allied air forces were able to intervene. The German advance was already flagging owing to growing resistance, the sheer congestion on the roads and chronic shortages of fuel. Once enemy fighter-bombers began harrying their supply columns, the last of these problems became critical. Running out of petrol, of which they required a great deal, Hitler's last Panzer reserves faced the same fate that had befallen so many units in Normandy. Accordingly, on 1 January 1945 the Luftwaffe committed every available fighter to a desperate riposte against the Allies' aerodromes. They destroyed 156 planes, but to no avail. Twice as many aircraft were lost, along with almost all of the precious tanks.[28]

The Luftwaffe's casualties were irreplaceable. Indeed, the damage it sustained here accelerated the relentless collapse of Germany's aviation. While debate might continue as to the true efficacy of much of the strategic bombing offensive, its value in terms of opportunity costs and the morality of 'blanket' bombing operations, by mid-1944 their round-the-clock attacks on the Luftwaffe and its industrial foundations had secured the Allies virtual command of the skies. This air superiority turned to utter supremacy in March 1945, when, in just four days, 42,000 sorties were launched against the remnants of Hitler's air force and its supporting infrastructure, effectively obliterating it. So far had circumstances altered that, during these raids, the RAF's Bomber Command undertook diurnal sorties for the first time in almost five years.

Air power also made a huge contribution to the outcome of the war in the Pacific. When consulted over whether Japan should resort to using force in her growing dispute with the USA, Admiral Isoroku Yamamoto, head of her navy, had cautioned the Prime Minister, Prince Konoe: 'We can run wild for six months or a year, but after that I have utterly no confidence. I hope you will try to avoid war . . .'.[29] Such was Yamamoto's scepticism that plots to assassinate him arose among some of Japanese society's more bellicose factions. His assessment of the strategic situation proved fairly accurate, however. For five months after Pearl Harbor, his carrier battle groups were to operate with virtual impunity, mounting forays against targets as far apart as Australia's northern coastline, the Bay of Bengal and Ceylon (Sri Lanka). During this period Japan's soldiers, too, proved unstoppable. Amphibious units overran a host of Pacific islands, while her armies not only poured across Malaya but also seized the Victoria Point Aerodrome at the southernmost tip of Burma, thereby severing the air-bridge linking the British and Commonwealth garrisons in India and Singapore. Similarly, in January 1942, Menado Airfield, on Celebes in the Dutch East Indies, fell to an assault by paratroops, as did the oil wells at Palembang, Sumatra. Indeed, together with their desire to molest India and to cut the flow of supplies to their implacable Chinese foes, with whom they had been fighting since 1937, their quest for oil, rice and other precious resources gradually lured the Japanese ever-deeper into Burma. Greatly assisted by their command of the skies, which was initially incontestable, they were to reach the Indian frontier by the spring of 1943.

In the interim, air power acquired immense significance in the battle for control of the Pacific, its fringes and its numerous islands. The sheer enormity of this ocean is difficult to comprehend. Amounting to over 69 million square miles, it is nearly double the size of the mighty Atlantic and covers almost half of the Earth's surface. In such a theatre, anchorages and aerodromes from which military operations could be mounted came at a premium, accentuating the need not just for aircraft carriers but also other vessels that were as capable of supporting them logistically as tactically.

In December 1941 Japan possessed the world's third largest navy. It already included ten carriers. Four more, together with the two biggest battleships ever built, were under construction. The fleet air arm's front-line strength comprised 1,750 torpedo-bombers, fighters and dive-bombers, backed up by a further 550 float planes and flying boats that were primarily intended for scouting missions. Besides numerous surface vessels that were purpose-built to carry troops, munitions, fuel and other supplies, there were vast submarines, notably the I-400 class, which was so capacious that it could accommodate a large cargo along-side its three reconnaissance aircraft. Moreover, although neither the design of its planes nor the training of its crews made it ideally suited to long-range maritime operations, the Japanese Army Airforce was also drawn into the fighting in and around the Pacific's rim. Some of its planes were assigned to escort carriers that protected merchant shipping, while others were deployed on the larger islands, notably Formosa (Taiwan) and New Guinea, and along the littoral of Indo-China (Vietnam). It was from the first of these locations that, on 8 December 1941, the USAAF's principal aerodrome in the Philippines – Clark Field – was subjected to a crippling attack, while, from the last of them, the Japanese could strike seawards – as they did to sink HMS *Repulse* and *Prince of Wales* – or inland against China and the Allied forces in Burma.

Certainly, if air power's role rapidly came to be seen as critical to the outcome of the Battle of the Atlantic, in the Pacific its influence was identified as being potentially crucial from the outset. Even prior to Pearl Harbor, the Americans, who had but a handful of shore bases in the entire region, had already invested a lot of thought and resources in creating carrier task forces that, backed up by a 'Fleet Train' of tankers, and repair and replenishment vessels, were both largely self-sufficient and able to conduct operations over long distances. By late 1944 they disposed of nearly 100 carriers of varying sizes, while, thanks to the USA's industrial muscle, an additional one was being launched almost every week. Japan could not possibly keep abreast in the production of new nautical and aerial platforms and, in fact, had always assumed that her forces as a whole would be numerically infe-rior. However, the balance proved far too asymmetrical, not least because Japan extended her defensive glacis dangerously beyond the reach of what land-based aircraft she had.

Since, by fighting within its perimeter, where they might have mustered sufficient quantitative and qualitative advantages for success, the Imperial Japanese Navy had hoped to wear down their opponents before dealing them the *coup de grâce*, this proved especially counterproductive. But other serious mistakes were committed as well. Besides a failure to train enough replacements for the many aviators they were bound to lose in the envisaged attritional contest, Japan's forces invariably emphasized the offensive to the detriment of passive and active defence, the importance of which was being starkly demonstrated by the ongoing struggle in the Atlantic. Whereas they neglected the significance of electronic detection and warfare, the Americans, aided by the British, were quick to exploit ship-mounted centimetric radar and, for anti-submarine operations, its cousin, sonar, which used underwater sound pulses to get a 'fix' on the target. Too often, the details of Japan's plans were also revealed by the Allies' radio-monitoring and code-breaking teams, while her own intelligence-gathering services lacked not only structural and doctrinal cohesion but also enough material and trained, human resources. They were badly misled on several occasions by their opponents' deception schemes. Likewise, the defence of both merchant shipping and combat platforms was undervalued. Frequently, individual cargo vessels and capital ships were not afforded sufficient protection, while convoys were poorly organized and furnished with inadequate or no escorts. American submarines alone inflicted immense damage, accounting for two-thirds of the naval vessels that were sunk, including eight carriers, and a similar proportion of Japan's total merchant tonnage. In fact, this proved the most successful campaign of its kind in history, not least because of the exploitation of radar, which was used by the submarines to locate targets before they dived to attack them. More generally, loss rates were augmented by a lack of investment in survivability and an ethos that dismissed concern with self-preservation as dishonourable. Just as many of their soldier colleagues preferred death to surrender, Japan's pilots seldom requested – or received – simple, life-saving devices such as parachutes, while her submariners too readily embraced rashly aggressive tactics. In any event, Japanese warplanes and ships were mostly designed with offensive capabilities and speed in mind, with little attention being paid to their vulnerability. For instance, only one of the navy's aircraft carriers had a fully armoured deck to mitigate the effects of any bomb or shell that struck it. The consequences could be, and frequently were, catastrophic. Fires and explosions, exacerbated by the fuel and ammunition stocks on board, would quickly spread out of control, engulfing the ship, its sailors, planes and pilots.

On the whole, Allied vessels were better designed for, and their crews proved more adept at, damage limitation. Despite the pounding that she took from Japanese planes during the Battle of Midway of 4–7 June 1942, the carrier USS *Yorktown*, for example, stubbornly remained afloat until she was torpedoed by a submarine. Still, carriers were appreciably more vulnerable than the battleships they were now challenging for the leadership of fleets. During the inter-war period, it had become common practice to equip capital warships with a catapult-launched seaplane that, after use, usually for reconnaissance missions, could be retrieved by a crane. Nevertheless, the trend towards constructing larger and ever more sophisticated carriers was a tangible acknowledgement that, first, surface superiority was intrinsically linked to air superiority, and secondly that the battleship was no longer the most flexible means of projecting power available to maritime forces.

This represented more of a tactical change than a strategic one. Although a battleship's main armament might be capable of hurling huge shells fifteen miles (24 km) or more, aircraft could project differing types of firepower – torpedoes, bombs, depth-charges and so on – over still greater distances and were better able to engage a broader spectrum of targets, including submarines and hostile planes. Indeed, whereas in theory the range at which a warship might inflict damage was primarily determined by the calibre of its guns, the reach of aircraft was constrained only by the size of their fuel tanks and payload and by the prevailing weather. As with shore-based planes, sortie rates were influenced by the quality and numbers of technicians and other support personnel, but carrier-centred operations also called for both exceptionally good flying and navigational skills as well as suitable environmental conditions, notably favourable winds and adequate visibility. In order to launch or recover fixed-wing aircraft, a carrier had to be turned into the wind. Even at the best of times, alighting in a controlled fashion on a platform that is itself moving constitutes one of the trickiest manoeuvres that any aviator can undertake. If the plane is not to overshoot the runway, it has to be caught by arresting wires that need to be engaged at the right point in time and space. Taking off from a rolling, pitching ship can also be very taxing and, depending on the length of the flight deck, the wind strength and the weight of the machine concerned, the aircraft's engines might have to be assisted by means of a catapult mechanism. Of course, once airborne, it must then be able to find the carrier in order to land. In the interim, however, the latter's location will vary according to its course and speed, thereby altering the distance between it and the plane and thus complicating any calculation of the period for which the aircraft might safely remain aloft. At the climax of the Battle of the Philippine Sea in 1944, for instance, numerous American planes had to ditch since, confronted with fading light and empty fuel tanks, they failed to regain their carriers. Most of their crews, however, were subsequently plucked from the waves by air-sea rescue units.

Not least because of the battleship's superior ability to absorb punishment, the US Pacific Fleet did not lose one during the war, other than in Nagumo's raid on Pearl Harbor. Moreover, four of those that did founder there were salvaged and eventually returned to service. The three carriers that were based at the anchorage were fortuitously at sea when it was attacked and thus evaded immediate destruction. While the rest of the fleet was being reconstituted, they harried the Japanese with a series of blows that gradually grew in scale and significance.

The damage done by the first of these was more psychological than physical. On 18 April 1942 sixteen USAAF B-25 Mitchells, all that could be crammed onto her flight deck, took off from the USS *Hornet*. She was 600 miles (965 km) from Japan, seeking to avoid patrols by land-based planes. Indeed, her own naval aircraft could not have reached the selected targets and returned. Medium bombers, the Mitchells by contrast had an appreciably greater range and, after disgorging their small payloads – four 500-pound (227 kg) bombs per plane – on Tokyo and other cities, headed for Chuchow Aerodrome in China, allowing *Hornet* to make good her escape. Surprise was largely achieved: none of the B-25s was intercepted or shot down over Japan itself, and most of their crews survived the raid. After crash-landing on Chinese soil or bailing out, however, some men were captured by the Japanese occupation forces and, on the grounds that civilians had been deliberately killed in the attacks, subjected to a show trial and condemned to death. Furthermore, both as a reprisal for the raid and to prevent any recurrence, the Japanese overran another chunk of eastern China, seizing several airstrips.

Nevertheless, this foray did embarrass Japan's government and demonstrated that she was not immune to aerial attack. Pressure duly mounted on the navy to entrap and destroy the American carriers, an objective that was nearly fulfilled early in May 1942 at the Battle of the Coral Sea. USS *Lexington* was lost and the *Yorktown* mauled by torpedo and dive-bombers. Their Japanese counterparts did not escape unscathed, however. The *Shoho* was sunk and the *Shokaku* damaged, while heavy losses among her aircraft incapacitated *Zuikaku*. As a result, these last two carriers could not participate in the subsequent, critical clash off Midway, the US forces' most westerly outpost, when the Japanese sought to invade it at the beginning of June. Although the *Yorktown* finally met her end here, the absence of *Shokaku* and *Zuikaku*, combined with tactical miscalculations by Admiral Nagumo especially and superior intelligence work on the part of the Americans, led to four Japanese carriers being lost. Together with their superb, experienced pilots, even the planes that did not go down with them eventually finished up in the sea.[30]

The major naval actions of the Pacific war – those of Pearl Harbor, the Coral Sea, Midway, the Philippine Sea and Leyte Gulf (1944) – were essentially contested and decided by aircraft engaging one another and the ships that they came from. Consequently, the fighting centred on the two sides' respective carriers. In fact, in these great battles, which often extended over hundreds of square miles of water, it was unusual for the opposing vessels to get so much as a glimpse of one another. Most played no active part in the fighting other than to fire their AA weapons in a bid to ward off torpedo and dive-bombers. Exceptionally stable, battleships made particularly good platforms for large numbers of AA guns and were thus valued for carrier defence. Their main armament, on the other hand, proved of little use except for coastal bombardment. By contrast, air power's flexibility, reach, comparative speed and potential ubiquity made it adaptable to a broad spectrum of operations.

Not the least among these were combat and transport missions that were undertaken within the China–Burma–India triangle. Apart from via the so-called Hump – an extremely perilous air corridor that, stretching for some 500 miles (800 km) over daunting mountain chains, linked eastern India with Kunming – supplies despatched by the British and Americans to their Chinese allies had to be fed in through Burma. Japan had first made serious inroads into China in 1931, when she had conquered Manchuria and established the vassal state of Manchukuo. Hostilities had begun afresh in 1937 and had continued ever since, embroiling large Japanese forces in an escalating conflict. The US and UK were as eager to keep these troops tied down as they were to aid the Chinese, whose airstrips would also prove very useful for the mounting of strategic raids against their common enemy's homeland. To increase the flow of aid, it was planned to construct an oil pipeline and an improved roadway across Burma. First, however, the Japanese would have to be evicted from that country.

Bounded to the south by the sea and with its northern reaches dissected by a great crescent of mountainous spurs, Burma was a vast bowl of sprawling jungle that, particularly during the monsoon, filled with mud. Not least because overland travel was so difficult and commensurably slow, air power – and the runways it depended upon – soon acquired particular significance.[31] Whether small strips of grass located in clearings amidst the rice paddies and forests, or something rather more elaborate, aerodromes became the hinges of the battle for Burma, a fight that was as much against Nature as it was against any human foe. Indeed, disease alone was a formidable opponent. Teeming with mosquitoes, the region was infested with malaria. The Allies sought to combat its spread by having specially adapted aircraft spray DDT on the insects' breeding-grounds.

In February 1943, four weeks before a plane carrying Admiral Yamamoto was shot down by Allied fighters over the Solomon Isles, killing its occupants, the first of the so-called Chindit expeditions began in Burma. Organized and led by Orde Wingate, the Chindits were British and Commonwealth infantry units trained to carry out 'butcher and bolt' raids deep inside enemy-held territory. The first of their long-range penetration operations involved just 3,000 men, yet it presented the Japanese with a novel problem. Whereas the positions of so many Allied forces had proved vulnerable to infiltration and outflanking attacks, the Chindits, who waged a mercurial style of warfare in classical, light-infantry style and were re-supplied from the air, were not susceptible to such stratagems. Unburdened by the need to protect overland lines of communication and supply, they struck their opponents where and when it was least expected before melting away into the jungle. Although the Chindits lost as much as a third of their number in their debut campaign, they were able to test and hone their modus operandi, learning useful lessons about the practical difficulties involved in aerial re-supply especially. They subsequently developed the integration of aviation and ground forces beyond anything that had yet been seen.

During the opening weeks of 1944, General William Slim's Fourteenth Army began a counterstroke from India into north-west Burma. Seeking to retake the local airstrips from which a further push down the coast could be supported, elements of the Allied forces, including the headquarters of the Seventh Indian Division, soon found themselves ringed by hostile troops, who had been probing towards the borderlands to forestall Slim's offensive. In the ensuing fighting for the 'Admin Box' and the wider battle around Ngakyedauk Pass, the Japanese were thwarted by a combination of stout resistance on the ground and the Allies' domination of the skies. Not only were the encircled units sustained by supply drops that went on day and night, but also their attackers were strafed and bombed by planes.[32] Slim's offensive resumed while, in its support, 'Merrill's Marauders' – some 3,000 American volunteers – joined with five Chinese divisions under a fellow countryman, General Joseph Stillwell, to threaten the crucial aerodrome at Myitkyina further north. Simultaneously, the Chindits mounted another campaign to distract and harass the Japanese in this area.

This time, Wingate's forces amounted to 10,000 men. Besides 1,000 pack animals laden with rations, munitions and equipment, a customized 'Air Commando' was earmarked to support their endeavours. Extemporized from USAAF units, it included 30 fighters, 225 gliders, and 100 reconnaissance and other light aircraft, together with twelve bombers and six helicopters. Whereas the gliders enabled the bulk of the troops to be ferried directly into the selected zone of operations, flying over and landing in such rough terrain was difficult and perilous, particularly during the monsoon, as underscored by Wingate's death in an air crash on 24 March. The aviation element was also dependent on servicing, rearming and refuelling facilities that the Chindits' handful of mobile workshops could not provide unaided; forward bases that were sufficiently close to the scene of action yet secure from Japanese attack were essential. On the other hand, the advantages flowing from the use of air power were considerable. Their activities coordinated by radio with those of the ground forces, the aircraft appreciably enhanced the Chindits' reach and punch. Reinforcements and additional supplies could be flown in if needed, while the combat planes furnished firepower that was far more mobile and flexible than any artillery could have been. Sick and injured soldiers were also evacuated by air, not least by the helicopters.[33]

A novel form of technology at this juncture, helicopters merit further discussion. The basic concept was a very old one. Leonardo da Vinci was long thought to have been its originator, but both the Chinese and, during the Renaissance, various Europeans devised toy helicopters well before he drew his celebrated sketches. However, transforming the imaginary into reality proved a lengthy undertaking, for the production of an effective rotary-wing aircraft called for the surmounting of two obstacles that were as fundamental as they were formidable. These problems were: first, that of developing an engine that was sufficiently powerful to generate enough vertical thrust to lift both its own weight and a load from the surface; and, second, that of controlling simultaneous vertical and horizontal movement. Although as early as 1907 Paul Cornu, a Frenchman, had built a machine that managed to hover a couple of feet above the ground for a few seconds, it was not until 1923 that the next breakthrough occurred, when Juan de la Cierva, a Spanish aviator, constructed a viable autogiro. Having elaborated on his seminal ideas and technical innovations, Igor Sikorsky, the Russian aeronautical engineer who was then working in the USA, eventually produced a single-rotor helicopter, the VS-300, during the late 1930s.

Thereafter, the development of rotary-wing aircraft proceeded apace. The Germans were to perfect two versions with military functions in mind, while Sikorsky produced several hundred 'choppers' for the USA's armed services. However, the crippling damage done to Germany's aviation industry by the Allied aerial offensive hampered the manufacture of her Kolibri and Drache machines in any quantity. All helicopters were, in any event, dismissed as too vulnerable to be of much use in actual combat. They were mostly reserved for casualty evacuation assignments, as in Burma, and for maritime rescue, communication and reconnaissance missions. As we have noted, before and during the Second World War many capital ships were furnished with seaplanes that fulfilled such duties, but helicopters were seen by the British especially as possessing great potential in this regard. Rotary-wing aircraft promised to be much easier to house, refuel, rearm, launch and retrieve, and might be accommodated on even quite small vessels. During the early 1940s the Royal Navy duly began conducting trials in which a converted merchant vessel, the *Dagheston*, served as a pad for an embarked helicopter to take off from and alight on. More generally, the sheer versatility of rotary-wing aircraft – their ability to hover over a given point and to take off from, and land on, constricted areas that were inaccessible to fixed-wing planes – made them as ideal for monitoring work as they were for embarking and disembarking personnel and *matériel*. Although hopes of using them as weapon platforms over both sea and land lingered, the fragility and poor power-to-weight ratio of early machines ruled this out until improved models were available. Indeed, as late as the Korean War – almost twenty years after the successful integration of controlled vertical and horizontal flight had first been accomplished – helicopters had still to make an impression on actual combat, though they reaffirmed their value in scouting and – as depicted in the film and TV series *M*A*S*H* – casualty evacuation operations.

Despite Stillwell's march on Myitkyina and the distracting raids of the Chindits and their Air Commando, by early April 1944 the bulk of the Japanese troops in Burma were lunging westwards, bent on overrunning the Indian frontier, notably the town of Kohima and Slim's foremost supply depots at Imphal. Having emerged victorious from the fighting around the so-called Admin Box, during which they had defeated the Japanese offensive's northernmost tentacle, two of his divisions were now free to bolster their hard-pressed colleagues further south. Several units were promptly airlifted to Imphal, where they arrived in the nick of time. The RAF then sustained the garrison throughout a four-month siege by flying in 6,250 tonnes of food, more than a million gallons of fuel, tonnes of ammunition and thousands more troops, as well as evacuating 13,000 sick and wounded soldiers and numerous non-combatants. Similarly, air power often proved the salvation of Kohima's few defenders until substantial reinforcements could arrive by land.[34]

The invaders recoiled from Kohima on 31 May, not least because of their own logistical difficulties, which had turned acute with the onset of the monsoon two weeks earlier. With his capture of Myitkyina's aerodrome on 17 May, Stillwell had opened up a new aerial link with Chiang Kai-shek's Chinese forces, to whom thousands of tonnes of supplies were delivered over the next few months. The Japanese, by contrast, having hoped to replenish their stockpiles from the depots they had anticipated capturing at Imphal, found themselves at the end of an overland supply route that was as precarious as it was lengthy. The divisions assailing Imphal clung on until mid-July, when, caught between ever stronger Allied forces and starved of food, ammunition and other necessities, they also withdrew.

With enemy fighter-bombers and troops snapping at their heels, their retreat degenerated into a catastrophic rout.[35] The greatest defeat ever suffered by the Japanese Army, it left much of central Burma at Slim's mercy. But by this time the Chindits were in a parlous situation, too. On 1 May their 'Air Commando' had been switched to other duties, leaving them with insufficient logistical support and firepower. Kept in the field by Stillwell until late August, when the survivors were finally airlifted to India, they became embroiled in the kind of fighting they were not configured for and suffered accordingly. Over a third of the 10,000 men who had set out with Wingate either never came back or did so injured.[36]

When they first ventured into Burma, the Japanese had enjoyed overwhelming strength in the skies over that country. The RAF had but five squadrons of ageing planes based in eastern India with which to oppose them. By 1944, however, the Allies could muster more than 1,000 modern aircraft in this theatre,[37] whereas their adversaries were down to just 200 increasingly obsolete machines. Among other failures, they were to prove incapable of preventing either the fall of Meiktila – the crucial logistical node of the Japanese in central Burma – in March 1945, or the aerial re-supply of the Allied division that captured it. Moreover, the collapse of Japan's land-based air power coincided with the demise of her once mighty naval aviation. Equipped with a new generation of fighter aircraft and radar that was far superior to anything their opponents possessed, the American carrier groups were now more powerful and numerous than ever. In the so-called Great Marianas Turkey Shoot during the Battle of the Philippine Sea in June 1944, they dealt a crushing blow to the Japanese, whose losses included three carriers, more than 400 aircraft and, perhaps more significantly, some 460 pilots. Nearly all of these men were the novices who made up the bulk of their country's dwindling reserves of trained air-crew. With them, Japan's fleet also lost its ability to domi-nate the sea's surface beyond the reach of land-based planes and to maintain the defensive glacis that it had helped to carve out around her. This made the war's outcome something of a foregone conclusion, for it meant that Allied air and maritime power could, in conjunction with amphibious units leapfrogging from one island to another, squeeze the remaining Japanese forces into an ever-smaller perimeter where they would be exposed to relentless bombardment.

The Allies' nautical blockade, not least their submariners' campaign against Japan's merchantmen, was already biting hard when the bomb-ing of her cities started in earnest. Established in spring 1944, the Twentieth USAAF, under General Curtis LeMay, began operations in mid-June, initially relying upon bases in China and India. From here, with a reach of 1,600 miles (2,575 km), its huge Superfortresses could mount forays against targets in Manchukuo, Korea, Formosa (Taiwan) and along the south-western fringe of Japan itself. By August, however, Allied forces had seized all of the Mariana Islands, the northernmost of which, Tinian and Saipan, lay just 1,200 miles (1,900 km) from Tokyo. Control of their airstrips offered the opportunity to extend the offensive to the enemy's heartland. The necessary masses of munitions, fuel, rations and other equipment and supplies were easily brought in along sea lanes over which the Allies had established indisputable mastery. Indeed, North Field on Tinian was swiftly transformed into the world's largest aerodrome. Raids duly began late in November.

The Japanese were barely able to resist them at all. Whereas the ageing Zero was a poor match for the Americans' Hellcat, Tigercat and Corsairs, Japan's latest fighters, the impressive Shiden and Hayate, were few in numbers. This was not merely because of attacks on the production lines but also owing to a shortage of raw materials, which was largely caused by the maritime blockade, and qualified aeronautical engineers. Supplies of spares and aviation fuel were no less limited, while Japan's electronic detection and warfare capabilities lagged far behind those of the Allies. Furthermore, by this time she was also running low on pilots who were capable of getting the optimum performance out of any aircraft, let alone out of the more sophisticated ones. Again, the courage of despair was looked to for salvation. Alongside the celebrated kamikaze, whose suicidal attacks in explosive-laden planes sank dozens of Allied ships and damaged hundreds of others,[38] were the less well-known Tai-atari squadrons, who sought to ram their aircraft into B-29s.[39] The only other active defences comprised AA guns, of which Tokyo, Kawasaki and Yokohama had approximately 500 apiece. These proved ineffectual, however, not least because of the jamming of their guidance radars, which prevented them from focussing their appreciable firepower.

This problem intensified during the opening months of 1945, as did the raids. Mitchell had predicted that, against Japan, a country where wood, bamboo and thick paper were widely used as construction materials, bombing would be particularly devastating.[40] So it proved. Often attacking from as low as 7,000 feet (2,130 m), the B-29s methodically rained incendiaries onto 66 cities, ultimately laying waste two-fifths of their buildings. Further damage was done by the authorities, who, in desperate bids to contain the flames, systematically demolished more than 500,000 properties. Whereas losses among the Superfortresses averaged less than 1 per cent, the intrinsic vulnerability of her urban centres, combined with the flimsiness of their active defences and the paucity of adequate passive ones, notably air-raid shelters, left Japan's inhabitants woefully exposed. Approximately eight million of them became refugees. Simultaneously, industrial and manufacturing out-put, already badly affected by the Allies' naval blockade, dwindled remorselessly as workers fled into the countryside in droves. In all, there were nearly 250,000 fatalities, while many more people were left injured.[41]

All of this was achieved with a fraction of the tonnes of bombs and thousands of planes that were used in the strategic air offensives in Europe. Indeed, a single raid on densely populated Tokyo during the night of 9 March 1945 claimed the lives of more civilians than had the entire Blitz. For two hours, nearly 300 Superfortresses rained some 2,000 tonnes of incendiaries from just 5,000–9,000 feet (1,525– 2,750 m) on to the crowded city. In the ensuing firestorm, 85,000 of its inhabitants perished, while scores of thousands more were hurt. Roughly a quarter of its built-up area – around 16 square miles (41 sq. km) in all – were destroyed, including twenty important industrial targets.

Yet, horrifying though this was, it did not convince the Japanese of the futility of further resistance. This was only to come with the dropping of atomic bombs on Hiroshima and Nagasaki. In both these operations, solitary aircraft, armed with a single weapon, inflicted comparable destruction in a matter of moments. Arguably the single most decisive use of air power ever seen, the nuclear attacks achieved what the gradual strangulation imposed by the Allies' maritime blockade, the fall of Okinawa, conventional bombing raids and the Russians' rather opportunistic declaration of war had not: they emboldened the advocates of capitulation within the Japanese cabinet in their struggle with their fanatical military colleagues, and helped to persuade Emperor Hirohito – who had always doubted that his country could sustain a prolonged, attritional contest and had favoured the acceptance of the Allies' demand for unconditional surrender issued at Potsdam on 26 July – that he should exceed his allotted constitutional role and order his bickering advisers to sue for peace. This was bound to – and did – provoke a backlash among some of the die-hard elements within the military, but it was the only way to save Japan and her people. By demanding her unequivocal capitulation, the Allies had indicated a willingness to go on inflicting casualties and material destruction to, if necessary, the point of annihilation. In an unprecedented radio broadcast on 15 August 1945, the mikado duly urged the nation to 'endure the unendurable', the acceptance of defeat.

This spared both the Allies and their adversaries the horrendous ordeal that a full-scale invasion of Japan would have entailed. To claim that air power alone brought the country to its knees would be to disregard the cumulative effect of numerous circumstances. However, its contribution to the securing of victory in the Pacific was manifestly of even more significance than it had been in Europe, and the Allies' domination of the skies – and, by extension, the waves – might fairly be seen as the single most decisive factor. For sure, air superiority had emerged as a sine qua non for the successful employment of both land forces and sea power, although command of the air was insufficient by itself to secure victory in either Europe or the Pacific, it had proved an essential prerequisite for that in both theatres. While, as in the inter-war era, there would continue to be debate in several countries about how aviation should best be organized and controlled – the US Air Force, for instance, finally become an autonomous service in September 1947, but decentralized aerial elements were retained within both the US Navy and Army – there were few analysts who did not now regard it as occupying a pivotal position in military power. Certainly, the atomic bombing of Japan helped to end the Second World War sooner than would otherwise have been the case, thereby averting still greater human suffering and material destruction. It also ushered in a new era; for if, in recent years, advances in, above all, information and aerospace technology have spawned talk of a 'revolution in military affairs', it was apparent that one had occurred in August 1945. Indeed, the advent of nuclear armaments must surely rank as one of the great milestones of history, an event that truly changed the world.

It is often overlooked that, by this juncture, the Japanese themselves had a fledgling nuclear research programme. The dying Nazi regime had sought to nourish this through the provision of technical data and raw uranium. The latter was en route to Japan aboard the U-234, but fell into American hands when the submarine surrendered as part of Germany's general capitulation. The material was duly refined and, somewhat ironically, might well have been incorporated into the bombs dropped by the USA on Hiroshima and Nagasaki.

However, it was actually in the UK four years previously that an atomic bomb had first been recognized as a device that might win the war. In the light of their pioneering research, by 1903 Rutherford and Soddy had concluded that atoms contained colossal quantities of energy. As early as the following year, Soddy suggested that atomic fission might yield extraordinarily destructive armaments. After Rutherford had also established that an atom's nucleus comprised the bulk of its mass, Arthur Eddington – by combining this disclosure with Francis Aston's measurements of the masses of helium and hydrogen nuclei and with Albert Einstein's formula that equated mass and energy – realized that either the fusion of light or the fission of heavy nuclei might be exploitable as weapons. Since the neutron is capable of penetrating nuclei, James Chadwick's discovery of this particle at Cambridge in 1932 was the next major breakthrough. Indeed, when the German scientists Fritz Strassmann and Otto Hahn bombarded uranium with neutrons in 1938, creating fission products that had a smaller mass than a uranium nucleus, the Austrians Lise Meitner and Otto Frisch made two crucial deductions: that, accompanied by a tremendous release of energy, the uranium nuclei were being split; and that, if there were neutrons among the resulting fragments, the makings of a chain reaction were also present.

Within a year, the distinguished Danish physicist Niels Bohr had concluded that it was the lighter isotope U235 that had been split, and thus might be harnessed as a weapon. Although by this juncture many British scientists were preoccupied with the pressing need to develop radar and electronic warfare systems, some fugitive Jewish Germans and Austrians, notably Rudolph Peierls and Frisch, who were now working at Birmingham University, continued to explore the feasibility of building an atomic bomb. In March 1940 they produced a memorandum showing how a warhead might be constructed using a relatively small quantity of U235 and outlining the devastating effects that its detonation and the concomitant radiation would be likely to have. By May 1941 a group of experts had reported to the Committee for the Scientific Survey of Air Warfare that a uranium-based weapon was indeed a viable concept and had recommended the development of such a device. A panel assembled by the Department of Scientific and Industrial Research was subsequently entrusted with the coordination of nuclear research in Britain, but Patrick Blackett – then scientific adviser to the head of the Anti-Aircraft Command – argued successfully that any such bomb should be built in the USA, not least because it might fall into Hitler's hands should the UK be invaded. Furnished with the reports and findings of the British, the Americans were suitably impressed and, spurred on by their own entry into the war, initiated the Manhattan Project the following year.

Within six months, it had become apparent that only the USA could spare the colossal financial and other resources necessary to complete the development of nuclear weapons. While British scientists and engineers contributed significantly to the perfection of the first atomic bombs, London's influence inevitably began to wane once the Manhattan Project gathered pace and Washington assumed an ever-greater role in the struggle against the Axis. In fact, because of a variety of concerns, including Congressional worries about the UK's post-war ambitions, the Americans limited the exchange of nuclear secrets for a time, reverting to their former openness only with the signing of the Quebec Agreement of 1943. This pledged the signatories to refrain from employing nuclear weapons against another state without one another's consent, or from using them against each other. Similarly, information relating to atomic energy was not to be passed to other parties without prior agreement. The British also undertook to exploit any post-war commercial or industrial opportunities flowing from the research in accordance with presidential stipulations. Moreover, anxious to see collaboration continue after the Axis's defeat, at Hyde Park in September 1944 Churchill persuaded President Franklin D. Roosevelt to initial an *aide-mémoire* to this effect. The document also identified Japan as a possible target for atomic attack. Incorrectly filed and forgotten about for a period after Roosevelt's sudden death on 12 April 1945, the Americans' copy of this memorandum – drawn up by two men who were not only the West's most prominent wartime leaders but also close friends – was destined to cause some controversy between his and Churchill's respective successors.

This contretemps between the British and American governments was coincident with and influenced by a far greater and more sinister problem, namely the mounting tension between the Occidental Allies and the USSR, not least because of their contrasting visions of the European post-war order. As early as the Placentia Bay conference of August 1941, Churchill and Roosevelt had compiled the Atlantic Charter that was subsequently to form the core of the United Nations Declaration. However, even before the end of the Second World War, the Russian government – which was not accountable to a free electorate and, in the light of recent experience, equated security with the occupation of territory – had predictably insisted that the practical application of the charter's ideals would 'necessarily adapt itself to the circumstances, needs and historic peculiarities of particular countries'.[42] This boiled down to the creation of a Soviet sphere of interest in Eastern Europe, which involved the redrawing of frontiers in line with the Red Army's strategic concerns and the imposition of 'friendly' administrations and Stalin's own brand of authoritarianism, quite regardless of the indigenous population's wishes.

Powerless to prevent this, Churchill and Roosevelt, had they remained in office, would have ultimately faced the unpalatable choice of renouncing either their erstwhile Russian allies or the very principles they had espoused in the charter. Roosevelt's death and Churchill's defeat in the general election of 1945 spared them this dilemma, but their successors could not evade it. If George Kennan's 8,000-word 'Long Telegram' from Moscow on 22 February 1946, Churchill's 'Iron Curtain' speech at Fulton, Missouri, on 5 March and the Iranian crisis of that month sowed suspicions about Soviet aims in the minds of US policy makers, then Stalin's behaviour with regard to divided and occupied Germany seemed to confirm them. Whereas the USA and Britain concluded that Germany's economic regeneration was essential for the revival of Europe as a whole, the USSR was pardonably anxious to prolong her weakness. Notwithstanding the Red Army's apparent strength, Stalin was fearful both of the possibility of German recidivism and of the technological superiority – epitomized by the atomic bomb – of the US especially. Although prepared to abide by much of what had been agreed at the wartime Yalta and Potsdam summits, he was bent on establishing and preserving a *cordon sanitaire* for the USSR in Central Europe. If that aim necessitated confronting the West, he was willing to do so, regardless of its military might.

This quest for security ultimately proved counterproductive in that it alienated both the Occidental powers and much of Central and Eastern Europe's population. The USSR's attempts to consolidate its grip on these regions were pardonably seen as threatening and expansion-ist, provoking the French, British and Americans to redouble their efforts to defend and develop the territories they controlled in Germany and elsewhere along the falling 'Iron Curtain'. Amidst the general demobilization that had followed the end of the Second World War, much of the web of military bases that the USA had established over the British Empire had been dismantled, not least in the UK itself. A cursory report in *The Times* of London on 23 February 1946 had noted that 'the last Flying Fortress bomber under American control in this country' was preparing to leave Honington Aerodrome. 'Its departure will mark the end of the US Eighth Air Force in Britain.' The UK, however, economically exhausted by the war, quickly acknowledged that she was no longer capable of coping with the demands imposed by her new commitments on the European mainland and simultaneously fulfilling the global responsibilities and obligations she had incurred as the greatest of the imperial powers. In many places, the Americans had to step into her shoes, notably in the eastern Mediterranean in early 1947. Indeed, just over a year after the winding down of the 'Mighty Eighth', unfolding events here had begun convincing the US Government that the rush to 'bring the boys back home' from Europe might be somewhat premature. Seeking Congressional aid for crisis-torn Turkey and Greece, President Harry Truman declared: 'It must be the policy of the United States to support free peoples who are resisting attempted subjugation by armed minorities or by outside pressures.'[43]

Stalin, dismissing this and the incipient Marshall Plan in general as a crude attempt to extend American influence, responded with the creation of Cominform, thereby reinforcing the splitting of Europe into two, ideologically hostile camps. By mid-March 1948 Britain, France and the Benelux states had signed the Brussels Pact on mutual defence and had pledged themselves to maintain garrisons in Germany for the next 50 years. Washington, meanwhile, had started discussions with London over the establishment of what, in 1949, was to become the North Atlantic Treaty Organization (NATO). A new currency, the Deutschmark, was also secretly prepared for use throughout Western Germany and scheduled for introduction in June 1948, whereas the Russians were bent on imposing their Ostmark in both the Eastern zone of Germany and the divided city of Berlin.

These rival bids at currency reform triggered the Berlin blockade. When the municipal assembly voted to accept the Deutschmark in the Western zone and the Ostmark in the Soviet sector, the whole city, which lay isolated within the half of Germany that was occupied by the Red Army, was sealed off. Over the preceding weeks, ever more petty restrictions had been applied to canal, rail and road traffic traversing the Russian-held territory between West Berlin and the rest of the Western zone. On 24 June, however, all of these routes, together with electricity supplies generated in the city's eastern reaches, were severed completely.

Imposing a counter-blockade on all rail traffic leaving their zones for that of the Russians, the Occidental Allies began to airlift supplies to their garrisons and the 2,300,000 inhabitants in the beleaguered half of the city. It was an early, striking example of the use of air power in a humanitarian aid operation. The Americans used C-47 and C-54 Skymaster transporters, while the British employed a great variety of planes, including a fleet of converted Halifax bombers owned by one Freddie Laker, who later became a champion of low-cost air travel. By the middle of September, 203,000 tonnes of supplies had been flown in, some 60 per cent by the USAF and the balance by the RAF. As peaceful as it was successful, not only did the operation sustain the West Berliners for months on end, it also put the Russians in a dilemma: suffering badly from the counter-blockade's effects and with their attempt to coerce the West foiled, they were left to choose between reopening the overland routes into the city or resorting to violence.

While their fighters frequently buzzed the Allies' cargo planes, however, the Russians were not willing to fight. This decision can probably be at least partly explained by the Occidental powers' evident resolve, which was underscored by a subtle bit of sabre-rattling. During the summer of 1948, 60 Superfortresses flew to the UK at the British cabinet's invitation and amidst a blaze of publicity. Predictably, it was widely assumed that these massive bombers were carrying nuclear payloads, a perception that the American and British authorities did nothing to dispel. In truth their bomb bays were empty, if only because stockpiles of atomic armaments had yet to be created, a fact that was among the West's most sensitive secrets and was kept from all but a few of the UK's most senior ministers and officials. The Russian government, thanks to their excellent spy network, were probably aware of it too, but the underlying message of the B-29's deployment was not lost upon them.

Although the Red Army's bid to strangle Berlin was subsequently abandoned, these events highlighted the collapse of the partnership between the liberal democracies and the Communist USSR that had triumphed over Fascism in the Second World War. The West now perceived a new threat to its hard-won security, with the American National Security Council, for instance, insisting that 'Soviet domination of the potential power of Eurasia, whether achieved by armed aggression or by . . . subversive means, would be strategically and politically unacceptable . . .'.[44] With the onset of the Cold War, much of the world divided into two ideologically hostile blocs, each of which was bent on preserving, if not extending, its own sphere of influence. This was particularly so in Europe, the division of which was increasingly set in concrete, both figuratively and literally speaking. By 1955 Western Germany had been formally admitted to NATO and the Russians had established the Warsaw Treaty Organization as a counterpoise to the transatlantic alliance. The two camps were as heavily armed as they were suspicious of one another; and, once the USSR had successfully tested its first atomic warhead in 1949, thereby ending the Americans' monopoly on such weaponry, nuclear armaments incrementally came to form the centrepiece of their respective arsenals.

The actual use of atomic bombs during the Second World War had ushered in a new era of strategic thinking. Indubitably, nuclear and, later, thermonuclear – which were derived from atomic fusion rather than fission – weapons were to transfigure, among other things, the whole notion of strategic bombardment in a way that was to dominate relations between the great powers for decades to come. Yet beneath all of this lay an acknowledgement on the part of all but a handful of extremists that humankind was confronted with perhaps the greatest transition in military precepts ever witnessed. 'Thus far', wrote Bernard Brodie, a prominent Western commentator on strategic affairs, 'the chief purpose of our military establishment has been to win wars. From now on its chief purpose must be to avert them. It can have almost no other useful purpose.'[45] While, as always, those self-same military establishments had to try to prepare themselves for possible conflicts, regardless of how unlikely they appeared, it was quickly recognized that the active use of atomic armaments in any quantity was almost impossible to reconcile with any classical definition of the concept of warfare. As one very early American memorandum concluded, it might be possible to 'stop the Soviets from overrunning Europe by resorting to the use of nuclear weapons, although, of course, this would kill millions of people. Moreover, we might have to give up our bases in Europe, . . . a hell of a problem.'[46] Equally, Nikita Khrushchev – who had eclipsed Georgi Malenkov to succeed Stalin as the USSR's leader and who, when the mood took him, had a taste for very bellicose language – candidly agreed with some US officials that '[W]e will make . . . missiles but we won't use them. . . . [I]t would be silly. Who would lose the most? Let us keep our rockets loaded . . . [I]f attacked, we will launch them.'[47] In looking back at the Cold War era in general and at the doctrines surrounding nuclear armaments in particular, one should neither confuse capabilities with threats, nor forget that, as Carl von Clausewitz discerned, war is – or at least ought to be – the 'continuation of political intercourse, with the addition of other [namely violent] means, . . . [which] does not suspend political intercourse or change it into something entirely different'.[48] Those who are tempted to dismiss the policy of the great powers by encapsulating it in the unfortunate acronym 'MAD', which they explicate as 'Mutual Assured Destruction', miss the point: the objective, surely, was mutually assured deterrence.

The principal peacetime *raison d'être* of military power is deterrence. Although in practice this abstract view might require refining in the light of exactly who is to be deterred, how and from doing what, all armed forces exist to persuade any would-be adversary that a resort to violence as an instrument of policy, even defence policy, would be counterproductive: the opponent would lose any conflict that ensued, or winning it would prove prohibitively costly. While it can seldom be conclusively demonstrated that deterrence has succeeded, the consequences of its failure are all too apparent. Whereas mere bluffs might sometimes ward off a putative foe, the credibility of any policy of deterrence is dependent upon an evident physical capacity to react to any challenge and the political will to do so. Deterrence may thus be based on an implicit or explicit threat, but such a stance does suggest that retaliation of some kind will follow any provocation. Indeed, the simplest form of coercion is a threat that does not have to be implemented because it is credible and feared.

Varieties of military power that might be of utility in deterrence are, however, not necessarily of use in coercion, where there is an implicit bargain between the party meting out the violence and its victim. Here, the very versatility of conventional forces offers obvious advantages. On the other hand, whereas deterrence based exclusively on such strength is inherently contestable, that founded on weapons of mass destruction (WMD) is far less so. There can be no question that the two blocs' military capabilities, especially their nuclear arsenals, played a major role in shaping the Cold War. Yet this was by no means the only factor that moulded events. That, during the Korean conflict of 1950–53, the Chinese – who did not possess nuclear arms at this juncture – fought the Americans – who did – to save a Communist regime, whereas Stalin – whose broad, strategic interests were just as much at stake – was desperate to conceal the active participation of Soviet pilots and planes;[49] that, at other times during the 'East–West' confrontation, the Russians and 'Red' Chinese competed with one another in actively wooing the USA; that the presence of, not just the capitalist enclave of West Berlin behind the 'Iron Curtain', but also of an American base at Guantánamo Bay, Cuba, was tolerated; that the major powers were happy to enter into various formal accords with another, which effectively regulated their rivalry: all of this suggests that the international situation was often more complex than it might appear at first glance. (In fact, the regrettable tendency to view everything through the prism of a bipolar Cold War led, among other things, to the USA's misguided decision to intervene militarily in what was a purely regional dispute in Vietnam.) Above all, unlike imperial Germany in 1914 or Japan in 1941, for most of the duration of their protracted rivalry neither the USA nor the USSR had any real grounds for thinking that their status as the world's most influential states was in genuine jeopardy. Although each of them tended to overestimate its own difficulties and weaknesses while simultaneously magnifying the other's strengths and advantages, generally they both believed that time was on their side and were primarily concerned with consolidating their respective positions. The prevailing balance of power might not have been ideal, but it was far from intolerable either. They were uppermost in an international pecking order that could have been altered significantly only through a major war in which both of them stood to lose far more than they could ever hope to have gained. Indeed, even when it became apparent that, contrary to Marxist calculations, history was not unfolding in the USSR's favour, that after decades of trying to rival the West she was losing and might actually be facing extinction, her leadership still rejected armed conflict as a viable solution to her problems.

Nevertheless, if only through some technological mishap, or because of a loss of control either between one side's political and military hierarchies or within them, there remained the possibility that the Cold War might degenerate into an actual clash of arms. Accordingly, both Moscow and Washington drew up contingency plans as best they could, with the task of ending civilization being entrusted to, above all, air power. For instance, at the height of the Berlin crisis in 1948, the US National Security Council produced NSC-30, a top secret report that called on America's armed services to prepare for and, at the President's direction, be 'ready to utilize promptly and effectively all appropriate means available, including atomic weapons, in the interests of national security'.[50] Concluding that matching and challenging the USSR's massive conventional forces was, at this juncture, not practicable,

Western thinking was predicated upon peripheral strategies: skeletal conventional units would offer token resistance to any Soviet incursion into Western Europe while gradually withdrawing to the Pyrenees and North Africa. In the interim, the Strategic Air Command (SAC) would pound the Russian homeland with atomic bombs, a process that, it was estimated, would take all of two years, not least because of the small number of warheads available. In order to do this, the SAC would also need bases within striking distance of the USSR. But too many potential sites in continental Western Europe were dangerously exposed to a sudden Russian thrust or were incapable of accommodating fleets of large bombers. In these and other regards, however, the UK especially was seen as having much to offer. Already dotted with sizeable airfields – relics from the Second World War – that could be easily and inexpensively adapted, Britain itself would serve as an excellent platform for raids against Central Europe and the Ploesti, Donbass and Moscow industrial areas. Similarly, her numerous overseas possessions might be used in menacing the USSR's southern and eastern flanks.

To begin with, manned aircraft remained the means of delivering these awesome weapons to their intended targets, and masses of material and intellectual resources were devoted to the creation of successive generations of jet-propelled bombers. Among them were the British Canberra, which appeared in 1951 and was followed by the Victor and Vulcan, and the American B-52 Stratofortress, the gigantic airframe of which first saw service with the SAC in 1955 and, suitably refurbished, remains in use with the USAF to this day. However, once refined, technological developments that had first emerged in the Second World War were harnessed together to produce a formidable alternative to inhabited platforms. Certainly, within a few years of that conflict's end, rocket technology was exerting a momentous influence on warfare in general and on the concept of air power in particular. Weapons had always been a major determinant of tactics, but, with the advent of long-range missiles, especially those bearing nuclear payloads, they also became crucial determinants of strategy, not least because intercontinental missiles and bombers appeared to release air power from any residual dependence on the enabling, essentially sequential actions of surface forces. Moreover, as the selfsame rocket technology was employed to start the human exploration of space, definitions of 'air power' had to be rethought and new environmental challenges, such as weightlessness and deadly solar radiation, overcome.

The launch, in October 1957, of the Sputnik satellite seemed to confirm the USSR's perceived lead in long-range rocketry, particularly in the perfection of boosters, and in the development of an aerospace industry. This clearly had implications in terms of military capabilities, for the Soviet Semyorka rocket could just as easily be fitted with a warhead as with a satellite. Indeed, in January 1960, the Russians successfully launched an intercontinental ballistic missile (ICBM) that travelled more than 7,000 miles (11,250 km) to a target in the Pacific. Furthermore, in May that year, the growing sophistication of their tactical rockets was underscored when an American U-2 high-altitude reconnaissance plane, which, piloted by Francis Gary Powers, had taken off from Pakistan, was brought down near Sverdlovsk by the latest S-75 surface-to-air missile (SAM). Perfected in 1955, the U-2 was primarily designed to conduct aerial photography runs over important Soviet military installations, notably suspected ICBM sites. Flying at up to 75,000 feet (22,360 m) – well above the ceiling of the Red Army's fighters and AA guns and rockets – several of them had been spying on the USSR with impunity for four years. Telling his Kremlin colleagues that these illicit flights 'spat in the face' of the Soviet people,[51] Khrushchev had ordered their interception. The development of ground-based missile technology that could accomplish such a feat was a milestone achievement and suggested that, as such systems proliferated, the employment of crewed aircraft in military operations was likely to become commensurably more hazardous.

Events during the Second World War had already contradicted Stanley Baldwin's confident prediction of only a few years before that 'The bomber will always get through.'[52] Ballistic missiles, in the form of the Germans' V-2, had proved another matter, however. Against them there was no active defence, save bids to destroy them while they were still on the ground or to deny them suitable launch-pads. Indeed long-range rockets, still more than crewed aircraft, seemed to lend themselves perfectly to treacherous, unheralded and possibly over-whelming attack, a nuclear Pearl Harbor, the very fear that spawned the Cuban Missile Crisis of 1962.

The intelligence initially gathered by the U-2s revealed that, more than a decade after she had first successfully tested an atomic weapon, the USSR's nuclear forces were neither as large nor as sophisticated as her leaders' rodomontade implied. While there had been intermittent popular anxiety in the West about bomber and missile 'gaps', in reality the Russians were lagging badly, not least because their own posturing had spurred their rivals into making fresh additions and refinements to their own nuclear arsenals. The British, who had first conducted an atomic test in 1952, had perfected a hydrogen bomb within five years and, by 1960, were abandoning static, ballistic missile systems, notably their Blue Streak project, in favour of strategic bombers. They also deepened their collaboration with the USA, not least by granting basing-rights to America's brand new Polaris submarines, which were both nuclear-powered and armed. Moreover, when Washington cancelled the Skybolt air-launched missile, with which the UK had been planning to equip her bombers, Polaris was offered – on extremely favourable terms – and purchased instead. France, by contrast, alienated by the Americans' behaviour during the Suez Crisis of 1956, sought to reduce her military and political reliance on them and NATO. In February 1960 she became the world's fourth nuclear power when she successfully tested an atomic bomb and, before the year was out, had announced her intention to create an independent *force de frappe*.

Indeed, Khrushchev's boasting had, if only at times, beguiled friends and foes alike. Recalling the crisis of 1962, Fidel Castro, Cuba's revolutionary leader, once emphasized how 'Nikita said that the Soviet Union had missiles that could hit a fly in the air. I thought [he] . . . had several hundred intercontinental missiles . . . We imagined thousands, even more, because that was the impression that was created.'[53] In fact, the ratio of American strategic warheads to Soviet ones remained at around seventeen to one, much as it had been in the early 1950s.[54] Furthermore, the Western powers, with their ocean-going fleets and global network of bases, could threaten and, if necessary, strike at the

USSR along several axes using an assortment of missiles and manned aircraft.

Among the former were Thor and Jupiter intermediate-range ballistic rockets that, in response to the Sputnik scare, the Americans had offered to base on European soil, essentially in a bid to reassure their NATO allies until the USA's ICBM inventory could be enlarged. The negotiations over this politically sensitive step had dragged on, as had the actual stationing process, with the result that these aging rockets were teetering on obsolescence by the time they were being deployed. Ultimately, only the British, Italians and Turks accepted some. The UK, for instance, did so under an agreement concluded in 1958, which stipulated that the missiles would be manned by British personnel. The crews would be trained by the USA, who, in accordance with her domestic laws, would retain 'ownership, custody and control' of any nuclear warheads provided under the accord. However, whereas the USSR consistently refused to share – even in principle – atomic armaments with her Warsaw Pact partners, any launch of the missiles would, the agreement stipulated, be a 'matter for joint decision by the two Governments . . . in the light of the circumstances at the time . . .'.[55] After much prevarication, the fifteen Jupiter rockets in Turkey likewise became operational early in 1962. Initially under American command, they were put under joint control the moment the Cuban Crisis erupted in the October of that year.[56]

Eighteen months earlier, counter-revolutionaries had made an abortive attempt to bring down Cuba's Communist government. Although he was eager to shield Castro's regime from any fresh attack, particularly one actively backed by American military might, Khrushchev's decision to dispatch substantial Soviet forces to the Caribbean was primarily motivated by his mounting concern over the growing asymmetries in the superpowers' nuclear inventories. Among the mass of troops and equipment surreptitiously imported aboard Russian freighters were IL-28 medium bombers. These were capable of carrying small atomic payloads and, in fact, had six nuclear bombs at their disposal. However, what first caught the Americans' attention and really alarmed them was the detection, by U-2s, of several ballistic missiles. Although the rockets concerned were only medium-range systems, from Cuba they could reach parts of the continental USA. Indeed, with their stockpile of more than 30 nuclear warheads, they doubled or tripled the number of Soviet atomic weapons trained on America.[57]

President John F. Kennedy's administration had a chequered history, not least in its conduct of foreign relations. Among several questionable moves was his decision to embroil the USA in actively supporting the Republic of South Vietnam under Ngo Dinh Diem, a policy that his successor, Lyndon B. Johnson, perpetuated after 'JFK' was assassinated in November 1963. Kennedy's handling of the Cuban Crisis is also a matter that continues to divide commentators, but has frequently been depicted as his finest hour. Certainly, his brinkmanship led to the USSR – despite protests from Castro, who felt, with some justice, that he had been sidelined – pulling out not only the offending rockets but also the IL 28s and much of the paraphernalia and most of the personnel that had accompanied them. Her bid to establish a bastion deep in the Western hemisphere and reduce the missile 'gap' had failed. On the other hand, Khrushchev did secure a public undertaking from Kennedy that Cuba would not be invaded and, in secret, a pledge that the Jupiters would be decommissioned.[58]

These few, old-fashioned rockets made a negligible addition to NATO's nuclear firepower, and their withdrawal had been on the cards for some time. They evidently proved a useful bargaining chip in defusing the Cuban Crisis. Far preferable though it was to fighting a war, Khrushchev's climb down was a humiliation. Nevertheless, he could blunt any criticism from his Kremlin colleagues by claiming that he had obtained important concessions, as had Kennedy. Unlike the Soviet premier – who was neither troubled by the need to accommodate the concerns of his (mostly reluctant) international 'comrades' nor accountable to a free electorate that was kept informed of events by uncensored media – the latter had to assuage public opinion throughout the West while avoiding any step that might have undermined NATO's cohesion. At the very least, he could not afford to be seen to be acting under duress.

For most of air power's history, the difficulties experienced by democracies in dealing with more autocratic opponents have had a profound impact on its use. An alternative to essentially attritional, sequential operations by surface forces, it has often been portrayed as the coercive instrument par excellence. Aerial bombardment, it has been claimed by a succession of theorists, can strike at the material roots of an adversary's martial might and conclusively demoralize him. Actual events have followed a more variegated pattern, however. As early as the Second World War, even some of air power's most prominent proponents realized that demoralization might all too easily prove an elusive goal. 'If the enemy is to be coerced', von Clausewitz had observed long before the era of powered flight, 'you must put him in a situation that is even more unpleasant than the sacrifice you call upon him to make . . .'. For war should be seen as 'an act of force to compel our enemy to do our will'.[59] The dilemma for the aerial strategist was identifying what act, precisely, might not only dishearten an opponent but also do so with exploitable ramifications.

'Bomber' Harris, for instance, favoured the destruction of the Germans' material capacity to wage war because he doubted that their society as a whole was susceptible to psychological pressure. Even if some of them could be dispirited, this accomplishment would be of little use against an authoritarian state that habitually eradicated dissenters and faint hearts.[60] After all, a common thread in the basic philosophy of so many Fascist movements was, as we have noted, that warfare was the great catalyst, the supreme test of any nation and its institutions. Hitler, for one, believed this and reasoned that the German *Volk* had to demonstrate that it was worthy of survival by triumphing in what he regularly described as a *Vernichtungskampf*, a battle of annihilation. If it failed, it *deserved* to perish. In *Mein Kampf*, for example, he asserted that 'Man has become great through perpetual struggle. In perpetual peace his greatness must decline.' 'The sacrifice of the individual . . . is necessary to ensure the conservation of the race', he continued. 'True idealism . . . is essentially the subordination of the life and interests of the individual to the interests and life of the community . . .'.[61]

While the Germans did form a clutch of volunteer pilots into a squad dedicated to suicidal *Totaleinsätze*,[62] in the case of the Japanese this ethos had been, if anything, even more influential. Indeed, rather too much significance was attached to the will to succeed. Although morale is the single most important factor in warfare, it is not the only consideration. The fighting spirit of Japan's armed forces had often proved unbreakable, but this had ultimately failed to offset the sheer material strength of the USA especially. In any event, by demanding the unconditional surrender of both Germany and Japan, the Allies underscored their own willingness to absorb the costs of an attritional strategy.

But this was, as the Nazis themselves had proclaimed, a 'total' war. Waging a conflict such as the one encountered by the Americans in Vietnam was a different matter. Here, they were not fighting for national survival. Day-to-day life in their geographically remote homeland continued essentially undisturbed. Indeed, this accounted for many of the difficulties that arose, for large numbers of American citizens, together with many other people around the world who likewise followed events on television and in the press, began applying what were really peacetime expectations and standards to the conduct of an armed conflict. If nagging fears of provoking the intervention of either 'Red' China or the USSR imposed some constraints on the US Government's actions in South-East Asia, worries about domestic political opinion proved more restrictive still.

From the outset, air power in general and strategic bombing in particular was looked to as a relatively cheap way of securing military and, thereby, political objectives. 'The . . . task confronting us', stated General LeMay, who had risen to the rank of chief of staff of the USAF, 'is to make it so expensive for the North Vietnamese that they will stop their aggression against South Vietnam and Laos. If we make it too expensive for them, they *will* stop.'[63] But therein lay the rub. LeMay and his colleagues were making a subjective judgement about the values of their opponents: what they would regard as important, what they would see as 'too expensive'. That the Communists' transport web and embryonic industrial base were selected as ideal targets for strategic bombing was partly because they were regarded by the Americans as essential to the North's war effort, but also because it was assumed that they were cherished assets. Start destroying them and, it was reasoned, the North's behaviour would be conditioned. This could be accomplished, moreover, through a short, intensive campaign à la Seversky. While the operation was not intended as a direct attack on civilians – not least because of public sensitivities in the USA – it was hoped that it would demoralize the North's population and thus distract the leadership in Hanoi.

In fact, Operation 'Rolling Thunder', as it was dubbed, dragged on from 2 March 1965 until the end of October 1968. It is estimated to have killed some 52,000 civilians,[64] despite defensive measures that included the evacuation of many people from major towns such as Haiphong and Hanoi to the rural villages where around 90 per cent of the population normally dwelt. This was largely because North Vietnam was an agrarian region, with topographical and climatic conditions similar to those encountered in Burma in the 1940s. There were few highways, rail links or other worthwhile targets for strategic bombing; raids inevitably focused on a handful of urbanized and industrialized patches and communication bottlenecks. Indeed, interdiction missions formed a major part of the aerial operations. Although much of the North's basic war matériel was produced by indigenous 'cottage' industries, the bulk of military supplies, together with many other commodities, came from 'Red' China and the USSR. However, whereas millions of Chinese soldiers and, more clandestinely, a few Soviet pilots had participated in the Korean War, neither of these major powers intervened in the conflict beyond sending financial and material aid to their Communist brethren. Preventing this without overly provoking either Beijing or Moscow formed part of the Americans' quandary.

Striking efficaciously at hostile soldiers proved difficult enough. During the Korean War, American air power had severely harassed the Communist ground forces, both by giving friendly troops close support and by hampering the enemy's with interdiction operations. But in Vietnam the battle lines were less clearly drawn. Operating alongside Hanoi's regular units were the Viet Cong, nationalist insurgents committed to the downfall of the South Vietnamese Republic. There were scores of thousands of these men and women, and they mounted a savage guerrilla war from within the civilian population. This ineluctably blurred the distinctions between combatants and non-combatants, creating an environment in which atrocities, such as that at My Lai in 1968, could all too easily occur. Coping with such a situation demanded the careful handling of civil–military relations and the judicious interlocking of political, including diplomatic, and military measures. Not least because of their vast experience as an imperial power, in dealing with the 'Emergency' in nearby Malaya between 1948 and 1965 the British proved quite adept at this. President Lyndon B. Johnson's administration, however, fared far worse in its handling of Vietnam's civil war, a conflict that, many Americans were persuaded, had its roots in Sino-Soviet plans for Asian hegemony.

The Tonkin Gulf Incident, which occurred in the midst of the presidential contest of 1964, not only provoked US air raids against North Vietnamese bases but also aggravated these fears to such an extent that the Congress mandated Johnson to prosecute the war as he saw fit. Emerging triumphant from the election, in February 1965, after a Viet Cong raid on their aerodrome at Pleiku left several Americans dead and more than a hundred injured, 'LBJ' responded by ordering further attacks on the North by carrier-based planes and by committing US marines to the land battle. Initially intended to protect airfields and other crucial installations, these soldiers were joined by ever more US military personnel as the fighting escalated. By April 1969 there were more than 543,000 here – more than were to be found in Europe. 'Rolling Thunder' had, in the meantime, contributed to a greater tonnage of bombs being disgorged on Vietnam than had been dropped on Germany and Japan in the Second World War.

Pentagon officials could scarcely believe that anybody could withstand this sort of onslaught. Concentrated firepower, however, was largely ineffectual against dispersed opponents who, matching the duration and intensity of engagements to their available logistical support, fought mercurial 'hit and run' actions before going to ground, both figuratively and literally speaking. As well as exploiting the natural cover provided by the jungle – which the Americans tried to reduce through the spraying of 18 million gallons of defoliants and by the use of 15,000-pound (6,804 kg) 'Daisy-cutter' bombs that, exploding 7 feet (2.1 m) above the ground, levelled trees by the hectare – the Communists made use of immense networks of concealed tunnels and

subterranean bunkers. Some of these were true feats of military engineering. Many were never unearthed, but even those that were still
screened any occupants from observation and fire. They greatly facilitated the surreptitious movement of infantry and supplies into the
South's heartland, not least during the Tet Offensive of January 1968,
when simultaneous attacks were staged within more than a hundred
towns, many of which had long been regarded as secure. This shattered
any illusion that the US was gaining the upper hand and thereby
destroyed Johnson's political ambitions. On 31 March, in a national
television address, he announced that, henceforth, bombing of the
North would be more circumscribed and called on Hanoi to discuss a
settlement to the war. He concluded by declaring that he would not
be seeking re-election in the presidential contest scheduled for 5
November.

That election was won by Richard Nixon a few days after 'Rolling
Thunder' subsided. Whereas some in factious America believed that an
intensification of the campaign would surely have yielded exploitable
results, others dismissed bombing as part of the problem, not the
solution. In April 1970 Nixon started disengaging US forces from
Vietnam, but simultaneously ordered an incursion into Cambodia in a
bid to staunch the flow of supplies to the Viet Cong. Although quite
short-lived, this exacerbated the bickering within the USA, as did the
resumption of large-scale aerial bombardments in April 1972. Begun
in response to an unbridled offensive by the North Vietnamese that
made appreciable headway, the brief 'Freedom Train' campaign, which
comprised attacks on a variety of targets, was quickly followed by
'Linebacker I', a grand interdiction operation that included more than
40,000 bombing sorties. Implemented by great flotillas of aircraft that,
throughout the summer, edged ever further northwards, this sought to
prop up the South's tottering divisions while depriving their assailants
of the means to maintain their offensive.

These objectives were achieved. Not least because of their need for
considerable logistical support, the North's regular forces were much
more susceptible to aerial attack than their Viet Cong comrades.
Concentrated infantry and armour; forward ammunition dumps; fuel
pipelines and depots; motorized convoys; railways and shipping laden

with supplies: all made vulnerable, worthwhile targets for scores of B-52s and fighter-bombers. However, the political impact of this military setback is harder to gauge. 'Linebacker I' ended on 23 October, just before the presidential election of 1972. That Nixon was anxious to secure a ceasefire before America voted increased Hanoi's chances of obtaining concessions, despite the failure of its offensive. Certainly, just ten days before the ballot, Henry Kissinger, the US National Security Advisor, notwithstanding Saigon's objections to the settlement negotiated by the North and Washington, told journalists: 'We believe that peace is at hand.'[65] It was not, but the promise of it can only have helped Nixon gain his electoral triumph.

With the prospects of peace fading, during December Nixon ordered a resumption of the bombing in an attempt to reassure the South Vietnamese and to force the Communists to accept the accords. This, incorporating some amendments, they did, clearing the way for the withdrawal of the few thousand US troops that were still in Vietnam. The last left on 29 March 1973. Just over two years later, the American embassy in Saigon was also evacuated as the South finally succumbed to the attacks of the Viet Cong and the North's regular forces.

The 'Linebacker II' campaign lasted for eleven days. As intensive as it was cursory, it was directed against the North's residual capacity to mount and sustain a conventional offensive. It did immense damage for the comparatively low cost of fifteen B-52s. Robert Pape, in his interesting study of aerial coercion, concludes that 'The effect of air power on Hanoi's behaviour is apparent from the course taken by the Paris peace talks.' Indeed, he is persuaded that, owing to 'the risk that American air power might return to the region', Hanoi delayed its final conventional offensive until after Nixon's fall in August 1974.[66]

Perhaps this was the case, but the history that we do not know is often as important as that which we do, sometimes more so. Certainly, considerations other than civilian or military vulnerability to aerial bombardment must have influenced events as well.[67] Shifting international allegiances, for instance, definitely played a part. Kissinger, while generally backing Nixon's military measures, went so far as to say that 'We demoralized Hanoi more . . . by sharpening differences between it and its patrons.'[68] They were the USSR and the 'Red' Chinese, the latter especially having helped to end French colonial rule in Indo-China during the 1950s. Since the rift of 1969, however, these two Communist powers had been squabbling, sometimes violently. In February 1972 Nixon made a conciliatory visit to Beijing and, within four months, had also signed the first Strategic Arms Limitation (SALT) accords with the Soviets. To Kissinger's delight, they were also busy courting Washington, not least because they feared a US–Chinese rapprochement. Leonid Brezhnev and Mao Zedong pressed Hanoi to show restraint, if only for a time. After all, it was apparent from the peace negotiations and the relentless extrication of US troops from combat in Vietnam that America's politicians were disheartened, despite her soldiers' numerous victories. If it clinched the latter's complete removal, a ceasefire was a price well worth paying by the North, while the accord left the South no more secure than before and, in the longer term, much less so.[69] First Johnson and then Nixon had tried to use bombing as a bargaining tool. Although aerial reconnaissance certainly suggested that the various raids had inflicted grievous losses, such intelligence can be cruelly deceptive, for it evaluates only material, not psychological, damage. It was surely apparent who had coerced whom.

Besides Détente, various intangibles must also have shaped the actions of the North Vietnamese throughout the conflict, notably patriotism, fear – if not of America then of some of their own 'comrades' – and ideological zeal. Yet, from the outset of his study, 'variables, such as domestic political, organizational and psychological factors' are treated by Dr Pape as 'exogenous in order to study the specifically military elements of coercion'. While acknowledging that such factors 'can affect outcomes', he is bent on 'developing propositions about military coercion that are generally applicable across space and time'. Analyses concerning specific events like Vietnam[70] do not, he complains, 'disentangle factors unique to a particular case from those common to a range of cases'.[71]

This quest for universal factors in warfare is scarcely new, and anybody who appreciates the true uniqueness of historical circumstances must remain sceptical about it and any 'lessons' derived from it. It has often led to tragic and foolhardy errors, not least in Vietnam, where they proved all the more tragic for being foolish. 'I'm not the village idiot', Dean Rusk, Johnson's Secretary of State, once insisted. 'I know Hitler was an Austrian and Mao is Chinese . . . But what is common between the two situations is the phenomenon of aggression.'[72] Had he highlighted not aggression, which is a subjective concept, but violence, the *only* universal characteristic of war, this remark might have been more perceptive. Alas, there were in any case innumerable, pertinent details that rendered his comparison invalid. While in practice war might not always fulfil the theoretical ideal of being the continuation of political intercourse, its parameters are hard to identify; for there are few things in human experience that have not influenced, or been influenced by, it. Certainly, a fixation with certain elements, notably technology, helped to doom America's efforts in Vietnam. LeMay might be pardoned for being tempted to believe that, by attacking much the same sort of target sets, he could replicate some of the success that he had enjoyed in the Pacific war. Indubitably, he was also anxious to justify the immense investments that the USA had made in air power in general and in the SAC in particular. But Vietnam was neither Japan nor Nazi Germany, any more than the 1960s and '70s were the 1940s. Expectations of what air power alone might accomplish were excessive, if only because any gains needed to be consolidated by land forces. This seldom occurred, not merely because of the essentially limited aims that the USA was pursuing but also because she tried to do so with limited means. Indeed, largely as a reaction to their experience here, for American politicians especially the strategic deployment of *any* ground units became a discrete act with its own ramifications. Where they might once have dispatched a gunboat as a means of showing resolve without necessarily shouldering commitments, after Vietnam they looked increasingly to air power for such leverage.

At the tactical level, interaction between aviation and surface forces was a prominent feature of the fighting in Vietnam. As had been witnessed in the Korean conflict – where the Soviets' MiG-15, which was powered by engines copied from Rolls-Royce's superb jet motor, had outclassed every British and American fighter except, perhaps, the F-86 Sabre – the ongoing substitution of jet for piston engines in most combat aircraft brought its benefits. Like most technological trends, however, it created new problems as well as possibilities. The ability, as in the MiG-15's case, to attain speeds approaching that of sound[73] and to climb very rapidly to altitudes as high as 50,000 feet (15,250 m) was clearly advantageous in dogfights, but it could greatly reduce an aircraft's utility whenever the provision of close support to ground units was called for. Travelling at, say, 600 mph (965 kmh), 10 miles (16.09km) per minute, a plane might have just a few seconds to distinguish friends from foes and identify and engage a given target. Over the jungles of Vietnam, it often proved impossible to see much at all from the skies, necessitating the blind bombardment of map coordinates that were relayed by radio from spotters on the ground. At best rather haphazard, because of the time lags involved this methodology could easily prove ineffectual, particularly against moving targets.

Whereas the bulk of the aerial operations over Vietnam were carried out by fixed-wing planes and were traditional 'strategic' bombing raids that probably cost more than the material damage they inflicted, the contribution made by rotary-wing aircraft in support of ground operations was as significant as it was unprecedented. The value of the helicopter's ability to take off from, and touch down on, confined spaces had long been recognized so far as the movement of personnel and *matériel* on the fringes of engagements were concerned. In Vietnam, however, where movement by land was slow and tortuous, and fighting could erupt almost anywhere, a new generation of more powerful machines supplanted the glider in facilitating the timely concentration of forces at threatened points. Some 7,000 Bell HU-1 'Hueys' saw service here, flying more than 36 million sorties, many of them to rescue wounded soldiers from remote battlefields where they would otherwise have perished for lack of medical care. Furthermore, the development of models like the 'Huey', which were faster and more agile than their predecessors, secured rotary-wing aircraft a role in actual combat missions. Not least because they could hover over a given point and duck behind terrain features, helicopters were seized on as ideal observation platforms and for the provision of mobile firepower in close engagements.

Indeed, as early as 1962, the US Army proposed establishing several air assault divisions equipped with them for transport, reconnaissance and fire support. Largely because of continuing inter-service arguments over the control of aviation assets, this particular suggestion was rejected, with the USAF putting forward counter-proposals for combined units of fixed- and rotary-wing aircraft in which the latter would fulfil an essentially auxiliary role.[74] This would offer a more cost-effective and flexible force structure, which would be of utility in a greater number of foreseeable scenarios. Certainly, its potential was underscored in December 1967, when the 101st Air Cavalry – some 10,000 personnel with more than 5,384 tonnes of equipment – was airlifted aboard C-141 StarLifters and C-133 Cargomasters directly from Kentucky to Vietnam.

During the early 1980s the US Army established several 'light' infantry divisions that were primarily designed with similar strategic mobility in mind. The requirement that they be air mobile and deployable in days through less than 500 sorties by C-141s severely constrained the quantities of armour, equipment and supplies that could accompany each division. This, in turn, posed potentially lethal problems with regard to their logistical sustainability in the field and their survival chances if pitted against adversaries equipped for high-intensity operations, notably Warsaw Pact armoured and mechanized forces. Many of the deficiencies in their capabilities were never satisfactorily rectified. However, attempts were made to strengthen their organic firepower and tactical mobility, primarily by attaching an aviation brigade to each of them. This comprised 68 differing helicopters, divided into transport, reconnaissance and attack squadrons.[75]

As technology had advanced, so too had the ability of rotary-wing aircraft to carry out combat functions. Whereas in Vietnam the 'Huey' had been prized as a platform for rockets and machine guns and for the insertion and retrieval of infantry, its light construction made it very vulnerable to AA cannon and missiles and even automatic shoulder arms. By the 1980s, however, the development of sturdy 'gunship' and 'attack' varieties had transformed the helicopter into a weapon system in its own right, creating the potential for so-called air-mechanized operations: the ability to manoeuvre in, and to fight mainly from, the air against hostile land forces and rotary-wing aviation. In such undertakings, the capacity to ferry air-mobile troops and their equipment into and out of a battle largely turns on the attack helicopters' effectiveness, for it is to them that the domination of territory, the securing of landing zones and the extrication or relief of surrounded units ultimately falls. Although technological evolution has improved the performance of the light artillery, man-portable anti-tank weapons and mortars that traditionally accompany airborne infantry, once on the ground such soldiers still have substantially less mobility, sustainability and punch than most motorized or mechanized units. Indeed, the helicopters' basic function is to enable the swift concentration or redeployment of soldiers and firepower in the course of an engagement, not least because maintaining an adequate concentration of strength – which is, in any case, a relative concept – at each and every point in time and space is often impossible. Attack helicopters especially can compensate for any deficiencies in punch and armoured protection among the troops they support. Robustly constructed and bristling with rockets and cannon, most are also capable of carrying 'stand-off' anti-armour missiles. These formidable projectiles can be unleashed from a safe distance and are either steered by a designator system aboard the aircraft to the target or, in the case of so-called fire-and-forget weaponry, by built-in tracking sensors.

Such 'gunships' were prominent participants in the fighting in the Beqaa Valley, Lebanon, during 1982, in Afghanistan between 1979 and 1989 and, above all, in the Gulf War of 1991. Here, the very first blow in the Allies' aerial offensive was struck by rotary-wing aircraft. During the early hours of 17 January 1991, having approached their quarry using high-speed, nap-of-the-earth flying, which was done without lights, American helicopters disabled two early warning radar installations, creating a chink in Iraq's armour. Thereafter, some 700 Allied planes poured into Iraqi airspace, followed by 151 Tomahawk cruise missiles launched from American warships, many of which lay hundreds of miles from their targets.[76] Subsequently, in air-mechanized operations, us Army Apaches especially wrought tremendous damage, destroying, among many other things, 521 tanks and 230 armoured personnel carriers.[77]

Air-mechanized operations are normally regarded as a dimension of land, rather than air, warfare. Nevertheless, the leadership and control of this type of undertaking has predictably and frequently been a matter of dispute between armies and air forces. Many navies have also been eager to exploit aerospace power, and this has coloured the institutional and command arrangements within the armed services of several states. The UK is perhaps the most notable of these, if only because, as an island nation, the British have had to rely on ships for the projection of military power for most of their history. The relationship between their generals and admirals, which had been shaped by centuries of implementing amphibious operations, became still more complex with the advent of air power.

The Royal Navy established an early lead in employing helicopters. Because of its extensive commitments and limited resources, it made more use of them than most fleets and, by the early 1950s, was striving to incorporate a flight deck into all its destroyer and frigate designs. From these and other platforms, a new generation of more powerful and capable rotary-wing aircraft, such as the Dragonfly, Whirlwind and Wessex, were able to undertake a growing spectrum of functions. The Whirlwind, for example, was extensively used in amphibious operations and, furnished with short-range, active sonar, for the detection of submarines. Day-and-night instrumentation and an automated hovering system permitted its successor, the Wessex, to conduct operations around the clock and, thanks to an enhanced sonar and radar suite, to scan both below and above the waves over an expanded radius. This brought with it a limited capacity for over-the-horizon targeting, which, as it increased, exceeded the range of the weapons mounted aboard ships. There was therefore a growing need either to develop armaments with greater reach and commensurable accuracy, or to install more firepower in the helicopters themselves.

While the British ultimately preferred the latter policy, arming Wasps with depth-charges, light-weight torpedoes or AS-12 air-to-surface missiles, they, in common with the Soviets and Americans, also experimented with torpedo-carrying rockets and drones, notably

Ikara. Although they provided an all-weather and almost instantaneous striking capability, these were expensive and not as flexible as rotary-wing aviation, which could, if necessary, shadow putative targets for lengthy periods. They were a relatively short-lived innovation, being steadily surpassed by ever-improving surface-to-surface missiles and helicopters. The Sea King, for instance, which first appeared in 1961, was a far better answer to a Soviet submarine challenge that was growing in sophistication, particularly when the introduction of sonar buoys endowed it and other maritime aviation with an additional passive-detection medium. Transmissions from these could be analysed either on board the helicopter itself, which could then react autonomously, or relayed to its parent vessels.

The former approach called for organic computing facilities which, as the areas under surveillance grew, had to be increased proportionately. The British especially overcame these problems by role specialization: dedicated Sea Kings were used for anti-submarine and, after the Falklands campaign of 1982, airborne early warning patrols, while Lynx helicopters – fitted with Sea Skua rockets, depth-charges and torpedoes as well as the Sea Spray radar for directing ship-borne surface-to-surface missiles – retained the flexibility to engage both submerged and surface targets.

Once the potential potency of air-launched, sea-skimming, stand-off weaponry had been underscored by the Exocet attacks mounted by the Argentine Air Force (the Fuerza Aérea Argentina) during the Falklands War, efforts to improve the defences of British vessels against this type of menace were promptly redoubled. New surface-to-air missile systems and automated, short-range cannon, notably Goalkeeper – which is designed to shred any approaching rocket with thousands of heavy bullets – were fitted to ships. However, the cardinal form of protection had to remain friendly planes keeping aerial threats at bay. This is not least because, unlike a missile, an aircraft is reusable, discriminating and capable of engaging a succession of targets at a variety of distances. Tactical missile systems are comparatively inflexible in that they not only have a much more limited reach but also need a certain amount of clearance in which to 'lock on' to, and then manoeuvre against, their quarry. They thus have both minimum and maximum effective ranges. Furthermore, their guidance systems are vulnerable to delusion by such simple measures as, in the case of heat-seeking varieties, the firing of flares as decoys. For air defence purposes, rockets are thus best combined with AA guns, which have contrasting performance characteristics. While even the largest of cannons or machine guns has a limited reach, they are mostly capable of engaging targets not only at a distance but also at very close quarters. By juxtaposing them with missile systems, a layered defence can be constructed that is capable of tackling an assortment of threats, making it possible for surface forces to dominate a fixed area of the surrounding atmosphere.

An aircraft-carrier battle group can do this supremely well. Certainly, Britain's carriers played a pivotal role in making the recovery of the Falklands a viable proposition. Despite their comparatively limited range and weaponry stocks, a relative handful of RAF and Royal Navy Harrier aircraft not only helped to vitiate attempts by Argentinean Skyhawks, Super Étendards and Mirages to assail the naval task force, but also provided invaluable support to British ground forces as and after these landed on the islands. In turn, the carriers' own security became an imperative. Indeed, while US carriers had performed a significant part in the Korean and Vietnam wars, their role was essentially intermittent and peripheral. Never since the defeat of Japan in 1945 had carriers been so central to the outcome of a war as they were in the Falklands conflict.

Since their first use in combat during the 1940s, such ships had undergone appreciable refinement. For instance, in 1960 the USA launched the first nuclear-powered carrier. This had no need for the oil tanks that had taken up so much room in conventionally propelled vessels. Modern gas turbines and other relatively compact but powerful propulsion systems yielded similar benefits, enabling proportionately more accommodation to be allotted to the ship's aircraft and their fuel and munitions. There were other changes, too, not least because of the proliferation of jets. These, because of their greater weight, which led to slower acceleration, higher landing speeds and increased fuel consumption, compounded some of the difficulties encountered in designing and operating carriers. British innovations especially helped to overcome some of them: a mirror landing-signal system and steam-propelled launch catapults were introduced, as were angled flight decks. Moreover, although carriers were generally much larger than before – modern big carriers are typically twice the displacement of their counterparts in the Second World War and yet cannot accommodate very much larger quantities of aircraft – smaller versions, such as the British Invincible class, one of which participated in the Falklands campaign, were developed with specific missions in mind. These were viable because, besides helicopters, they made use of planes capable of taking off either vertically or on very short runways, which the British supplemented with simple but ingenious 'ski' ramps.

Early attempts to devise fixed-wing aircraft with vertical take-off and landing (VTOL) capabilities foundered on a rudimentary problem. A plane flies because, as it moves forward, the passage of air across its wings generates lift. To travel vertically, it needs to be able to generate enough downward thrust to raise both its own weight and any load from the surface. Not least because bigger engines can increase the machine's overall weight commensurably, this can consume a disproportionate amount of the energy provided by even the most powerful motors, leaving comparatively little to propel it horizontally, as with the helicopter. Moreover, accommodating engines and their fuel deprives other cargoes, notably weapons, of room. These flaws marred designs such as the American Hummingbird, the British SC-1 and the French Balzac, the last two of which had five and nine motors respectively, mostly just for producing vertical thrust. The challenge was, therefore, to develop a so-called convertiplane that, once airborne, would be able to channel the power of its solitary engine into creating rapid, horizontal movement.

Because of their superior thrust-generating capacity, ever-improving turbojets with swivelling nozzles offered a suitably compact solution to the energy requirements for VTOL. By dramatically enhancing their power-to-weight ratio, the spread of new, light but sturdy alloys and composite materials throughout aeronautical engineering has also improved the speed of such planes as the Hawker Siddeley Harrier and the Russian Yak-36 Forager, though they remain subsonic machines. The former, for instance, is fitted with Rolls-Royce Pegasus engines that generate up to 24,000 pounds (10,886 kg) of thrust. This enables the aircraft to hover for brief periods, but devours large amounts of fuel and coolant. Short take-off and landing (STOL) is thus the preferred modus operandi where runway space is limited, notably aboard small carriers such as the Invincible class, where the flight deck's 'ski jump' helps a fully laden Harrier to get airborne.

That such planes are not necessarily reliant on vulnerable, purpose-built bases, be they ashore or afloat, makes them ideal machines for use in expeditionary warfare – an advantage recognized by, among others, the US Marine Corps, which currently has the world's largest force of Harriers. Certainly, in dogfights over the Falklands these splendid machines, armed with the latest air-to-air Sidewinder missiles, which used infrared sensors to home in on the heat emitted by their targets' engines, destroyed numerous Argentinean aircraft for no loss to themselves. However, flying a Harrier calls for exceptional dexterity. In its successor, the F-35, computers ease the pilot's burden, not least by automating such taxing manoeuvres as hovering.

This is symptomatic of a wider trend within military technology: the enhancement of human faculties through the substitution of electrical circuitry for muscle and mechanical engineering. While not exclusively dependent upon the calibre of its material machinery, any air force is largely so. Although the missions performed by aerial units remain the same as in the infancy of military aviation, the refinement of mature technologies and the adoption of nascent ones have not only radically altered air power's ability to carry out these functions but have also done so at a rate not seen across the gamut of armed forces.

The design of tanks and other fighting vehicles, for instance, improved substantially between the 1940s and '80s. Yet this was as nothing when set against the strides made in that of combat planes through the application of wings of variable camber and sweep, jet engines, ejector-seats, in-flight refuelling systems and, above all, precision-guided munitions (PGMs),[78] night-vision devices, image intensifiers and other avionics, and radar-absorbing 'stealthy' constructions and materials. There was no comparable development in maritime warfare either, despite the widespread replacement of mechanical with electrical engineering. Even during the Second World War, warships, for all their steel plating and often very strong, active defences, had too often proved vulnerable to attack by aircraft especially. Heavy metallic armour steadily became a rarity in the aftermath of that conflict, with the result that, as the Falklands campaign highlighted, modern vessels cannot withstand anything like the punishment that their ancestors were built to absorb. Moreover, although mostly physically smaller than their predecessors, today's warships are not generally faster; in fact, the top speeds of sizeable craft are much like those attained by similar vessels during the First World War. Most modern fixed-wing combat aircraft, by contrast, are capable of supersonic flight and routinely travel at speeds that would have been considered extraordinary in the 1940s. Furthermore, while attempts to bolster the warship's active and passive defences against aerial attack have included the addition of electronic warfare devices and sophisticated missile systems, as in the Second World War the principal form of protection still remains a screen of friendly planes that are capable of keeping those of an opponent at bay. Much the same remains true of land warfare. Such has been the degree of air cover enjoyed by the USA's ground forces in recent conflicts that, until 28 were killed during the Gulf War of 1991 by a Scud rocket – which, as much by accident as design, hit their barracks – no American soldier had perished in an air attack since 1953.[79]

Although by no means the only factor, the achievement and maintenance of a technical 'edge', especially in the air, have been crucial determinants in deciding recent conflicts. Nowhere has this been more vividly illustrated than in the various clashes that have occurred in the Middle East. In the Arab–Israeli War of 1967, the Israeli Air Force (IAF) achieved both strategic and tactical surprise, catching first most of Egypt's aviation and then that of Jordan and Syria on the ground. Within a few hours, the Egyptians alone lost 309 out of their 340 available aircraft. In all, some 500 Arab planes were destroyed, whereas the IAF lost just 20. With their command of the skies virtually uncontested and their own operating bases unmolested, the Israelis were at liberty to maximize their sortie rates and make optimum use of their air power in close support of their ground forces. This helped lead to the

Arab armies, despite their numerical strength, being routed in as little as six days.

Superior in design though the Israeli aircraft were, this outcome is not to be explained purely in terms of technological preponderance. In the final analysis, any equipment is only as good as its operators. As planes have become more sophisticated, a commensurably higher degree of skill among ground- and air-crews alike has become necessary for their effective use. Thus, much depends on the training and general calibre of personnel; and it was in this regard that the IAF's superiority over its Arab counterparts was most pronounced. Even when confronted with seemingly formidable technology – notably Russian-supplied SAMs of the type that, only a few years earlier, had proved capable of bringing down a U-2 – the Israelis prevailed through better tactics.

In the so-called Yom Kippur War of October 1973, the Arabs, however, having learnt from this experience, made every effort to blunt the impact that the IAF might have on the fighting. An integrated, well-sited and skilfully coordinated air defence network inflicted heavy losses on Israeli squadrons seeking to check the advancing Egyptian ground forces, while only the sacrifice of some 40 aircraft in desperate spoiling attacks enabled the Israelis to thwart the Syrians' bid to over-run the Golan Heights. Nevertheless, as the Egyptians ventured beyond the protection of their AA defences and as the network itself was gradually neutralized by Israeli tactical and technical countermeasures, the IAF was able to reassert itself. Once more, owing to a combination of Israeli preventative steps and a failure on the part of the Arab air forces to hinder the process, the IAF was left at liberty to 'turn around' its planes in the shortest of time spans and fulfil its role as the Israeli armed services' cardinal strike force.

The first half of the 1980s also witnessed exemplary applications of air power by the Israelis. When, in 1981, their intelligence reports suggested that Iraq was embarking on the construction of atomic weapons, the IAF performed a round trip of some 800 miles (1,287 km) to wreck her nuclear plant at Osirak. Complete surprise was achieved, and all the planes involved regained their bases safely. Likewise, in 1985, a handful of Israeli aircraft – which were refuelled in the air en route and had their approach masked by a Boeing 707 equipped for electronic warfare – skirted the Mediterranean for some 1,600 miles (2,575 km) to assail the Palestine Liberation Organization's headquarters at Tunis. Once more, surprise was achieved, the building was destroyed with laser-guided bombs and all the attackers returned home. By contrast, when the Americans followed suit with a raid on Libya the following year, the operation was far from blemish-free.[80] Nevertheless, the action did seem to have the desired effect of persuading Moamar Qaddafi that he could not promote terrorism 'without cost'.[81]

Impressive though the foregoing was, what was arguably the most spectacular display of the IAF's technical and tactical pre-eminence during this period occurred in the Beqaa Valley in Lebanon during 1982. Here, the Syrians had erected a large and carefully integrated web of surface-to-air weapons in a bid to impede collaboration between Israeli aviation and ground forces. However, after employing Scouts – remotely piloted vehicles equipped with electro-optical sensors and digital communication systems – to scour the valley and reconnoitre the Syrian airfields and SAM batteries in the vicinity, the Israelis launched several unguided drones that could mimic combat planes electronically. Compelled to keep their target-acquisition radars switched on in order to engage this apparent threat, the SAMs were themselves then assailed with missiles that homed in on their own radar beams. Simultaneously, the Syrians' communications and attack radars were jammed by Boeing 707 airliners and CH-23 helicopters that had been equipped with electronic warfare devices, while Israeli E-2C reconnaissance planes monitored the enemy's airspace, guiding IAF fighters to intercept hostile machines the moment they took off. Neither could the numerous Syrian AA cannons and man-portable rockets molest the Israeli planes much either, for they operated at ranges and altitudes beyond the reach of these armaments, using their advanced avionics and PGMs to pick off their targets.

The outcome was a disaster for the Syrians. In under a month, approximately twenty SAM batteries were destroyed, together with 85 of their MiG fighters, whereas only two IAF planes were lost. The element of technical surprise had been as significant, if not more so, as operational surprise. The Israelis' mastery of the skies was again preserved and, with it, their ability to mount effective ground operations, even against numerically superior opponents. Indeed, air power has been the key to Israel's survival throughout her history. It formed, and forms, the cornerstone of her military might, with her strength in this regard compensating for her vulnerability in others.[82]

Not least because it left them feeling vulnerable, for much of the Cold War many people were pardonably critical of the policy of nuclear deterrence pursued by, above all, the two superpowers. Yet whereas the proliferation of atomic armaments and the concomitant rise of a polycentric international order intensified the fears of some, others welcomed these trends as a guarantor of stability. It was, in any case, difficult to suggest a viable alternative to MAD, regardless of how one explicates that acronym. The scientific discoveries that had led to nuclear weapons could hardly be forgotten, any more than the rivalry between the various powers could be conjured away, dangerous though it sometimes appeared. However, alongside those few radicals who either wanted to blow up the world or, through unattainable, total disarmament, hoped to save it were those who sought to use arms control measures and technological innovations to underpin deterrence and, should that fail, to mitigate any war's destructive effects.

Together with China's perfection of an atomic bomb in 1964, the Soviets' rapid enlargement of their ICBM stockpile in the aftermath of the Cuban Crisis ignited the first debate in the USA about some form of active ballistic missile defence (BMD). Faced, on the one hand, with Congressional demands for anti-ballistic missile (ABM) interceptors and, on the other, with the USSR's initial reluctance to commit itself to bilateral talks over strategic weaponry and the curtailment of the erection of ABM networks, Defense Secretary Robert McNamara was in a dilemma. For a time, he felt that the USA would be left with no alternative other than to construct a national ABM system. There were concerns about the impact that such a step would have on the Non-Proliferation Treaty negotiations, however. Moreover, likened to hitting one bullet with another, BMD appeared to be as technically challenging as it seemed financially prohibitive. With McNamara concluding that the best way to counter any Soviet defences was with more and better offensive missiles, the often heated discussions eventually yielded a compromise proposal.[83] An ABM system, Nike-X – later known as Sentinel – would be developed to counter any emerging Chinese rocket threat.

Announced in 1967, this decision was to be echoed by NATO's Nuclear Planning Group the following year, when it rejected the suggestion that a European missile shield should be devised.[84] Meanwhile, the Soviets' deliberations about ABM defences were proceeding much like the Americans'.[85] Indeed, anxious to preserve the status quo, both superpowers were in the end content to accept the ABM and SALT Treaties of 1972, whereby they pledged essentially not to do what they had no overwhelming desire to do anyway. Indubitably, the costs of the projected ABM defence networks outweighed their likely advantages, while SALT I left both sides free to refine and expand their nuclear forces in a more selective fashion, notably through the procurement of systems that might survive, and then respond to, any initial attack with a crushing, retaliatory blow.[86]

Costly though they were, submarine-launched weapons were among those most likely to evade destruction and, consequently, were invested in heavily. The USSR took the lead in equipping submarines with ballistic missiles. The ill-fated K-19, which foundered in 1961, was one of a class that carried three. Whereas early rockets relied upon volatile, liquid propellants that had to be pumped into them before use – a process that could take twenty minutes or more – the advent of 'plasticized' fuels reduced both launch times and the space needed to accommodate such armaments. Although the Soviets persevered with liquid propellants, employing them in both their R-21/SS-N-5 and R-27/SS-N-6 rockets,[87] the Americans used this innovation to ease the incorporation of Polaris, Poseidon and, later, Trident ballistic missiles into their submarine fleet's arsenal. Combined with the fitting to such rockets of several warheads – each of which could be programmed to descend on a different target if desired – this enabled a colossal amount of firepower to be housed aboard a solitary vessel. Moreover, both the USA and the USSR perfected compressed-air booster mechanisms that could thrust ballistic rockets from submarines to the surface, where their engines ignited, thereby creating the capacity to mount attacks from beneath the waves.

That submarines of the time could remain submerged for relatively short periods had often proved a fatal limitation during the Second World War. However, the eradication of this drawback through the substitution of atomic for diesel propulsion was highlighted in 1960, when the USS *Triton* circumnavigated the Earth, travelling 41,519 miles (66,804 km) in 84 days without surfacing. Whereas static, land-based missiles, even those in deep, 'hardened' silos, remained vulnerable to location and pre-emptive destruction, submarines were much less likely to be found. Not only were they able to exploit the third dimension, but also the only restraints on their freedom of movement were the reach of their missiles and communication systems. Provided they stayed within range of their targets and in touch, at least passively, with their high command, they could disappear into the deep ocean and await the order to unleash their lethal cargoes.

But whereas in 1955 Churchill had expressed the hope that, within this deterrence framework, safety might prove 'the sturdy child of terror, and survival the twin brother of annihilation',[88] sooner or later there were bound to be others more reluctant to acquiesce in such an unpalatable situation. In 1983 the US President, Ronald Reagan, unveiled his vision of an alternative security arrangement, the Strategic Defence Initiative (SDI), which was widely dubbed 'Star Wars' after the popular science-fiction trilogy. The unveiling of this plan for exotic, space-based defences that might intercept incoming ICBMs was coincident with, and influenced by, a marked deterioration in East–West relations as a result of the deployment of a new generation of intermediate-range missiles. In response to the Soviets fielding the mobile, nuclear-armed SS-20 ballistic rocket in Central Europe, NATO had started basing new Pershing and cruise-type Tomahawk missiles in Britain, West Germany and Italy. These, too, could be fitted with atomic payloads and, like the SS-20, fired from transporters. This rendered them harder to target and made their launch sites difficult to predict. Moreover, the Tomahawks, essentially versatile descendants of the wartime V-1, posed any defender with complex, novel challenges. With a reach of up to 1,000 miles (1,609 km) and guided by on-board artificial intelligence devices that were small but sufficiently sophisticated to 'read' the underlying terrain, they did not follow a fixed trajectory. Rather, they hugged the ground's contours, despite travelling at considerable speed. They could thus, if only to some extent, mimic manned aircraft without suffering from the drawbacks attached to any inhabited platform. Not only could they follow flight paths of a kind that would have defied even the most accomplished of human pilots, as machines, cruise missiles could not tire or be frightened. This made them ideal for assailing heavily defended targets with a high degree of precision.

Alongside the planned SDI, there were also calls for a European Defence Initiative (EDI), with, among others, Manfred Wörner – West Germany's Defence Minister and, subsequently, NATO's Secretary-General – advocating the enhancement of the alliance's existing air defences so that they would be able to counter cruise and tactical ballistic missiles.[89] NATO's growing fascination with the concept of Follow-on Force Attack (FOFA) – whereby the rear echelons of Warsaw Pact ground forces would, from the outset of any conflict, be pounded by highly accurate conventionally armed rockets – also testifies to the perceived potential of modern missile weaponry during this period. For their part, the Soviets, too, were anticipating a time when improved technology would enable missiles to replace inhabited platforms in many missions, releasing them for other assignments. Pointing to 'the emergence . . . of automated reconnaissance-strike systems, long-range high-accuracy terminally-guided weapons, unmanned aircraft, and qualitatively new electronic systems', Marshal Ogarkov, Chief of the Soviet General Staff, argued that missiles and uninhabited aerial vehicles (UAVs) could eventually become global in their reach and capable of such accurate targeting that the use of conventional warheads would be sufficiently destructive for most purposes. Whereas mounting a large aerial offensive with planes would demand both a high degree of coordination and the suppression of NATO's air defences, missiles, Ogarkov reasoned, could be manufactured and used en masse with relative ease and would be more likely to reach their targets. This would permit the exploitation, to an unprecedented degree, of the capacity of air power to avoid protracted, sequential operations and rapidly inflict damage that might be politically exploitable.[90]

Yet this very quality troubled the Soviets, for it blurs the once neat distinctions between war's tactical and strategic levels. Like the Cuban Crisis, the deployment, in the 1980s, of cruise missiles on one side of the Iron Curtain and ss-20 rockets on the other, both of which were armed with nuclear warheads, created a dilemma for friend and foe alike. Whereas NATO's Tomahawks and Pershings were capable of hitting 'strategic' targets not merely in the Soviets' glacis of Central Europe but also in the western reaches of the USSR itself, the ss-20 could only directly threaten the territory of America's European allies, not the continental USA. While this engendered fears among some Western Europeans that their security and that of the Americans could be 'decoupled', to the Russians it appeared that these inter-mediate-range weapons jeopardized the strategic balance between the superpowers. Accordingly, on becoming Soviet leader, Mikhail Gorbachev quickly began negotiations to secure their withdrawal in return for the destruction of all the ss-20s. This rather asymmetrical deal was formally ratified in 1987 and was followed in 1989 by a treaty between Washington and Moscow concerning reductions in strategic arsenals.

Gorbachev, on the other hand, was unable to persuade Reagan to abandon the SDI. Although this particular scheme never came to fruition in the form originally envisaged, the militarization of space was already well under way. As early as August 1960, just three months after Powers had been shot down, the USA had substituted a much more efficient and less provocative intelligence-gathering device for its u-2 aircraft. Launched on a Discovery rocket, the Corona spy satellite was virtually invulnerable to attack and, from the supreme vantage-point of space, could take pictures of as much as one million square miles (2.6 million sq. km) of Soviet territory. Although the picture resolution – which was sufficiently good to reveal objects as small as 20 feet (6.1 m) across – was slightly poorer, this was many times the area covered by the u-2's cameras. In fact, a solitary reel of film, shot in a single day, could yield more coverage than had all of the u-2 flights put together. Initially, capsules of exposed film were automatically dispatched from such observation platforms by parachute and, on re-entering the Earth's atmosphere, were intercepted and reeled in by a specially adapted c-119 aircraft.[91] However, the subsequent development of digital and other suitable transmission media greatly speeded up and generally facilitated the whole process of collecting information about putative foes.

Indeed, within 40 years of the end of the Second World War, the exploitation of breakthroughs in electrical engineering, not least the miniaturization of components and exponential increases in the processing capacity of computers, was transfiguring the day-to-day existence of millions of people. That the (then state-of-the-art) flight-computer which, in 1969, guided the lunar-module from Apollo 11 to the Moon's surface possessed a smaller memory than most mobile telephones have today is testimony to the sheer pace of this change. But nowhere was this transformation more dramatic than in the sphere of military power, where the inexorable enhancing of human faculties through the replacement of mechanical engineering with electrical circuitry played a significant part in ending the protracted Cold War.

For much of its duration, the competition between the West and the USSR had essentially been confined to the military arena, as the Soviets had steadily fallen behind politically and economically, if not culturally. The possession of immense armed forces in general and nuclear ones in particular had, however, enabled them to maintain their image as a superpower. Yet, by the 1980s, the façade was crumbling. As early as October 1982, Brezhnev was openly expressing fears that 'Technological advances necessitated by future military requirements might be beyond the sophistication of ... [our state-controlled] economy.'[92] It was the nature and structure of that economy that were the fundamental problems, not a lack of investment in the armed services as such. In fact, one knowledgeable member of the Congress of People's Deputies stated in 1990 that, contrary to official figures, the military had been devouring between 20 and 25 per cent of the GNP,[93] while those sectors of the economy that had built a formidable war-fighting machine and had enabled the dispatching of scores of cosmonauts on eye-catching space missions had long been the repository for the USSR's very best administrators, scientists and technicians. Now, impressive though it seemed, her existing martial strength and her capacity to preserve it in the face of an ongoing arms race were being undermined by the ability of the West's entrepreneurs to mass-produce computer chips and other electrical components that, steadily shrinking in size and cost yet increasingly refined, would clearly revolutionize many aspects of both quotidian life and warfare. Indeed, by the time he came to power, Gorbachev had concluded that the Soviets could not hope to keep abreast of the relentless harnessing of multifarious sensors, computers and other convoluted circuitry to an ever-wider range of armaments, command, control and communication systems, weapon platforms and military activities, such as intelligence-gathering, targeting and electronic warfare. If the USSR was to remain a great power and her citizens' demands for consumer goods were to be met, the regeneration of her industrial base, the channelling of resources from the military into the civil economy and the embracing of a more conciliatory foreign policy were all essential measures.

By the end of the 1980s, air power seemed poised to fulfil the promise that generations of visionaries had glimpsed in it. Certainly, the Gulf War of 1991 witnessed the realization of aspects of Ogarkov's prophecy. When, in 1961, Iraq had first threatened to seize the oil-rich sheikdom of Kuwait, the British had reacted with an impressive airlift of troops and supplies. Although it stretched the RAF's transport capabilities, it underlined the mobility that air power could bestow and, executed at great speed, was a salutary act of power projection.

What was to occur some 30 years later, however, was to dwarf this undertaking in both scale and complexity. No sooner had King Fahd agreed to the deployment of US troops in Saudi Arabia than the Americans and their allies began a huge airlift. On 9 August 1990 – the day that Saddam Hussein proclaimed the establishment of a 'provisional government of Kuwait' – the Fifteenth Tactical Fighter Wing, having flown for more than fourteen hours from the USA, necessitating seven aerial refuelling operations, started patrolling the Saudi frontier. Within 24 hours, they had been joined by a squadron of

RAF Tornado air-defence fighters that had travelled to Dhahran. More personnel and *matériel* followed at the same rapid tempo. American strategic transporters mounted 91 missions to Saudi Arabia during the first two days alone, and more than 70 on each day for the remainder of the month.[94] Many of these trips originated in the USA, with the planes taking just fifteen hours to deliver a cargo 8,000 miles (12,872 km). In-flight refuelling operations were on a commensurate scale, with some 12,800 tonnes of kerosene being dispensed to RAF and other friendly aircraft by British tankers alone.[95] Meanwhile, large numbers of American Civil Reserve and other privately owned planes joined in helping to transport thousands of troops and their paraphernalia, a process facilitated by the quality of Saudi Arabia's airfields, which, like her ports, were among the world's largest and best developed. In fact, the airlift was larger than that used to sustain Berlin in 1948–9 and, during the crucial 30 days following the decision to intervene, enabled Iraq's adversaries to rush in 38,000 soldiers together with 39,000 tonnes of supplies and equipment. Its very size and speed, combined with the presence of substantial naval units, probably deterred Saddam from making further aggressive moves that might have disrupted, if not halted, the influx of hostile surface units. Certainly, even at this early stage he ceded the strategic initiative. While the opposing coalition was left to concentrate overwhelming strength, his forces focused on consolidating their grip on Kuwait.

Ostensibly impressive though they were, Saddam's armed services were ill-prepared for the storm that was about to engulf them. Nowhere was this clearer than in the realm of aerial operations, on which control of both land and sea largely depended. The Iraqis' recent, attritional conflict with Iran offered few lessons as far as the large-scale use of modern air power was concerned, and they sorely underestimated the impact it would have on the impending confrontation.[96] Although their air force mustered more than 600 combat planes – many of them MiG-29s, Mirage F.1s, SU-24 ground-attack aircraft and other advanced machines – it had negligible electronic detection and warfare capabilities. Indeed, too much faith was invested in firepower alone. Having wrapped their heartland in an integrated air defence web – comprising 16,000 SAMs and 7,000 guns – the Iraqis misjudged their opponents' ability to penetrate it in strength and, often using stand-off and other PGMs, to strike at targets by both night and day. Iraqi command, control and intelligence-gathering mechanisms were as inflexible as they were rudimentary, too.[97] Certainly, there was nothing that could even begin to compare with the Allies' Airborne Warning and Control System (AWACS), or the Americans' brand new Joint Surveillance and Target Attack Radar System (JSTARS). Mounted in E-8 aircraft, the latter could monitor most of the theatre of war with a radar that could sweep almost 11,000 square miles (28,500 sq. km) of territory twice a minute. Likewise, the USA's reconnaissance, communication and navigational satellites were assets that their adversaries could only envy. By enabling users to calculate their bearings to within 15 feet (4.6 m), the Navstar Global Positioning System (GPS) rendered, for instance, the traversing of essentially featureless deserts – which, furthermore, were sporadically swept by blinding sandstorms – a far easier and safer undertaking.

In practice, much of this equipment's very sophistication barred all but the Americans themselves from using it. Indeed, many of the coalition members' contributions to the air campaign especially were of more political than military value. Still, tactical adroitness was as much a hallmark of the operation as superior technology. Allied planes predominantly attacked in 'packages' comprising several dozen machines with complementary capabilities. While this modus operandi helped to bewilder opponents and compelled them to divide their fire among numerous, fleeting targets, it demanded extraordinary organizational skills. That hundreds of planes could be committed either simultaneously or nearly simultaneously to raids is testimony, not only to air power's capacity to combine speed, reach and omnidirectional approach to achieve an adequate concentration of strength, but also to the unified and dextrous nature of the Allied air forces' high command. Although he did not enjoy direct control of those units that were not from the USAF, in his capacity as Joint Forces Air Component Commander, General Charles Horner shouldered the responsibility of managing the war zone's airspace. While some squadrons from the coalition's eleven national air arms occasionally rejected specific assignments, he achieved a remarkable degree of collaboration among

them. Any other considerations aside, this kept the chances of colli-
sions or inadvertent exchanges of fire between friendly planes to a
minimum, making his direction of some 110,000 sorties as exemplary
a feat of choreography as it was militarily telling.

The number of sorties undertaken is a reflection of the sheer size
of the task that confronted the Allied aviators. Neutralizing Iraq's own
air force was but one of their objectives, for the aerial offensive was
always envisaged as part of a wider, joint operation, even though there
was some hope that it might reduce the scale and intensity of any
surface combat. However, Iraq possessed no fewer than 24 major aerodromes, as well as various secondary installations. That at Talil alone
covered an area twice the size of London's Heathrow Airport, while
nearly all of these bases were furnished with multiple runways and
taxiways, numerous hardened shelters for aircraft and active defences
of such lavish density that they even surpassed anything that NATO's
pilots had anticipated encountering in the event of a war against the
Warsaw Pact. Putting these aerodromes and their planes out of action
and then keeping them that way were demanding assignments. The
RAF Tornadoes, for instance, executed daring raids in which, from a
few score feet above the ground and employing techniques and technology originally devised with Cold War adversaries in mind, they
carpeted runways with anti-personnel and other mines fitted with
an assortment of fuses. Almost inevitably, some planes were lost.

Nevertheless, these and other attacks swiftly yielded results. It had
been assumed that, once hostilities began, the Iraqi Air Force would
be able to mount a 'surge', which, until the Allies' aerial campaign
began to bite, would peak at between 900 and 1,000 combat sorties
each day.[98] Yet, not least because they were lulled into a false sense of
security by elaborate deception schemes, on the eve of the coalition's
offensive, the Iraqis' aerial activity had already declined to as little
as 100 sorties per day. In fact, their forces were even more taken aback
by the Allied onslaught than had been hoped. Far from the anticipated
'surge' occurring, their daily sortie rate actually dwindled further in
the first 72 hours of the campaign and, by day four, had slumped to
only twenty.

Indeed, Iraq's air power quickly succumbed to a combination of its own flaws and the Allies' technological, tactical and managerial prowess. The Americans' few 'stealth' planes, for instance, had an impact disproportionate to their numbers. Darkness, weather fronts, camouflage, jamming devices and sheer speed had long been used to screen the movements of military aircraft, but efforts to counter the detection of both surface and aerial platforms – be it by optical instruments (including the human eye) or by acoustic, infrared or other sensors – had been redoubled during the 1960s, yielding, among other things, the world's first 'stealthy' aircraft, the SR-71 Blackbird, which entered service in 1966. Ingeniously shaped, constructed from titanium and composite materials and clad in radar-absorbing paint to give off the smallest echo possible, this remarkable machine could, moreover, attain velocities in excess of 2,000 mph (3,200 kmh) and altitudes of 80,000 feet (24,400 m), making it very hard for even the most sophisticated of radar-guided weapons to spot – let alone strike – it. However, whereas the SR-71 was, for all its versatility in this role, purely for reconnaissance, the generation of 'stealth' planes that emerged in the 1980s comprised bombers and fighter-bombers.

Furthermore, they emitted, at most, miniscule radar 'signatures'. Although subsonic, F-117 Nighthawks, for instance, could scarcely be detected electronically and were commensurably versatile, particularly if used in nocturnal raids. Besides being able to penetrate even the best protected of areas without the support of the usual 'package' of escort and jamming planes, they were more likely to destroy any target in one fell swoop with their laser-guided weaponry. By severing the knots within the Iraqi AA web, they unravelled much of it. Other platforms and weapon systems then overcame the remaining air defences by alternative means: Tomahawks, for example, flew too low and fast for the opposition to engage them efficaciously, whereas manned aircraft could, once the comprehensive SAM network had been neutralized, operate above the ceiling of most guns. With virtual impunity, they concentrated on wrecking hardened shelters with suitably powerful bombs. More than 370 were destroyed or badly damaged, many with aircraft inside them. Faced with annihilation, Iraq's residual planes sought cover elsewhere. By the ninth day of the offensive, many had been dispersed within woods and settlements, while 148 had sought sanctuary in Iran and had been interned. Thereafter, there was negligible Iraqi air activity.[99]

By the time that major Allied ground units were unleashed against the enemy's positions, the air offensive had done immense damage not only to Iraq's aviation and its bases but also to targets across the length and breadth of her military, industrial, governmental, transport and energy-generating infrastructure. Alongside more than 320 Tomahawk attacks, manned aircraft had undertaken more than 100,000 sorties. These had rained down roughly 85,000 tonnes of bombs, including 6,250 tonnes of PGMs.[100] The latter and the cruise missiles proved especially deadly, highlighting the strides made in accuracy and, consequently, lethality. Laser-guided bombs dropped by Nighthawks, for example, were almost invariably accurate to within ten feet (3 m), whereas only 7 per cent of the bombs disgorged by B-17s during the Second World War had landed within 1,000 feet (305 m) of their target. Often, a solitary, sophisticated aircraft using 'smart' munitions could prove more destructive than a 'package' of planes seeking to saturate a target with hundreds of 'dumb' ones. It could achieve its objective, moreover, with minimal risk to itself. Indeed, owing to their 'stealthy' design and ability to employ 'smart' weaponry, it fell to less than 3 per cent of the coalition's available planes to assail more than 30 per cent of the strategic targets attacked, including 80 per cent of those in Baghdad.[101]

While such attributes further endeared air power to those elected politicians who craved exploitable military results for few, if any, casualties, even within NATO there was but a tiny handful of states that actually possessed the requisite technology. 'Stealth' aircraft were – and remain – uniquely American, while, at this juncture, only the RAF and the French Air Force (Armée de l'Air) had any capacity whatsoever when it came to mounting 'surgical' strikes with precision weapons. Indeed, some of their senior officers candidly acknowledged an emerging 'differential' between their own units and those of the USAF.[102]

No sooner had air power 'come of age'[103] in the Gulf conflict than these intertwined problems were being highlighted in the skies over the disintegrating Federal Republic of Yugoslavia (FRY). As the Cold

War petered out, several of the international organizations that had been spawned by it found themselves in a Darwinian race for survival. One after another, they and others endeavoured to bring peace to the troubled Balkans and, by so doing, justify their own continuing existence. Interlocking in the eyes of their advocates and mutually obstructive in those of their critics, all that is certain is that they failed and handed the task to the United Nations Organization (UNO).

What ensued was really an effort to manage, rather than end, a civil war. The 'peace-keepers' found, often to their bitter cost, that there was no peace to keep. Yet, several 'safe havens' were proclaimed by the UNO, an institution that had neither the will nor the means to protect them adequately. Although sizeable ground forces were eventually provided by member states, these seldom clashed with the belligerents at all. Rather, NATO – as a regional security organization – was mandated to use its air power to condition the warring factions' behaviour. A no-fly zone, akin to those imposed on Iraq after her defeat, was introduced over Bosnia in 1993, and, with the UNO's express permission, several pinprick attacks were made on – mostly Serbian – land units that were threatening the integrity of the havens. These proved ineffectual. Not only were the Serbs not coerced, but also their opponents were encouraged to go on resisting by the expectation that the great powers would, if only to salvage their own credibility, have to intervene decisively sooner or later. Sure enough, with acrimonious disagreements emerging between the USA and her NATO partners as well as between the West and the Russians, the Americans – who had tried to remain aloof and whose sporadic efforts to broker a peace had been resented by some of the more ambitious polities and institutions – seized control of the situation by effectively subordinating the tarnished UN to the transatlantic alliance.

So it was that NATO, in a policy redolent of the 'air control' of the 1920s, embarked upon Operation 'Deliberate Force' in August 1995. Political 'burden-sharing' and the avoidance of 'collateral damage' were accentuated, sometimes at the expense of military effectiveness. More than 3,500 sorties were flown, including several reconnaissance and electronic warfare missions that, in its first combat assignment since 1945, were executed by the Luftwaffe. For the sake of solidarity, the alliance's other air forces were also urged to participate in some 850 bombing raids, though the vast majority could do no more than drop 'dumb' bombs on appropriate targets. In all, 1,026 weapons were released, of which 708 were PGMS. These were used by American and British aircraft against, above all, the nodes of the Bosnian Serbs' command and communication network. This eroded their leaders' ability to control and coordinate their forces' activities, thereby preventing them from pursuing their strategy. Powerless to ward off the aerial attacks either, they faced the distinct possibility that their adversaries on the ground would exploit this situation. Under these circumstances, agreeing to a ceasefire was their least unpalatable option. They duly grasped it on 15 September 1995.

In so far that it helped towards the achievement of the political objective – the imposition of an armistice – 'Deliberate Force' was a successful strategic bombing campaign. Yet it also exemplified some of the conundrums encountered in trying to use aerial attacks as a coercive tool. Whereas in land combat territory gained or ceded furnishes at least a crude indication as to who is making headway, progress in air warfare is frequently much harder to gauge. While NATO's air raids certainly compounded the problems confronting the Serbs on the ground, as in other conflicts economic sanctions and diplomatic initiatives also contributed to the outcome.

This was indubitably the case with Operation 'Allied Force', the 78-day aerial campaign over Kosovo in spring 1999. Another corner of the collapsing FRY, this province of Serbia was predominantly populated by ethnic Albanians, who were bent on gaining independence from Belgrade. From their midst emerged the 'Kosovo Liberation Army' (KLA), the aspirations of which included the unification, by violent means, of all the Albanians of the Balkans within a single polity. Just as had occurred in Vietnam and elsewhere, the rise of guerrilla warfare blurred the distinctions between combatants and non-combatants, creating scope for a spiral of atrocity and counter-atrocity. Certainly, as the Serbian security forces resorted to increasingly repressive measures, the struggle within Kosovo became ever more barbaric, notwithstanding NATO's 'solemn warning' to President Slobodan Milošević, the shuttle diplomacy of the USA's special envoy, Richard

Holbrooke, and the avuncular – and often competing – efforts of the UN, the European Union, the Conference on Security and Co-operation in Europe and a 'Contact Group' of six major powers. By mid-September 1998 scores of thousands of people had either abandoned or been driven from their homes in Kosovo, and the crisis was jeopardizing the fragile stability of neighbouring states.

In an undertaking that was never formally endorsed by the UN Security Council and was criticized by many as a violation of the UN Charter, NATO assailed the FRY in March 1999 in a bid to hamper the Serbs' molestation of the Kosovo Albanians.[104] Although troops were also accumulated along the FRY's borders, drubbing Milošević into good behaviour was ultimately left to the transatlantic alliance's air forces. In all, they mounted 38,004 sorties, including 10,484 bombing raids that devoured 23,614 munitions between them. In addition to attacks within Kosovo, AA defences in Montenegro and bridges and other targets in Belgrade were hit, much to the concern of French and Russian ministers especially. With several other governments, notably those in Germany and Italy, already fearful of the potential electoral costs of this controversial conflict, politicians strove to control every detail of the military operations. Although ordered to remain beyond the reach of AA guns and missiles, pilots were also instructed to avoid 'collateral damage' through 'surgical' strikes, a particularly taxing requirement from 15,000 feet (4,572 m) and in changeable weather or darkness. Counterproductive incidents included the bombing of the Chinese Embassy and a convoy of refugees.

In fact, the location, identification and targeting of Serb units frequently proved impossible. During the Cold War, the FRY had intermittently feared forceful incorporation into the mainstream Communist bloc and had prepared passive and active air defences geared to countering a Soviet aerial onslaught. In the event, it was NATO's aerospace power that was neutralized. The FRY's army was skilled at dispersal and concealment tactics, including the use of electronic decoys to delude 'smart' weaponry. Consequently, many bombs were expended on barracks that were empty and on dummy, wooden tanks. Indeed, the aerial bombardment was far less effective than NATO planners and politicians believed. It did, however, prevent their opponents from concentrating their forces to deal with the KLA's incursions, a dilemma that could only have been exacerbated had NATO's waiting troops joined the fray. Like Rommel's soldiers in Normandy in 1944, the Serbs might evade or survive air attacks by scattering, but this left them vulnerable to other threats and incapable of staging offensives.

The suicidal attacks mounted against targets in the USA on 11 September 2001 provoked President George W. Bush to proclaim what he termed a 'war against terrorism'. This 'war', like the ones against drugs and crime, is a political metaphor. But whereas these last two struggles command the instinctive support of most people, any bid to subdue terrorism is essentially a battle for hearts and minds; for one man's terrorist is another's freedom fighter. Certainly, Bush's announcement was not much of a guide for action. It could not provide a foundation on which to build a coalition for the longer term, any more than it could furnish military leaders with attainable strategic goals. Beyond the initial preoccupation with capturing or killing Al-Qaida members and those sympathetic to them, there was no defined enemy and no definable objective. On the other hand, use of the term 'war' aroused calls and expectations for the employment of armed forces against some such foe in a dramatic and, above all, decisive fashion.

After an ad hoc coalition – including the indigenous Northern Alliance and other factions opposed to the Kabul regime – had ousted both Al-Qaida and the ruling Taliban from Afghanistan, Washington turned its attention to Iraq, part of what President Bush had now dubbed the 'axis of evil'. Unperturbed by its failures in the Balkans, the UNO had persisted in issuing decrees that it had neither the will nor the capacity to implement. Among these were numerous resolutions concerning the disarmament of Iraq, some of which dated back to the Gulf War of 1990–91 and reiterated the provisions of the ceasefire agreement that had concluded that conflict. Fearing that Iraq already possessed mass-casualty weapons in the form of biological and chemical agents and was seeking to develop nuclear armaments – some or all of which she might be tempted to pass to terrorist movements like Al-Qaida – the USA and the UK especially had consistently evinced a willingness to compel her to comply with these resolutions by all necessary means. Whereas maintenance of the *Pax Britannica* of the nineteenth century largely fell to the Royal Navy, enforcement of the *Pax Americana* that has emerged since the end of the Cold War has mostly been entrusted to aerospace power. Predictably, after UN inspection regimes had failed to yield satisfying results, during December 1998 RAF and American planes razed a number of Iraqi installations that were believed to be clandestinely producing proscribed weapons and delivery systems.

Operation 'Desert Fox', as these raids were known, was at best a partial solution to this problem, however. Accordingly, in March 2003 British and American forces, with some active support from Australian soldiers and planes, embarked on an invasion of Iraq, regardless of the strident objections of several UN Security Council members and millions of demonstrators across the world. Nevertheless, from the very beginning, the political complexities surrounding Operation 'Iraqi Freedom' had a profound impact on its conduct. The absence of a lengthy, aerial campaign to 'soften up' the opposition was particularly conspicuous. The need – because of the volatility of domestic, public opinion – to be seen to be making rapid progress through the apparent conquest of Iraqi territory; the imperative of minimizing 'collateral damage'; the anxiety to afford 'liberated' civilians and valuable infrastructure – notably petroleum plants – at least some protection against attack by factions loyal to the Baghdad regime; the wish to overthrow that hierarchy and seize the reins of government as swiftly as possible; the desirability of preserving at least some Iraqi security units to help underpin the post-war order; the longing to capture, intact, the port of Umm Qasr to ease the importation of, not just *matériel*, but also humanitarian aid supplies: all of these considerations compelled the coalition's members to commit their land forces from the outset of the conflict.

Some of these factors, moreover, prevented the Allies employing much of their military muscle in the most economical and effective way. This was particularly true of the aerospace power with which they had inflicted such damage in the first Gulf War. Whereas, not least because of UN inspections and economic sanctions, the Iraqi armed services had generally undergone further atrophy since that conflict, the capabilities of British and American aviation, above all, had improved appreciably. In 1991 just 10 per cent of all the bombs dropped were PGMs. In 2003, with most of their aircraft equipped with the necessary targeting aids, and the crews trained and experienced in their use, the Allies were able to undertake 'surgical' strikes on a much greater scale. For instance, all of the fighter-bombers based on the US Navy's carriers had been fitted with precision ordnance and furnished for all-weather and round-the-clock operations, while the RAF and Royal Navy had also invested heavily in armaments steered by satellites and lasers. Similarly, Tomahawk missiles had been installed in British attack submarines, and the RAF's inventory now included the Storm Shadow PGM. New 'area' weapons had been added to the armoury as well, notably the Americans' 21,000-pound (9,525 kg) MOAB (Massive Ordnance Air-Blast), the largest conventional bomb ever manufactured. Furthermore, the ability to locate targets and focus all of this destructive power against them in a timely fashion had been enhanced through the introduction of better UAVs, such as Predators, and augmentations and refinements to the USA's eavesdropping and other satellite constellations. Drones were often used to probe well-defended positions, while the latter helped to monitor the Iraqis' communications and movements.

Certainly, foremost among the quandaries facing the Iraqi high command was one that, incrementally exacerbated by technological evolution, had frustrated a succession of generals: how, in the face of American air supremacy, might operations be successfully executed and maintained on the ground? Iraq's own air force could offer only negligible assistance, for it had never recovered from the beating it had taken in 1991. Crucially, it could neither contest control of the skies, nor interdict the streams of enemy vehicles – many of which would indubitably have proved very vulnerable targets – that converged on Nasiriya, Baghdad and Basra, nor furnish friendly soldiers with close support. Neither was it possible to regain lost soil. In fact, any surface units that assembled for defence or attack in open countryside would be too exposed to detection and, above all, to aerial bombardment.

Executed by aircraft ranging from A-10 'tank-busters' to Apaches and B-52s, this threatened to obliterate even entrenched forces. The only promising strategy to hand was that of relinquishing indefensible territory and sucking the Allies into battles for built-up areas, the garrisons of which would be partially screened from observation and – not least because of the propinquity of civilians – fire.

Sure enough, this approach soon yielded both military and political dividends. Their air power constrained, if only by their own rules of engagement, the coalition partners were too often left with an unpalatable choice between street fighting and sealing off entire towns to prevent their defenders – many of whom wore civilian dress – from mounting forays against the Allies' lengthening supply lines. Whereas both these courses of action invariably call for very large numbers of troops, the second is as potentially sanguinary and destructive as it is labour-intensive. However, although the Pentagon especially had reasoned that America's command of the skies would reduce the need for surface combat units dramatically, Washington was as anxious as London to avoid costly urban warfare.

Indeed, the absolutes of the coalition's liberalism withered amid the realities of armed conflict, particularly when, after nearly a week of fighting, the Allied air forces began shifting their weight against Iraqi units embedded in the outer crusts of Baghdad especially. Up until this point, most air strikes had been directed against the Iraqi hierarchy's command and control nodes. An attempt to 'decapitate' the regime by killing Saddam Hussein began this process, which climaxed in a tremendous bombardment of governmental offices in the capital. By now comparatively cheap and plentiful, a thousand Tomahawks alone were expended on this in one night, most of them unleashed by ships and submarines. Spectacular though it appeared, rather than causing the 'shock and awe' predicted by American officials, the onslaught seems to have engendered more shrugs and yawns. While few nearby residents can have slept through the explosions, ravaging buildings that had almost certainly been cleared of everybody and everything of value beforehand appeared, at best, otiose. Even before the fighting started, Saddam, recognizing the threat posed by his adversaries' aerospace power, had disclosed that he had set up a decentralized political and military command system. Certainly, unlike the fourteen civilians who died when a marketplace was hit, he emerged unscathed and as defiant as ever, thereby underscoring the fact that bomb-damage assessments, however accurate, merely evaluate the physical destruction inflicted by a bombardment, not its psychological impact.

More generally, too many Americans struggled to comprehend the collective psyche of those whose country they had invaded. With the likelihood of the easy victory anticipated by some in the Pentagon beginning to fade, the ruffled coalition partners had to make some hasty adjustments to their calculations. Iraqi television studios and telecommunication networks were suddenly deemed to be 'dual function' facilities and attacked as the bombing of Baghdad intensified. Tellingly, Tony Blair, Britain's Prime Minister, dashed to Washington for a cursory meeting with President Bush, while 110,000 more American soldiers set out for the Gulf to join the struggle to contain and defeat hydra-headed opponents. Meanwhile, civilian casualties continued to mount. Alongside those inflicted by stray bombs and Tomahawks were the victims of 'collateral damage' to life-supporting infrastructure, notably electricity-generation and water-purification plants, much of which had still to be repaired many weeks after the fighting was officially deemed to be over. Other Iraqis suffered or perished as a result of the anarchy and looting that erupted once much of the country was left with neither military nor civil law. Indeed, as the secular authorities collapsed, the only order remaining was that furnished by Muslim clerics, few of whom regarded the interloping infidels and their reforming agenda with anything other than suspicion. Even the Allies' policy of supplying food to win over towns – which, in any traditional siege, would have been starved into submission – went awry, not least because of the difficulties in distributing aid to communities that, already suffering deprivations because of economic sanctions, were now caught up in what was as much a civil as an international war – a war that highlighted both the strengths and weaknesses of aerospace power, though ultimately successful in ending Saddam's brutal reign.

Part Two

Issues

Chapter 3

Aerospace Power's Evident Nature and its Impact on War and Peace

Fearful of the risks, expense and technical challenges inherent in the arms race that was underway as the twentieth century dawned, the Russians persuaded the Hague Peace Conference of 1899 to accept a five-year moratorium on the use of airships as weapon platforms. By the time that the ban lapsed, the Russian Empire was grappling with Japan in a struggle that presaged the First World War in so far that the spectra of technology employed in these conflicts were largely identical. Dirigibles and fixed-wing aircraft were among the handful of exceptions, not least because attempts to constrain the military's use of aviation through international accords had been abandoned by the time of the second Hague Conference in 1907. This was partly because a description of 'air power', particularly one that was sufficiently holistic and sound for use in legal documents, was almost as elusive then as it is today.

Writing shortly after the Second World War, one commentator stressed that:

> Air power is the ability of a nation to fly . . . [It] is indivisible; military and civil air power, so called, are nothing more than different uses of the same dynamic force. [T]he ability . . . to use controlled flight . . . is part of national power. . . . It is not . . . [necessarily to] be used as an application of force. Air power is simply the ability to act in the airspace.[1]

Since then, just as the development and proliferation of missile technology and helicopters have intensified debates about the institutional and command arrangements for military 'air power', so too have such trends exacerbated the problem of defining it. In 1993 the RAF's doctrinal manual *AP3000* summarized it as:

> The ability to use platforms operating in or passing through the air for military purposes. The means of exercising air power are many and include any system which can be used to wage warfare in the air: for example, manned or unmanned aircraft (fixed or rotary wing), guided missiles, balloons and space vehicles.[2]

This was fairly typical of the expositions used by air forces at this juncture, but they were barely rigorous. They could, after all, be applied to just about any 'system', except perhaps a submarine, torpedo or land-mine. Anti-tank or any other category of missiles would certainly have to be included under this rubric. On the other hand, such definitions did not cover aerospace capabilities particularly well because of the characteristics of most contemporary space platforms and their modus operandi. In any event, such a comprehensive approach was and remains a matter of dispute within armed services other than autonomous air forces. Air-mechanized operations, for instance, are regarded by soldiers as a dimension of land battles, not air engagements. Likewise, mariners would see many uses of aerospace assets as facets of naval warfare.

Certainly, the search for an all-embracing and acceptable statement of its meaning has been bedevilled by air power's relatively acute sensitivity to technological change, the growing incidence of joint-service and humanitarian-relief operations, and the diverse fashion in which differing countries set the parameters for the various branches of their armed forces. Bids to solve this conundrum are perhaps best exemplified by the lengthy clarification resorted to by the heads of the seventeen national air forces that meet within the forum of the European Air Chiefs' Conference (EURAC). In June 2001 they concluded that air power was: 'The ability to protect and employ military force in air or space by or from an air platform or missile operating above the surface of the earth', in which military force is to be understood as 'all military strength dedicated to offensive and defensive missions as well as all other non-destructive, supporting duties, such as reconnaissance or airlift'. An air platform, the definition continued, is 'any aircraft, helicopter, unmanned air vehicle, spacecraft or satellite'. Moreover, it added:

> Air Power is not only delivered by Air Forces but also includes the aerial capabilities provided by the other services (Army, Navy, Marines), and even by civilian aviation. . . . [It] is not only composed of weapon systems, but relies on personnel who employ it, infrastructures to operate from, or spare pieces vital for its use.[3]

Indeed, during recent years there has been an appreciable increase in the amount of theorizing about air power's nature and functions. We have already noted the impact of early hypotheses by the likes of Douhet and Mitchell. Nevertheless, until the late 1980s, it remained hard to disagree with David MacIsaac's ageing observation that thinkers had had 'only limited influence in a field where the effects of technology and the deeds of practitioners have from the beginning played greater roles than have ideas'.[4] However, once the Cold War – which had dominated strategic thinking for some fifty years – finally fizzled out, a new fascination with theory arose. The RAF, for instance, had spent half of its history preparing itself, both psychologically and materially, to meet the same challenge, that from the Warsaw Pact, and had scarcely concerned itself with the updating of doctrinal manuals. The AP1300 version of 1957 was withdrawn during the early 1970s, but a new one was not issued until 1991. This coincided with the appearance of similar works in several other countries and the establishment of new institutions such as the School of Advanced Airpower Studies at USAF Maxwell, Alabama.

This was partly a reaction to the disarmament race that ensued after the demise of the Cold War. Western armed services found themselves under ever more pressure to justify their budgets and force structures. There was, therefore, much to be gained by highlighting both their general utility and the specific contributions they might make within the 'new world disorder'. The British Army, for instance, astutely stressed the accumulated experience it had in 'constabulary' missions, producing a new field manual on 'wider peacekeeping' in order to be visibly prepared for UN assignments in particular. Similarly, the potential applications of aerospace power in crisis management and in war and peace ('duality') were accorded a higher public profile through conferences and publications, not least those of the EURAC, which was first formed in 1993. Its *Air Power Paper* of 2001, for instance, argued that 'the military instrument of first political choice' would remain that of air power.[5]

Just as many early theorists were fascinated by the potential of aviation and saw it as the very embodiment of modernity in an epoch that, they were persuaded, would be shaped above all by scientists and technocrats, so too are many of today's commentators convinced that aerospace power has come of age, not least in warfare. It is now widely regarded as a genuine alternative to attrition – as *the* means to make armed conflicts briefer, more humane and less costly. Whereas Mitchell once opined that aerial warfare might spawn 'a special class' like 'the armoured knights in the Middle Ages' who would do all the actual fighting,[6] some now sense that the broader mechanization of combat means the end of the heroic warrior; tomorrow's battles will be waged by unfeeling machines and by technicians who will be emotionally if not physically divorced from events on the field.[7] Certainly, aerospace power is currently seen as not just the dominant form of military might, but also as one of the crucial indices of state power per se. Several factors help to account for these perceptions.

If the preceding overview of the history of military aviation is considered as a whole, it can be deduced that air power has several intrinsic and synergistic qualities. First among these is its capacity to exploit the third dimension, height. Armies have, of course, frequently sought to benefit from elevated positions through the occupation of high ground or the construction of fortifications. Aircraft, however, are matchless in their ability to exploit gravity and attain better fields of fire and observation. (Indeed, the development of spacecraft and satellites can be seen as the logical continuation of this quest for the ultimate vantage point.) Moreover, since they can manoeuvre in three dimensions rather than just two, aircraft can prove evasive targets. This enhances their chances of survival in combat, particularly when combined with another basic characteristic, their speed.

Although this is no longer the foremost criterion of quality that it once was – nowadays, the calibre of, say, an aircraft's avionics and weaponry might be accorded more significance in this respect – modern fixed- and rotary-wing aviation can achieve tremendous velocities. Typically, fixed-wing combat planes can travel at between Mach 2.0 and 2.4, while light helicopters mostly have top speeds of between Mach 0.24 and 0.3. Higher velocities not only permit the projection and redirection of military power with greater celerity, but also enable missions to be accomplished in less time. Consequently, more assignments can be undertaken in a given period. Besides the purely operational benefits of this attribute, the ability to react promptly and with celerity can offer political advantages too, not least because a shortage of time can result in the first satisfactory, rather than the best possible, course of action being pursued. For instance, anxious to avoid so-called collateral damage, democratically accountable leaders might seek an unusually high degree of control over the selection of targets, as occurred in the Bosnian and Kosovan campaigns, ineluctably slowing down the process of planning and actually implementing any use of armed force. Once a mission has received political endorsement, however, aerospace power is peculiarly equipped to execute it in a rapid, timely manner.

Speed is, of course, relative. Whereas the capabilities of aircraft have substantially advanced in this regard, the performance of surface forces has increased only marginally. Few modern ships, for instance, have a top speed that is very much better than that of the fastest in service in 1914, and whereas there has been a prodigious increase in firepower on land, motorization and mechanization have not led to a proportionate enhancement of battlefield mobility. It remains improbable that a fleet will cover much more than 500 miles (800 km) in 24 hours; indeed, reaching many destinations might take a month or longer. Likewise, armoured and mechanized ground forces might still manage to traverse no more than 200 miles (322 km) a day.

Planes, by contrast, can cover great distances in a matter of minutes or hours, with their innate reach extended by air-to-air refuelling. For example, to attack targets in Yugoslavia during Operation 'Allied Force', American B-2 bombers flew round trips amounting to as much as 10,000 miles from their home bases in the USA; by repeatedly rendezvousing with tankers while on the wing, they were able to stay aloft for some 30 hours at a stretch. Aerospace platforms are in any case virtually unfettered in their scope for movement. Aircraft are almost unimpeded by topography and, these days, often prove less susceptible to adverse climatic conditions than surface forces. Amidst fog, ice and storms, when ports, shipping and road networks are all too frequently paralysed, suitably equipped planes and aerodromes often continue to function, while helicopters – because of their capacity for slow and vertical flight and hovering – can frequently operate with still greater safety than fixed-wing aircraft. Similarly, as technology has advanced, poor light has not only become less of a hindrance to aerial operations but has also been turned to advantage. Aircraft, furnished for night-time and all-weather flight, have used darkness and bad weather to help conceal their activities from opponents.

Another characteristic of air power is flexibility. Aircraft can perform a broad spectrum of functions that, with comparative ease, can be extended further to cope with changing conditions or unanticipated situations. Such is their versatility and adaptability that they can be entrusted with more than one role during a single mission and can be reassigned, if required, while aloft. This flexibility, together with speed, height and range, endows aircraft with ubiquity, responsiveness and the capacity to concentrate force in time and space. They can simultaneously, or near simultaneously, pose or counter threats across a far broader geographical area than is possible with surface forces, and are ideal for achieving concentrations of strength that are as relatively rapid as they are economical. Because of its reach, air power can respond swiftly, even from home bases, to near or distant developments, deterring aggression or providing explicit or implicit support, as circumstances dictate. In contrast to ground forces, it can do this without incurring the perils of a residual commitment, making its application more akin to the naval 'presence' that has long played, and continues to play, such a significant role in diplomacy, not least in crisis management.

The ability of aerospace platforms to monitor and even influence developments without actually venturing into a trouble spot is, on the other hand, frequently superior to that of maritime surface forces. The latter are unavoidably confined to suitable stretches of water and thus can exert little leverage over landlocked countries or even the distant hinterlands of those that do possess a littoral. Because of their ubiquity and ability to exploit height, aircraft, by contrast, suffer from no such constraints. The illicit flights over the USSR that were executed during the Cold War by American U-2 spy planes provided an early illustration of air power's potential in this regard. Whereas these encroachments violated the USSR's airspace, crewed or uninhabited reconnaissance and other aircraft can, while remaining outside its territorial limits, often 'see' deep into a country; for such missions, be they covert or overt, the human eye can be complemented or replaced by optical instruments, or by a variety of sophisticated electromagnetic and thermal sensors, all of which have their respective strengths and weaknesses. While it might be possible to jam the collection of information by such devices through various technological countermeasures, this can pose technical, if not legal, problems. The human eye and brain, on the other hand, are generally less easy to deceive than machines. The eye, for all its merits, has severe limitations, however. Anybody blessed with good vision who has tried discerning objects on the Earth's surface from a (relatively slow) passenger plane flying in clear weather at just 10,000 or 15,000 feet will appreciate how significant these can be. Even reconnaissance and eavesdropping satellites – the ultimate 'spies-in-the-sky', which are essentially immune to physical attack save by other space-going platforms – suffer from several drawbacks, not the least of which is the need for humans to interpret any data that their sensors gather. After all, information per se is not necessarily useful; and, just as the volume of material reaped by aerial intelligence-gathering platforms is continuing to grow, so too is the task of sifting the chaff from the wheat.

Indeed, much as it has to recommend it, air power is not without its limitations, first among which is its impermanence. Capable though they are of dominating the surface beneath them, aircraft cannot stay aloft indefinitely; even if refuelled by tankers (and not all types can be), they still require servicing, rearming and fresh crews, none of which can be provided while they are airborne. The resulting demand for bases – be they for missiles and aircraft, or concomitant surveillance and targeting installations and replenishment and repair facilities – gives rise to an unavoidable restriction that can often have political as well as practical dimensions. Even when located on home soil, the presence of military personnel and equipment can be a controversial issue. An understanding for the armed forces' need to prepare for and practise their wartime assignments in peacetime is seldom encountered in wider society. Whereas many people claim to favour disarmament, but, because of the implications for the local economy, would be reluctant to see a nearby weapons factory or military base close down, combat training is something that almost everybody believes would be better done in some other neighbourhood. Low-flying aircraft in particular are a common cause of complaint, while air forces in general tend to be unwelcome in this regard. Since they often exercise at some considerable distance from their stations, they are likely to be perceived as bringing nothing to the locality except noise and a fear of accidents. Likewise, whether it stems from the armed services of other states or from terrorists, the possibility of attacks on military installations can alarm those living in the vicinity, a dilemma encapsulated by an old jingle about Polaris:

> Put the missiles out to sea
> Where the real-estate is free
> And they're far away from me.

Furthermore, the quest for convenient bases can, and frequently does, lead to the stationing of one state's armed forces within the territorial limits of another, a matter that can all too easily prove troublesome to hosts and guests alike and which will be examined in more detail in the next chapter. Yet, even where the use of air power might not entail the potential political or military liabilities of a residual commitment, it can have only an ephemeral operational impact. All aircraft have to land, if only intermittently. Even if, as in the case of helicopters, they do not need runways, they still require considerable logistical and other support. This consideration has restricted the assimilation of aviation into army units, for instance, while, despite the difference that in-flight refuelling has made to the reach of many machines, the distance between the battle zone and the nearest base clearly remains paramount in determining how frequently and for how long they can participate in a given assignment. The proximity, quality and security of bases are, therefore, factors that have to be taken into consideration in any calculations about the sustainability of aerial operations. Since missions have to be repeated in order to prolong any effect, the holding of ground, for example, by aircraft alone is scarcely feasible. Air power's impermanence also means that, however physically devastating aerial attacks might prove, it is improbable that in isolation they will achieve the political impact necessary to bring about whatever the use of military force is expected to accomplish.

In any event, success in war has normally been achieved by those who develop and exploit synergy, combining military units with complementary qualities – as is found in a 'package' of aircraft – and, moreover, drawing on moral, legal, economic and diplomatic instruments as far as possible. Impressive though the achievements of aerospace power in the recent campaigns in Bosnia, Kosovo and Afghanistan are, they must be seen in context to be explicable. Since the payloads they can deliver are, generally speaking, far more limited than those carried by ships or land vehicles, missiles and aircraft are at their most economical when they are able to focus potent firepower on targets of relatively high value. In each of these campaigns, the potential or actual threat posed by the presence of hostile surface forces effectively compelled the opposing side to concentrate its martial strength in a fashion that made it that much more vulnerable to aerial attack, including bombardment with cluster and, in Afghanistan, 'Daisy-cutter' bombs. The Serbs' various adversaries in Bosnia; the KLA in Kosovo; the Northern Alliance fighters in Afghanistan: all of these – together with putative or actual interlopers in the form of foreign states' special forces and other ground units – left the nominal government concerned struggling to control what was supposedly its own territory. When, in addition, aerospace power was brought to bear, often with the assistance of targeting data furnished by friendly surface forces, this political and military dilemma was intensified.

Air power was once summarized as 'the ability of a nation to fly, [which partly depends on whether] . . . a nation has the *right to fly*'.[8] As early as 1909, Blériot's cross-Channel journey raised perplexing questions regarding the freedom of aerial navigation and, on the other hand, a state's entitlement to control the airspace adjoining its territory, not least because of security considerations. The Paris and Chicago Conventions of 1919 and 1944, respectively, erected political barriers where it was not possible to construct physical ones, insofar that they codified the right of each state to exclusive control over its own airspace, as well as that of unimpeded passage in the skies over international waters. The no-fly zones established over Bosnia and Iraq in the 1990s thus constituted a peculiar challenge to the legitimacy of their rulers, since claiming responsibility for a particular piece of the Earth's surface and the adjacent skies and evincing at least some determination and capacity to protect them are basic tests of sovereignty and governmental authority, respectively.

Equally, however, the degree to which aerospace power can influence events on the ground depends upon the interaction between essentially static technological capabilities and political intentions that all too often fluctuate. Whereas surface units, both on land and sea, can often be employed in more subtle and discriminating ways, air power can prove a somewhat unwieldy instrument, particularly if used alone and as a display of resolve rather than as an active tool of martial strength. This prompts questions as to its overall utility in, for instance, UN 'peace support' missions. Just as Saddam Hussein used 'human shields' to try to deter aerial attacks on crucial installations during the Gulf War of 1991, the Serbs also intermittently offset the threat of NATO air strikes in Bosnia by taking UN personnel hostage. In any case, the spectacle of swarms of planes being scrambled to find and destroy a Serbian tank or two as they violated the UNO's 'safe havens' not only suggests that the utilization of air power suffers from limitations in an operational, military sense but also in a political one.

Although their sheer speed and agility, together with their capacity to gain height, makes them difficult targets to engage, and any adversary's problems can be compounded by the use of active and passive defence-suppression measures, aircraft are more fragile than ships or many land vehicles. The skies are a pitiless environment, and planes are vulnerable to a broader spectrum of weapons than most ground vehicles or maritime platforms. Exposing them to fire is always a risky undertaking. Certainly, even moderate damage to, say, the flight computers of a sophisticated plane could have lethal ramifications. Yet, the success of Western, particularly American, aerospace power in recent conflicts has tempted many to believe that its use is a relatively painless course of action – hence its frequent depiction as the 'military instrument of first political choice'. The very act of choosing this easy option can, however, betray a lack of resolve. Indubitably, losses need not be all that great in absolute terms for the public to begin to question the relative value of the political object at stake. Precisely because of their image as knights mounted on high-technology steeds, the slaying or capture of air-crew can be a coup with greater political than military significance. The show trial of Gary Powers in the USSR spawned horror and outrage across the USA, as did the treatment of captive American aviators amidst that orgy of violence and destruction, the Vietnam War. Similarly, the spectacle of the dead crew of a helicopter being dragged through the streets of Mogadishu in 1993 not only sealed the fate of the American intervention in Somalia but also inspired Mark Bowden's book *Black Hawk Down* (1999) that subsequently formed the basis of a film. Likewise, when his F-16 was shot down over a Serb-held corner of Bosnia in 1995, so politically sensitive did the fate of Captain Scott O'Grady become that it jeopardized the Americans' participation in Operation 'Deny Flight', if not their wider efforts to smother the Balkan crisis as a whole. Certainly, the US Government went to extraordinary lengths to rescue the stranded pilot. While President Clinton issued several statements in a bid to soothe the frayed nerves of the American public, the US armed services mounted a rescue mission that involved the deployment of a team of 43 marines, who were transported and supported by a synergistic 'package' of 40 aircraft, to extricate just one man. With the mission successfully completed, no less a figure than the President himself telephoned the captain's family to advise them of his safe return.

It is revealing in this regard that, just eight weeks before the presidential election of 1996, Clinton, in retaliation for Saddam Hussein's assault on the Kurdish enclave of Sulaymaniyah, authorized attacks on southern Iraq with, not crewed aircraft, but Tomahawk missiles. Indeed, the growing use of drones, uninhabited aerial vehicles (UAVs), flight computers, multiple sensors and other artificial intelligence devices forms part of a broader automation process that has numerous implications for the use of aerospace power in both peace and war, not least because novel problems invariably accompany new possibilities. If the scope for contention between people is considerable, the extent of that in relations between machines and humans is potentially greater, particularly in warfare, an activity peculiar to *Homo sapiens* and one that, consequently, has both psychological and physical dimensions. However sophisticated technology might be or might become, the quality of its manipulation by people – whose endurance has fairly static limits that are soon reached – is likely to prove an abiding factor in its overall effectiveness.

For instance, combatants have always derived a degree of protection from the limitations of their opponents' weaponry. As the quality of the latter has improved, however, vulnerability has increased, fuelling interest in the substitution of technology for people. Indeed, air power's initial development for military purposes owed a great deal to a quest for an alternative to sanguinary, surface warfare, while as early as the 1920s Mitchell foresaw the use of 'gliding bombs' and pilot-less machines to assail well defended targets.[9] Yet, tempting though it is, reducing the vulnerability of a given group of belligerents through a reliance on 'smart' or other technology has often been achieved at the cost of increased risks to other members of one's own armed forces and to innocent bystanders. Combat theatres are, by definition, dangerous environments, and instances of 'collateral damage' and 'fratricide' are as old as soldiering itself. Even in situations where humankind has retained a significant degree of control and, thereby, some scope for discrimination, such tragedies have all too easily occurred, not least because of the 'fog of war'. The celebrated aviator Italo Balbo, for example, met his death when he was shot down by his fellow Italians while trying to land at Tobruk in 1940. Similarly, one British lieutenant who found himself caught up in the long retreat across Burma two years later has described how he and his colleagues came under attack from RAF planes that feared they were Japanese invaders:

> Pilots . . . queried the targets, saying they looked like British vehicles, [only] to be told it was captured British transport. We had heavy casualties from our own aircraft. We fired at . . . and hit [them] . . . Many of the problems were caused by poor communications. The radios were useless.[10]

The Gulf War of 1991 and the campaign in Afghanistan in 2002 likewise gave rise to 'friendly fire' incidents. During the Gulf War, nine British troops were killed and eleven injured when an American A-10 Thunderbolt attacked their vehicles, having perceived them to be Iraqis. In the course of the Afghanistan campaign, four Canadians perished and eight were wounded when the crew of a USAF F-16, mistaking what was actually a nocturnal exercise for an attempt to shoot them down, released a laser-guided bomb in what they evidently believed was an act of self-defence. Similar confusion also led to an American AC-130 gunship firing on a wedding party north of Kandahar, killing some 50 Afghan civilians, some of whom had apparently been discharging rifles into the air as part of the festivities. Allied operations during the invasion of Iraq the following year were also marred by numerous 'blue-on-blue' mishaps.

The growing public awareness of such incidents owes much to the so-called CNN Factor, an unprecedented capacity for journalistic intrusion into ongoing military operations. This potentially contentious phenomenon is itself very largely a by-product of aerospace capabilities, insofar that it stems from communication devices, notably mobile telephones and video apparatus, the transmissions of which are often relayed by satellite, as are those of the global television broadcasters. If the introduction of Morse-code telegraphy in the middle of the nineteenth century had a profound impact on the conduct of warfare, not least in terms of public accountability,[11] then the perfection and spread of instantaneous communication devices have proved little short of revolutionary. What began with crude, bulky radios that had a very limited range has recently led to a plethora of portable gadgets that can reach across continents and are used on a daily basis by military personnel and civilians alike. Among the latter are war correspondents, whose 'live' reports to audiences worldwide can not only endanger the security of the belligerents if uncensored but can also prove paramount in moulding public perceptions of any conflict.[12]

Predictably, this has had a greater impact on those states that are most susceptible to public reaction, be it at home or abroad. Whereas, for instance, the Russian Confederation has shrugged off international disquiet about its frequently incautious use of force in the continuing civil war within Chechnya, in recent years[13] more mature democracies have intensified their efforts to avoid mishaps such as 'collateral damage'. Pressed by their political masters to do so, this, in turn, has compelled armed services to be that much more sensitive to public and legal opinion, sometimes to the detriment of military efficiency. Of the conflict in Vietnam, for example, President Johnson once boasted that 'The US Air Force cannot even bomb an outhouse without my approval.'[14] Indeed, when it was discovered that he had ordered several unsanctioned attacks between November 1971 and the following March, General John Lavelle was removed as commander of the American Seventh Air Force, demoted and retired. However, as one embittered aviator observed, the rules of engagement were 'created by US [politicians] . . . to cover themselves; then each subordinate commander added a few more rules to cover himself; and pretty soon everyone was covered – except the . . . pilot, and he had to know all the rules'.[15] While, together with national military codes, the Geneva Conventions and their protocols seek to mitigate the impact of armed conflict by outlawing certain excesses – something that is in everybody's interests – the recent establishment of the International Criminal Court is likely to inflame the controversy surrounding this issue. Certainly, the USA, fearful that this body might claim jurisdiction over her forces, has refused to recognize its legitimacy.

If only because it is a political activity, war is, as Georges Clemenceau famously opined, 'much too serious a thing to be left to the generals'. Yet, amidst the 'blame culture' that prevails in so much of the developed world today, the very nature of civil–military relations and of the communication systems upon which both parties rely can all too easily thrust servicemen and women into invidious situations. Just in case something goes awry, air-crew are tempted to create an 'audit trail' so as to be able to disclaim responsibility for any misfortune. On the other hand, such is the speed with which news now travels that their political and military masters might face questions from correspondents regarding a mission from which the participating planes have not returned, or about which their crews have not yet been debriefed. Similarly, the 'live' reporting of accidents, such as the collision between two British Sea King helicopters at the outset of Operation 'Iraqi Freedom', can expose governmental and military spokesmen to journalistic interrogation about incidents of which they know little, if anything.

Armed services, like any other branch of society, are not immune to disease and accidents, each of which can occur in peace and wartime. Campaign conditions, however, tend to increase the propensity for both. Moreover, although the technology employed might vary, violence remains war's great constant. It is, alas, ineluctable that it will be misdirected, if only occasionally. Whereas *Homo sapiens* is subject to psychological strains that can lead to all sorts of shortcomings – not least errors in the manipulation of technology, such as the programming of targeting computers with incorrect coordinates – machines lack human discretion and can suffer technical malfunction, in which event a 'smart' weapon's behaviour can prove that much more unpredictable and dangerous than a 'dumb' one's. (In the Gulf War of 2003, for instance, several wayward cruise missiles unleashed against targets in Iraq exploded in Turkey and Iran.) Not only is war a uniquely human activity, it is also the most intractable in which we engage. Nobody with any awareness of its realities would expect it to be consistently undertaken with a degree of perfection that is so seldom encountered in any other sphere of human endeavour.

While there would be little point in having combat aircraft without armaments, the development and procurement of both lethal, accurate weapons and platforms capable of delivering them is, like so many other aspects of acquiring and maintaining an air force, a dauntingly expensive business in terms of both money and time. For example, it took McDonnell Douglas and the US Army more than twelve years and some three billion dollars to perfect the Apache helicopter, while the Eurofighter – which is just entering service with the RAF as the successor to the Jaguar and Tornado F-3 – has been gestating since 1985 and has become the most expensive procurement project in British military history. The RAF plans to acquire 232 planes in all, the development, production and initial support costs for which are currently nudging £22 billion. Similarly, in September 2002, the British Ministry of Defence announced that it was setting aside £10 billion to cover the costs of replacing its ageing Harrier fleet with 150 F-35 Joint Strike Fighters. Both the Eurofighter and the F-35 are 'stealthy' aircraft; planes that are fully endowed with state-of-the-art 'stealth' capabilities, such as the American Nighthawk and B-2 bomber, cost commensurably more.

This level of expense inevitably heightens anxiety not only about affordability, but also vulnerability and opportunity costs. Furthermore, air power is so much a product of technology and its capabilities are so markedly determined by it that, besides wealth, various material resources and technical skills are essential for its acquisition and preservation. For instance, various fuel oils and lubricants are as indispensable for the operation of aircraft and missiles as they are for the running of so many electricity-generating plants and manufacturing and industrial processes. The discovery of the world's principal oil reserves in the Persian Gulf in 1908 was both coincident with and essential for the rise of the internal combustion engine that ushered in the age of the automobile, the oil-fired ship and the aeroplane. The British campaign in Mesopotamia in Iraq during the First World War was an early, tangible acknowledgement of the developed world's spiralling dependency on oil, which, as we have seen, was soon to precipitate Japan's bid to conquer much of Asia, as well as German thrusts into the Middle East and the Caucasus.

The security of oil supplies has clearly been a major factor in recent wars as well, notably those in the Gulf in 1991 and 2003. Indeed, without kerosene – much of which needs to be produced to an advanced formula that, in turn, calls for suitably capable petrochemical industries – these conflicts, had they ever occurred, would have been very different.

Similarly, whereas in the 1930s wind tunnels – a particularly impressive example of which survives at Farnborough in England – were essential for the testing of a plane's aerodynamic qualities, today much of this work is done by means of extremely sophisticated computer simulations. Indeed, the feasibility of 'stealthy' designs in particular is rooted in computational aerodynamics, while the widespread supplanting of mechanical engineering and human faculties by electrical circuitry has made advanced computers part and parcel of modern air power in general. In combat operations, for example, the optimal use of PGMs and other 'smart' weapons calls not merely for the armaments themselves, but also sophisticated command, control, communication and intelligence infrastructure. At present, only the USA possesses these appendages to the degree necessary to support such operations on a grand scale.

More generally, air power, both civil and military, calls for a range of advanced industrial and manufacturing capabilities and their concomitant, highly skilled labour forces. The commercial use of aviation has matured from being a luxury to being a routine mode of transport that has transformed the world's patterns of social and economic activity, while access to space and the possession of telecommunication and surveillance satellites has become one of the foremost indices of state power. Consequently, the aerospace industries have become a lucrative and highly competitive sector of the global economy, in which one often sees governmental endeavours to mould or promote growth. Indeed, aerospace capabilities and their related manufacturing base are increasingly regarded as central to both national security and prosperity. It is revealing in this sense that the British Government exempted the massive Eurofighter project from its Strategic Defence Review of 1998. Equally telling is the somewhat paradoxical conduct of Russia and India. The former, for all her economic woes, maintained the space station Mir until quite recently and still disposes of substantial aerospace assets, including Glonass, a constellation of navigational satellites that is akin to the Americans' GPS. Likewise, although far from being a wealthy country that one instinctively associates with high technology, India has one of the world's most ambitious space programmes and has not only perfected the Agni II, an intermediate-range ballistic missile, but is also seeking to enhance her older Surya ICBM.[16] Similarly, most states, including many less developed ones, have deliberately fostered the growth of prestigious 'national' airlines. Although some were adversely affected by the commercial ramifications of the terrorist attacks in the USA in September 2001, and many face intense competition from rival 'budget' carriers, they still enjoy a certain totemic significance (and, in some cases, government subsidies) as national flag bearers.

Besides skilled workforces to design and build aircraft, literate, highly competent people are also essential to maintain and utilize them. While an air force's capabilities are, broadly speaking, dependent upon the calibre of its technology, the quality of personnel is also of crucial importance. In the final analysis, any equipment is only as good as its operators, and the ability to exploit advanced machinery to the full is reliant on air- and ground-crews being sufficiently fit, educated and professional. People of such distinction are difficult and expensive to recruit and hard to retain. Furthermore, the amount of training they require is proportional to the variety of tasks they are expected to perform and the exotic nature of the technology they are required to manipulate. Consequently, it can take some time, and more than a little money, for aviators to adjust to the demands of meeting novel assignments and, indeed, for new equipment to be successfully assimilated and exploited by an air force as a whole.

All of these factors make the possession of air forces – in the form of crewed, fixed-wing planes at least – an unappealing or impracticable proposition for many states. Those that do dispose of substantial inventories are predominantly reliant, not on indigenous manufacturers, but on foreign suppliers for 'off-the-shelf' purchases of such basic *matériel* as machines, spare parts and, in many instances, armaments. Moreover, even many of the world's more advanced air forces are struggling to keep abreast of the innovations in aerial warfare that have occurred in recent years. The large and growing gap between America's aerospace power and that of her European allies is causing particular concern. NATO is, after all, an institution that is supposed to facilitate cooperation between its members and thereby enhance their political influence and military assets. Alarmed by the increasing technological incompatibility of their respective air forces, the strategic 'de-coupling' of the USA and Europe and the reductions in the latter's defence expenditure and procurement programmes, the Americans launched the Defence Capabilities Initiative as long ago as June 1998. Nevertheless, Operation 'Allied Force' in Kosovo highlighted continuing European deficiencies in several crucial spheres. Among these were: intelligence, surveillance and reconnaissance capabilities; the ability to mount 'surgical' attacks against both static and mobile ground targets; secure data transfer and other communication links; and the capacity for efficacious defence suppression, not least through electronic warfare.[17]

As recently as the NATO Prague summit of 2002, these and other shortcomings had not been addressed by the overwhelming majority of the alliance's European members. In fact, that conference saw the setting of yet more force goals and the depressingly familiar reiteration of promises to meet them.[18] Even if these are at least partially fulfilled, however, NATO's expansion threatens to exacerbate the existing problem of interoperability, in so far that it will juxtapose integrated, well-trained and fairly well-equipped forces with others that have incompatible communication, in-flight refuelling and friend-or-foe identification systems, and differing doctrines, insufficiently experienced personnel and ageing or obsolete machines with few, if any, precision weapons. That, of NATO's members, only the Americans and British actively participated in the conquest of Iraq was a source of acute political embarrassment. On the other hand, it is improbable that the majority of their European partners could have made a militarily useful contribution to the campaign because of the relative obsolescence of their martial capabilities.

Those who favour the complete integration of Europe's nation states under the auspices of the European Union (EU) have long advocated the creation of a common foreign and security policy and armed forces that would rival, if not supplant, NATO as the protector of the continent. France has cast herself as the great champion of this cause and, ever since the mid-1960s, has intermittently endeavoured to undermine European reliance on the North Atlantic Treaty. Her blocking of Turkey's invocation of Article IV of that document on the eve of Operation 'Iraqi Freedom' in 2003 was thus widely perceived as contumacious opportunism. What is indisputable is that the divisions that the Iraq crisis caused within and between NATO and the EU have done both these institutions appreciable harm, underlining the fact that political postures can alter overnight. Military power, by contrast, can take decades to develop. Besides illustrating the difficulty a score of diverse nation states can experience in achieving consensus over such potentially contentious issues as security and foreign affairs, the Iraq débâcle highlighted the USA's incomparable economic, political and military might. Although not inconsiderable, European martial capabilities in general and aerospace ones in particular remain weak when set against those of the USA. Whereas a single American carrier group – of which there are twelve in active service – disposes of more advanced air power assets than the bulk of the European air forces put together, the USA also enjoys a virtual or actual monopoly over certain types of equipment, notably 'stealth' aircraft, space shuttles and some intelligence-gathering devices. Indeed, the inventories of many European countries include platforms, weaponry and sub-systems that originated in the USA and could scarcely be maintained or operated without American assistance. Trident, for instance, was purchased, on very favourable terms, by a British administration that was as eager to increase the political interdependence of the US and UK as it was to promote commonality and interoperability between the two countries' armed services. Moreover, while America evinces a willingness to go on investing the requisite resources to develop further her military capacity, in this as in so many other spheres European ambitions outrun achievements.

Historians and economists continue to argue among themselves about the economic merits of past and ongoing research into, and expenditure on, military capabilities. Two things are certain, however. First, that security is a prerequisite for prosperity. Secondly, that problems encountered in the course of either peacetime preparation for war or actual wars have engendered and accelerated a quest for solutions, many of which, together with their spin-offs, have found utility in other spheres. Indeed, ironic though it might be, the exigencies of armed conflict have often led to scientific and technical advances of great benefit to humankind.

A strikingly large number of these have stemmed from the development and refinement of aerospace power. For instance, the first electronic and other navigational and reconnaissance aids were initially created for use in connection with aerial warfare. Radar remains the pre-eminent illustration, but the German Sonne system also outlived the Second World War; preserved and expanded, the network was exploited by civil and military traffic for many years thereafter. More recently, navigational devices that draw on the GPS satellite constellation have become commonplace and are used in such quotidian activities as rambling and motoring. Likewise, aerial photography not only transformed battle-zone reconnaissance and damage assessment, but archaeology and cartography as well. Similarly, the need to provide armed services, particularly navies and air forces, with dependable weather forecasts gave meteorology a tremendous stimulus. For example, after the Japanese used a frontal system to help mask their attack on Pearl Harbor, the Weather Wing of the USAAF was expanded to include no fewer than 4,000 meteorologists who were scattered in data-collection stations throughout the world. Indeed, weather predictions are at their most accurate when based on information gathered from around the globe; and the television and radio forecasts that are a feature of so many people's daily routines and influence innumerable plans, both great and small, are founded on intelligence gleaned by dozens of terrestrial monitoring stations and satellites, such as MSG-1, that monitor developments with radar, thermal and other sensors. Much of this network was created for, and continues to be employed by, military forces.

So far as seeking ways of protecting people against climatic vagaries, noise, blast, radiation and extreme temperatures and pressures is concerned, nowhere has wartime innovation proved more important than in the field of aerospace medicine. Although the very first atomic weapons were delivered by long-range aircraft and the Nazis' rocket programme began the exploitation of space for military purposes that, with the subsequent amassing of intercontinental ballistic missiles, ushered in the lengthy reign of the 'balance of terror', these and related developments had compensating, peaceful applications as well. After Yuri Gagarin, in Vostok-1, became the first man to orbit the Earth in April 1961, President Kennedy, fearing that the USSR was winning the space race, pledged that the USA would land a man on the Moon 'before this decade is out'.[19] Sure enough, this goal – a fantasy for past generations of human beings – was achieved in July 1969, by which time the superpowers were undertaking a hundred or more space exploration missions between them every year. Both the Americans and Russians also began developing the first manned space stations – the Skylab and Salyut, respectively – while 1981 witnessed the successful completion of the inaugural flight of a reusable shuttle craft. Although manned space flight peaked with these endeavours, thanks to them and the various cosmological and astronomical programmes they spawned or nourished, our knowledge of Earth's solar system and the wider universe has grown tremendously.

Mitchell once observed that 'Transportation is the essence of civilization'.[20] Certainly, aerospace power has revolutionized the movement of information, goods and people, not to mention certain contagious diseases. Navigational, surveillance and communications satellites, originally developed for military purposes, have transformed our day-to-day lives, leading, in the course of just a few years, to now-familiar gadgets such as satellite televisions, together with their 'dishes', and portable telephones. Although, for the present at least, space travel remains the preserve of a tiny elite who can afford the immense charges involved, quite the opposite is true of air travel, with millions using both domestic and international flights to make either business or recreational trips. Vast amounts of freight – including perishable goods, such as exotic fruits and vegetables from distant lands – are also transported around the world in an increasingly 'globalized' economy, some of the principal nodes of which are the great international airports. These have arisen in the space of a few decades, with once obscure little aerodromes – like that at Ringway at Manchester in England, which was the headquarters of the parachute training school during the Second World War – mushrooming into vast complexes through which pass scores of thousands of passengers and cargoes every year. At Manchester and elsewhere, this dramatic growth has wrought great changes in the local and wider economy, many of which have proved beneficial. On the other hand, the relentless expansion of airports and the growth in aerial traffic – which can be a nuisance to nearby residents, particularly those unfortunate enough to live directly beneath a noisy flight path – has become one of the great environmental concerns of our age.

The wide-scale monitoring of that environment has been facilitated by aerospace power especially. Today, satellites, weather balloons and aircraft play a leading role in the observation of such phenomena as global warming. Similarly, the 'duality' of air power has secured it a prominent part in humanitarian relief missions of various kinds. Besides being used for the timely delivery of food, specialist rescue workers and other necessities to (often remote) parts of the globe that have been ravaged by famine, earthquakes or some other natural calamity, aircraft are used on a daily basis by emergency services all over the world. Among them are flying doctors and fire fighters, coastguards and mountain rescue teams. Police forces, too, make extensive use of aerial platforms, notably helicopters fitted with cameras and infrared sensors for surveillance missions. Recently, law enforcement officers in the USA also employed a sophisticated Predator drone to help search for a sniper who had murdered several people in the Washington area. Indeed, the miniaturization of components that has played a prominent part throughout the evolution of aerospace power and made such 'smart' machines possible has now reached the microscopic level. With the advent of 'nano-technology' – the engineering of individual molecules and atoms – incredibly small UAVs are becoming feasible. In time, they might well transform activities such as espionage.

Aerospace power, however, has already had a vast impact on the lives of so many people, not least in terms of the shaping of the towns in which they live and work. The building and expansion of both airports and their ancillary infrastructure – notably hotels and warehouse complexes, parking lots, and road and rail links – have had a profound effect and seem destined to continue to do so. In many places, moreover, new construction has been accompanied by reconstruction, often as a result of aerial bombardment. Between 1939 and 1945 especially, many of the world's greatest population centres were subjected to bombing raids that reduced much of them to ruins. London, Tokyo, Volgograd, Hamburg, Warsaw, Hiroshima and Nagasaki were among many cities transfigured by this process and the rebuilding that followed, while more recently the skylines of Belgrade, New York and Baghdad have been appreciably altered as a result of attacks mounted from the air.

The cultural change stemming from all of this has been no less tremendous than the alterations to trade patterns and other economic activity that aerospace power has spawned. Certainly, as what was once science fiction has turned into fact, fulfilling some of the visions of Jules Verne and H. G. Wells, artists as diverse as d'Annunzio and Stanley Kubrick have stressed the awful potency of military aviation. Writers such as W. G. Sebald have explored the impact that the experience of aerial bombardment and the ensuing rebuilding of cities have had on German society, for instance,[21] while mastery of the skies and space has proved an enticing theme for novelists and for radio, cinematographic and television studios. Popular, fictitious creations have ranged from the exploits of such mythical pilots as Biggles to *Star Trek*, the 'cult' television series. Even some ageing films based on real, heroic events – be they Lindbergh's transatlantic flight, or the raid by the 'Dambusters' during the Second World War– also continue to move audiences, not least because of the frequently atmospheric music of their soundtracks. For instance, the distinguished composer William Walton not only produced his acclaimed *Battle of Britain* Suite for the film of that name, but also furnished the *Spitfire* Prelude and Fugue that is used to such marvellous effect in *The First of the Few* (1942). This wartime movie tells the story of how the brilliant aeronautical engineer R. J. Mitchell – who is played by Leslie Howard – toiled night and day to perfect his Spitfire for the RAF as Hitler's Luftwaffe – the air force that, according to the Versailles Treaty, should never have been built – loomed on the horizon. His health destroyed by his selfless exertions, the anguish and feverishness of which are reflected in the background music, Mitchell dies at the end of the film, comforted by the knowledge that his task is complete. (In an eerie twist of fate, Howard met his own death while returning to the UK from the movie's Lisbon premiere in June 1943. The airliner that he was aboard was shot down by German fighters.)

The cultural impact of aerospace power reverberates far beyond artistic endeavour, however. As long ago as 1947 one writer expressed the fear that, as a result of it, 'Boundaries would cease to exist and commerce or terror might be overhead. The end of nationalism might result.'[22] Indeed, if only because it has effectively made the Earth a much smaller place, interlacing contrasting civilizations, it is both a cause and symptom of the amorphous phenomenon known as 'global-ization'. Although we have yet to witness the establishment of either Wells's universal republic or the utopian, international brotherhood envisaged by Verne, the world's various states have certainly become significantly more interdependent, not least in security terms, and the debate about whose values should prevail in an increasingly integrated world has intensified commensurably. It is unsurprising that some groups fear that the principles and precepts they cherish are being trampled over.

One such group is Al-Qaida, whose suicidal, indiscriminate blows against Washington and New York on 11 September 2001 earned its members enduring notoriety. For most of her history, geography has been the USA's salvation; Americans have been able to engage in armed conflicts abroad without having to worry much, if at all, about direct threats to their homeland. As aerospace power has matured, however, this situation has altered. Just as, by substituting duration for destruc-tion, nuclear deterrence, in the form of ICBMs and long-range bombers, prolonged the Cold War, so too does so much of the *Pax Americana* that has superseded the bipolar, international order rest on the USA's dominance of the skies.

Whereas many of its earliest advocates regarded air power as a supreme emblem of modernity, they were equally persuaded that the very sophistication of the advanced, industrialized societies that were best placed to acquire it rendered them that much more vulnerable to aerial attack than comparatively undeveloped ones. It is somewhat paradoxical that, in hijacking aircraft and crashing them into buildings, Al-Qaida exploited what is perhaps the greatest symbol of the very modernity that they loathe.

Chapter 4

Bases Ashore and Afloat

The impermanence of air power stems from a constraint that is as tangible as it is seemingly ineluctable: a reliance on bases. Although all forms of military forces are dependent, if only to some extent, on such nodes, the need of air power for specialist facilities and infrastructure, as well as ancillary services such as radar stations and command and traffic-management systems, is as fundamental as it is distinctive. Even outer space probes and other space-going platforms cannot entirely slip the bonds that link them to activities on Earth, if only because it is from them that they derive their very *raison d'être*. Tempting though it can be to speak of the 'dominance' of aerospace power in the light of recent events in the Persian Gulf and the Balkans, it should not be overlooked that such power is ultimately and unavoidably reliant on surface forces and installations without which it could not exist, let alone function.

The proximity, quality and security of bases are, therefore, factors that have to be reckoned with in any calculations about the sustainability of aerial operations, particularly those undertaken by fixed- and rotary-wing aviation. Not least because they might be sited in places that are very remote from the actual war zone, bases can be difficult for an adversary to locate. Generally speaking, however, the larger they are, the easier this task becomes. Furthermore, it is one that can often be undertaken in peacetime, at least as far as static bases are concerned. On the other hand, the bigger a custom-built aerodrome is, the harder disabling it can prove, as was found as early as the Battle of Britain. In October 1940 the Luftwaffe tried to paralyse an RAF fighter station by attacking it, not with the usual high-explosive bombs, but with SD-2 'Butterfly' mines that, suspended from little parachutes, scattered themselves far and wide. Fitted with a variety of fuses, these were difficult to clear and, in the interim, posed a serious hazard to personnel and aircraft alike. Similarly, some 50 years later, in the first Gulf War, RAF Tornadoes executed low-level attacks to shower crucial Iraqi airports with sub-munitions from JP-233 bombs – the sophisticated descendants of such devices as the SD-2. Nevertheless, by using angled, if relatively short trajectories, planes might still be able to take off from a runway that is quite liberally sown with mines or badly pitted with bomb craters. Helicopters and other machines that are capable of vertical flight might also defy immobilization, as might those fixed-wing aircraft that are built to operate from grass strips.

In any event, aerodromes contain many high value targets besides actual aircraft and their runways. Damage to command, control and maintenance facilities, or fuel or munitions depots, for example, could effectively render an airfield's aviation assets inoperable. Whereas both assailing and protecting satellites and other space platforms are really the preserve of machines of the same genre, attacks on surface stations could come in the form of aircraft, airborne-assault units or stand-off weaponry of various descriptions. This can make the provision of adequate passive and active protection a difficult undertaking, for it is rarely possible to gauge the size and nature of potential threats. Indeed, static bases can possess seemingly formidable defences that, if assailed, can nonetheless prove insufficiently strong: any concentration of force is, after all, relative, not absolute. If, however, they are not attacked, to all intents and purposes the resources devoted to protecting them are wasted.

In any case a balance has to be struck between sustaining an offensive capacity and defending the base. Carriers have been unfavourably contrasted with land stations in this regard. Although often much larger than their ancestors, today's carriers tend to accommodate fewer aircraft, since modern fighter-bombers are significantly heavier and bigger than their forerunners. Today's machines are far more capable, of course. Yet, when operating from the confines of an ocean-going platform, they are still unlikely to function as well overall as aircraft operating from dry land, not least because they are restricted in terms of their numbers and dimensions, which affects the quantity and types of ordnance they can carry. Whereas the payload of carrier-based planes rarely exceeds 5,000 pounds (2,270 kg), that of land-based bombers can be as much as 55,000 (24,950 kg). Sortie rates can also be influenced by the type of base being employed. Again, this can affect the amount of firepower available over a given period. In the Gulf War of 1991, for instance, although carrier-borne aircraft accounted for more than a fifth of the American-led coalition's disposable planes, they performed just 17 per cent of the strike missions involved in Operation 'Desert Storm'. By contrast, the US Marine Corps, with only 238 planes, half as many as the US Navy had available, executed 7,690 attack sorties, nearly 20 per cent of the total of 38,000.[1]

The marines were able to achieve this largely because they used land bases. Besides permitting faster 'turn around' rates, the accumulation of larger fuel stocks and more varied arsenals, and the accommodation of extensive repair and maintenance facilities, these are much more resilient to attack. Consequently, they can be defended with proportionately fewer resources. Today's carriers, on the other hand – despite the use of armoured flight-decks, water-tight bulkheads and advanced-formula kerosene, which is less volatile than older fuels and thus less likely to pose a hazard to the ship itself – are still quite vulnerable and need to devote perhaps half of their planes to defensive missions. (Normally, such capital vessels are also guarded by several escort ships and submarines.) After all, a state-of-the-art carrier might not be so easy to sink, but a solitary, well placed bomb on its flight-deck would still incapacitate it and might also destroy many of its aircraft.

That said, unlike a static base, a carrier can seek to evade detection and attack by shifting position. Furthermore, since it is essentially a mobile aerodrome, it has an attribute that no other platform can match, namely its ability to provide close and fairly comprehensive support to aviation, either from within a war theatre or from its rim. The ship's propulsion system – which can also generate electrical and heat energy for a host of other purposes – enables it to be moved to almost any location in suitably spacious waters in order either to complement land bases or to compensate for a lack or shortage of them. Indeed, besides housing at least some command, control and communication assets, as well as medical, meteorological and other specialist cells, a sizeable carrier – the British, for instance, have plans to lay down two of around 66,000 tonnes in the next few years – can offer essential material sustenance to other platforms. Not only are such a vessel's fuel and ammunition reserves normally large enough to enable its aircraft to conduct three or four days of very intensive combat, but also it possesses its own maintenance and repair bays, together with significant stocks of spare parts. The difficulties encountered in squeezing such logistical necessities and capabilities into land vehicles have truncated the assimilation of aviation units by ground forces. Alluring though the notion of operating helicopters and VTOL and STOL planes from motorways or clearings in woods might be, the practical problems in doing so are as complex as they are constraining. Whereas 'train' vessels can either accompany or be summoned to carriers to replenish them as and when necessary, safe rendezvous between flights of aircraft and ponderous, vulnerable convoys of trucks can be much harder to accomplish, particularly under combat conditions.

By prolonging the period that military aircraft can stay aloft, the adoption and refinement of in-flight refuelling techniques particulary since the 1970s has greatly extended the reach of the world's leading air forces. An early, dramatic illustration of this occurred at the outset of the Falklands conflict, when RAF ground-attack Harriers travelled 8,000 miles (12,900 km) from the UK to join the task-force that was assembling to retake the colony. Refuelled on the wing, they were able to complete this feat under their own power and in a matter of hours. Likewise, replenished by Victor tankers that undertook in excess of 600 fuel transfusions in more than 500 sorties, Hercules, Nimrod and Vulcan planes were enabled to perform the round trip of 7,000 miles (11,250 km) from the aerodrome on Ascension Island to the combat theatre. Large numbers of personnel and substantial quantities of equipment were also airlifted to Ascension Island, the fleet or the Falklands themselves, as circumstances required.[2]

Without sufficient logistical support – including the kerosene consumed in all these flights – aerial operations would have been unsustainable here as elsewhere. However, gauging the stocks of munitions and fuel required in a potential war zone and accumulating them there can prove a far lengthier process than deploying aircraft to it. In any event, bases, ashore or afloat, are indispensable, for aircraft regularly need not just refuelling and rearming, but also servicing and fresh crews.

Whereas a carrier might remain in international waters, the utilization of land bases often impinges on the sovereignty of other states. This can prove a particularly troublesome matter when the facilities concerned are to be used for military purposes, since the host can too easily become embroiled in far more than the granting of rights of passage. Indeed, serious legal and cultural issues can arise, occasionally spawning political and security quandaries. Although by no means as potentially lethal as the stationing of Soviet nuclear forces there in 1962, more recent events on Cuba, for instance, have caused appreciable controversy. In the aftermath of the conflict in Afghanistan, 'unlawful combatants' were interned there at the American outpost at Guantánamo Bay – a base deemed to lie outside the jurisdiction of the USA's own courts. If the treatment of these captives caused Western liberals especially some disquiet, the very presence of 'infidel' forces in Saudi Arabia and other corners of the cradle of Islam is regarded by some Muslims – not least Al-Qaida's members – as an affront. Indeed, Washington's bids to use the aerodromes or airspace of nearby countries – notably Turkey – during the invasion of Iraq in 2003 became a cause célèbre within the bitterest and most divisive diplomatic dispute since the Cold War.

Nevertheless, thanks to long-standing or ad hoc multilateral or bilateral deals – some of which were clinched through grants of financial or military aid – from the outset of the conflict, the American-led coalition forces were able to make use of a sprawling web of bases. Besides their headquarters in Qatar, this included the aerodromes at Ali al-Salem and Ahmed al-Jaber in Kuwait; the Prince Sultan Combined Air Operations Centre in Saudi Arabia; airfields at Seeb, Masirah and Thumrait in Oman and at Al-Dhafra in the United Arab

Emirates; several helicopter and aircraft carriers cruising in the Gulf and the Red and Mediterranean Seas; and the large base on Diego Garcia in the Indian Ocean. American airborne units were also flown in from Italy to secure an airstrip at Bashur in northern Iraq, while wounded and sick US personnel were evacuated to Ramstein in Germany.

It was, above all, the regular sorties by B-52 Stratofortresses stationed as far away as Fairford in the UK that caught the eyes and cameras of journalists, however. Mounted from an RAF aerodrome encircled by demonstrators, their spectacular bombing raids added to the furore ignited by Operation 'Iraqi Freedom' – a war that engendered as many political as military problems. Yet this was not the first time that the presence of US forces in the UK had provoked controversy. Nor is it likely to prove the last, if only because installations at Fylingdales and Menwith Hill form part of the national BMD network that the Americans began erecting in 2002 – a defence initiative that, widely dubbed 'Son of Star Wars', has aroused considerable, if sporadic, public concern in Europe and elsewhere. Although the precise details of the arrangements governing the Pentagon's use of facilities in the UK remain closely guarded secrets, from the official documentation that is available – most of it American in origin – an insight can be gained into the issues surrounding the basing of military units on foreign soil.

As we have already noted, the withdrawal of American air power from the UK at the end of the Second World War proved ephemeral; by the summer of 1948 the USAF had started to reoccupy aerodromes that it had left just 30 months earlier. Even before the 'Iron Curtain' began descending across Europe, however, the British cabinet had concluded that the mighty USA was the only country that could both help the UK regain her economic prosperity and guarantee her security. Ernest Bevin, the Foreign Secretary, had long regarded the offer of bases as a 'sweetener' with which a transatlantic treaty that would bind America to Europe's defence might be made more palatable.[3] As early as August 1945, when Britain approached the USA for a loan, the notion of such 'attractive appurtenances' loomed large, with Washington requesting facilities in, among other places, the Cape Verde Islands, Ascension

Island and nine Commonwealth-administered islands in the Pacific. Turning to Churchill for advice, Bevin was urged to seize 'this sublime opportunity': 'The long term advantage to Britain and the Commonwealth', wrote Churchill, 'is to have our affairs so interwoven with those of the United States in external and strategic matters that any idea of war between the two countries is impossible. . . . [W]e stand or fall together . . . [and] the more strategic points we hold in Joint occupation, the better.'4

The passing of the MacMahon Act by Congress in mid-1946 underscored the extent of enfeebled Britain's dependence on America. This law effectively ended nuclear collaboration between these erstwhile partners, undermining the UK's martial and international standing. In granting facilities to Washington, London glimpsed a chance to reinvigorate their relationship and preserve some influence over the USA. For their part, the Americans believed that fewer political obstacles to the establishment of bases would be encountered in Britain than in any other European state, not least because the UK's ongoing need for American financial, technical and military assistance could be used as leverage. Moreover, since much of the affinity that had developed during the war between the armed forces of the two countries remained, particularly within the higher command echelons, Washington hoped to conduct negotiations through military rather than through diplomatic channels – a proposal that France and Italy had already rejected, but which Britain accepted. So it was that Sir Arthur Tedder and Carl Spaatz were authorized to negotiate an administrative accord whereby a number of RAF aerodromes were to be modified 'for the support of atomic operations' and made available to US bombers in the event of an emergency. Even Clement Attlee, the UK's Prime Minister, remained aloof from these proceedings. He 'not only did not want to discuss European defense but positively eluded attempts to draw him into it, leaving discussion to his field and air marshals',5 observed Dean Acheson, the US Secretary of State.

Within a year of the agreement being concluded, units of the SAC had begun rotational tours of Europe. Three B-29 groups, including one from Germany, were dispatched to Britain at the onset of the Berlin airlift and dubbed the 'Third Air Division'. As independent American logistical and command networks began sprouting around their aero-dromes, the US Government asked Bevin if the squadrons could be permitted to stay indefinitely. He granted this request, approaching Washington for some sort of written agreement on the matter only after the establishment of NATO in April 1949. Shortly after, the Berlin blockade was lifted, kindling some hopes of an improvement in East–West relations. In September 1949, however, the USSR tested its first nuclear weapon. The US had lost its atomic monopoly, and the Cold War appeared commensurably more dangerous.

The Americans responded to the grim prospect of pre-emptive or retaliatory raids on 'Airstrip One' by seeking yet more aerodromes in the UK's western reaches, notably Fairford in Gloucestershire, where their bombers would be less vulnerable to attacks out of the blue. However, the incipient spread of US forces within Britain bedevilled the country's efforts to reassert control over them. Indeed, not least because the Treasury – fearful of the monetary costs of expanding and refurbishing bases – was bent on dominating the negotiations, the issues that really concerned the Foreign Office and Defence Ministry – what the details of the American Strategic Air Plan (SAP) were, and what would occur if the US was tempted to act unilaterally, or if the UK wished to terminate the stationing rights – were scarcely discussed. Although unwilling to risk causing 'suspicion or offence' through too strong a protest or a formal letter on the matter,[6] Bevin 'did not want to be telephoned by the American Ambassador one night and told: "Our planes are taking off from your fields in five minutes, do you mind?" Nor did [he] . . . want to read in the papers some morning that something of this kind [had] . . . happened'.[7] On the other hand, the Cabinet as a whole took the supremely pragmatic view that 'matters should be left as they stood . . . [since the danger of the Americans acting independently from their hosts] could hardly arise unless British policies had diverged so far from those of the United States that American use of the airfields would have to be reconsidered anyway'.[8] Nevertheless, whereas Bevin's own fears were allayed somewhat by an exchange of letters between the Air Ministry's Under Secretary and the US Ambassador in April 1950,[9] before the end of that year Attlee himself had been jolted into action. Such was Parliamentary and public reaction to President Truman's disclosure to journalists that he was giving 'active consideration' to using atomic weapons in Korea that the Prime Minister set out for Washington in search of a formal accord over the Americans' use of bases on British soil.

Truman and Attlee, together with their respective advisers, duly met in the White House on 7 December. With regard to atomic armaments and their possible use, the President assured the Prime Minister that Britain and America 'had always been partners in this matter, and that he would not consider any use of the bomb without consulting the United Kingdom'. Attlee was eager to have this on paper, but Truman demurred, observing that 'if a man's word wasn't any good it wasn't made any better by writing it down'.[10] Acheson, however, noted that Attlee 'never relaxed for a moment his determination to establish a British veto over American strategic action, particularly in the case of the bomb'.[11] Indeed, the following day the Prime Minister resumed this quest. While the other members of the negotiating teams pored over the latest reports about the Korean conflict, Truman took Attlee into his private study. Acheson, persuaded that they were merely discussing personal matters, was aghast when they emerged and the President announced: 'We've had a good talk about the bomb. We want to say in the communiqué that neither of us will use . . . [it] without prior consultation with each other.'[12]

Incurring a 'nasty look' from Attlee, Acheson hastily pointed out to Truman that such an undertaking would conflict with his constitutional obligations as commander-in-chief of the USA's armed forces and as the ultimate guarantor of his country's security interests. 'We were perfectly willing to talk about consultation', he stressed afterwards, 'but to require the agreement of the British . . . was a silly thing to do because [the bomb] . . . might have to be used at once. If . . . [Russian] missiles were coming, you didn't have time to go sending cables around asking for agreement.'[13] Moreover, Robert Lovett, the Assistant Secretary of War for Air, reminded everyone that, while the Quebec Agreement of 1943 had stipulated that atomic weapons would not be used against a third party without the signatories' mutual consent, this veto clause had been nullified by the *Modus Vivendi* of January 1948, whereby the British had surrendered it in return for closer cooperation over nuclear research. In fact, Lovett himself had subsequently assured the Joint Congressional Committee on Atomic Energy that: 'We have achieved more than we might have expected. . . . [The wartime agreements] . . . have been terminated by mutual consent.. . . All embarrassing political provisions such as that in the case of the bomb have been eliminated.'[14]

Although the *Modus Vivendi* had been left unsigned so as to circumvent the right of Congress to scrutinize treaties, both parties had pledged themselves to honour its terms.[15] Furthermore, as Sir Roger Makins of the Foreign Office, who had participated in the negotiations over the *Modus Vivendi*, now pointed out, the veto had been more apparent than real in so far that it was unenforceable. Trading it for an improvement in collaboration over nuclear research – which had been in the doldrums since the passing of the MacMahon Act – had thus been worthwhile, even if some British officials ineluctably felt that the resulting data exchanges were of minor importance when set against their country's loss of 'a contingent right to consultation before action was taken that might lead to her own annihilation'.[16] In any event, Acheson's prediction of Congressional 'uproar' unnerved Truman. He had already been subjected to rather hostile interrogation by the Atomic Energy Commission in 1947 when it had uncovered the existence of the Quebec Agreement.[17] He could not now risk making a similar arrangement, however well intentioned and informal.

Distinguishing between consultation and consent, the communiqué issued at the conclusion of the meeting duly and merely observed that: 'The President stated that it was his hope that world conditions would never call for the use of the atomic bomb. [He] . . . told the Prime Minister that it was also his desire to keep [him] . . . at all times informed of developments that might bring about a change in the situation.'[18]

American officials even insisted that Truman's ephemeral pledge to Attlee be expunged from the written record of the proceedings. One subsequently noted that the British 'did not accept this . . . so far as their file copies were concerned, but in the copy of their minutes which they . . . [exchanged] with us this paragraph is deleted'.[19] Still, London evidently sought comfort from Truman's fleeting promise, for it had to be reiterated to the UK's embassy in Washington that the official position, 'as agreed by the President and as accepted by Prime Minister Attlee, was set forth in the . . . Communiqué – no more and no less'.[20] Gordon Arneson, Acheson's Special Assistant, was also moved to write that 'Whatever might have passed between the President and Prime Minister in private talks prior to the issuance of the Joint Communiqué, . . . that document . . . represented the last and, therefore, authoritative statement on the matter.'[21]

In September 1951 Attlee entrusted a team led by Herbert Morrison, who had superseded the dying Bevin, with the task of trying to wring more concessions from Washington. Arguing that it was 'intolerable that Britain should risk annihilation without being first informed or consulted', Morrison pleaded for details of the SAP and a commitment to consultation.[22] Although he was rebuffed with the usual arguments, it was acknowledged, in what the Americans emphasized was an unbinding 'exchange of views', that their tenure of UK bases did impinge on Britain's sovereignty and that the US 'should seek acquiescence before launching a war from them'.[23] Indeed, 'On the question of whether we proposed to use UK bases without their consent', an internal State Department memorandum records: 'we stated . . . that prior consultation and agreement would obviously be required. . . . On the more general question of consultation', it continues, 'a real issue existed. . . . We wanted to talk as frankly . . . as possible, but . . . could not enter into an agreement or commitment or procedure that would imply . . . even a commitment to continue to talk or to follow any given procedure.'[24] The climax of the discussions came when Air Marshal Elliot enquired what would happen in the event of hostilities. Would the Americans 'consult with the UK in advance of taking action, or not?' Paul Nitze replied: 'Having a policy of desiring to talk . . . was something else than making a commitment.' Oliver Franks, the British Ambassador, then remarked that, while he understood that there should be no formal treaty, 'an expression of intent is in a certain sense a commitment'. Anxious to be 'absolutely clear about this', Nitze adamantly rejected this suggestion, stressing that an 'Expression of present intention . . . could in no way be a commitment for the future.'[25]

With Churchill turning the whole issue into a political hot potato at a time when a general election was impending, Franks sought to salvage what he could. The provisional text that he submitted to Washington concluded that the use of the bases in emergencies 'naturally remains a matter for joint decision in the light of the circumstances at the time'.[26] 'If Churchill is returned', the Americans reasoned, 'he will doubtless want a greater commitment from us. We would be in a better position to withstand his onslaught if this statement had already been agreed upon.'[27] Accordingly, in exchange for Franks acceding to their position on the wider question of consultation, the Americans evinced a readiness to approve the gist of his draft, subject to it being used exclusively in response to direct Parliamentary questions. A vague statement on this aspect of the Attlee–Truman 'Understanding' was duly endorsed by the President on 18 October.[28] Churchill, presented with a fait accompli, had indeed to accept it; and it was he, following his return as Prime Minister, who first revealed it to the Commons.[29]

As anticipated, Churchill did endeavour to tighten his control over US action. Meeting Truman in January 1952, he was briefed on the minutiae of the SAP, many of which were subsequently also disclosed to the British chiefs of staff. He had, however, to content himself with verbal promises of consultation over any employment of atomic weapons in particular. Insisting that written agreements would violate constitutional law, the Americans would not go beyond releasing a suitably nebulous communiqué at the conclusion of the summit. This reaffirmed 'the understanding that the use of the bases in an emergency would be a matter for joint decision by . . . [the two governments] in the light of the circumstances prevailing at the time'. The US also pledged to 'remain in close consultation on [any] . . . development which might increase danger to the maintenance of world peace'.[30]

When, in 1958, ballistic rockets were deployed alongside American bombers in the UK, it fell to Harold Macmillan as Prime Minister to ratify the relevant accord, such as it was.[31] The clause that regulated any unleashing of these missiles echoed the 'Understanding' that covered Washington's use of UK aerodromes and which had been arrived at earlier in the decade. While Macmillan was to speak on television of having 'an absolute veto', less publicly he was to grumble about the 'loose arrangements made by Attlee and confirmed by Churchill'.[32] Moreover, if the deterioration in East–West relations at the beginning of the 1960s compelled him to 'look carefully again at the precise terms of the agreement . . . to ensure that they were watertight',[33] he failed to record whether he found them to be so. In any case, as his predecessors had concluded, the value of any paper guarantees was essentially dependent upon realpolitik – on strategic and political considerations that might necessitate the use of military force in the first place.

It can be deduced that the Churchill–Truman 'Understanding' served as the basis for the use of British sovereign territory by the American armed forces for the remainder of the Cold War. Furthermore, it probably remains the quasi-legal foundation governing the US military presence in the UK. Certainly, during the Yom Kippur conflict of 1973, Edward Heath exercised the 'right of veto' when, along with several other European premiers, he refused the Americans permission to use British facilities in the Mediterranean for operations in support of Israel. (Indeed, as a report prepared for a Congressional subcommittee noted at the time, 'Portugal was the only NATO ally to permit US use of its military bases to resupply Israel. . .'.[34]) It is also revealing that, in 1983, Margaret Thatcher, speaking of the impending deployment to the UK of American Tomahawk missiles, stated that the governing conditions were 'the same as those of long ago between . . . Churchill and . . . Truman. They are arrangements for joint decision – not merely . . . consultation. . . .'.[35] Again, three years later, when the USAF's raid on Libya – in which fighter-bombers based on British soil participated – was being debated by Parliament, she stated: 'The Arrangements under which American bases are used in this country have been the same for well over thirty years. . . . Under [them], . . . our agreement was required. It was sought and, after discussion and question, . . . obtained.'[36]

By extending the reach of many weapon systems and sensors, technological evolution has reduced the need for the forward stationing of many armaments and ancillary facilities. Just as, today, free-fall 'dumb' bombs are increasingly being replaced with air-to-surface missiles that can be directed against remote targets with increasing accuracy, so too have crewed platforms often given way to rocket systems that are not only less vulnerable but also have greater – and, in many instances, increasing – ranges. Having already largely super-seded planes as the delivery platforms for nuclear weapons, us submarines, for instance, became still less reliant on foreign bases. Whereas the Polaris A2 missile could reach 1,500 miles (2,413 km), through the use of new, lighter construction materials – notably composites – smaller electrical components and better propellants, the range of the A3 version exceeded this by 1,000 miles (1,609 km), making it possible for submarines to strike many targets in the USSR from the Pacific as well as the Atlantic. In either case, they could exploit a larger operating area to help counter improving Soviet anti-submarine capabilities. With the supplanting of Polaris by Trident in both the US and Royal Navies, attack radii have expanded still further. Likewise, in-flight refuelling has extended the reach of crewed aircraft, as the USAF's raid on Libya underscored.

In the absence of any 'dual-key' technological constraint that might have enabled them physically to prevent the use of the F-111s that carried out this particular mission – or, for that matter, prevent the firing of the Tomahawks stationed at Greenham Common and Molesworth, or the missiles aboard US Polaris submarines then based on Clydeside – the British evidently put their trust in, not so much the wording of executive accords with no real standing in international law, as in a political constraint that had long since been recognized, not least by the Americans themselves. If 'agreements with [various] host nations give the United States the *legal right* to use military installa-tions', a report by the Congressional Committee on International Relations noted as early as 1977, '. . . the fact nonetheless remains that these countries have the effective means to prevent American usage of them should they determine to do so. . . . In the absence of a profound crisis it is difficult to envisage . . . the US Government . . . willingly [inviting] the serious political repercussions that would most likely follow [any] . . . attempt to use a base located in a friendly country against that country's will.'[37]

The ultimate 'profound crisis' would have been one that provoked the major powers into employing their nuclear arsenals. Had this occurred, it is improbable that what remained of the human race would have been preoccupied with the further pursuit of political and military objectives, still less with the possibility that some obscure, esoteric agreement had been flouted. Since the end of the Cold War, the danger of a genocidal nuclear exchange has receded. However, recent changes in the geostrategic environment have undermined the customary reliance on deterrence and engendered an increased propensity for pre-emptive action. Foremost among these are the resurgence of international terrorism and the USA's evident disillusionment with the disarmament and arms control regimes that, for several decades, have constrained the proliferation of mass casualty and mass destruction weaponry, and sought to mitigate their effects, should such armaments ever be used.

Chapter 5

Missile-Defence Dilemmas

In June 2002 the USA formally rescinded the ABM Treaty to which she had adhered for 30 years and began the construction of a national BMD system that might offer her some protection against attack, not least from 'rogue states', notably North Korea. This step formed part of a wider policy aimed at countering the proliferation of what are commonly referred to as weapons of mass destruction (WMD) and platforms that might be used for their delivery. Indeed, although Britain and the USA sought to justify the launch of Operation 'Iraqi Freedom' with various arguments, the core rationale for embarking on their invasion of Iraq remained their long-standing concern about Baghdad's WMD programmes.

To putative foes, all weapons appear threatening. Some are evidently more disquieting than others, however. Recently, American and British apprehension over Iraq's development of WMD has been pre-eminent, but the spread of such armaments was already causing appreciable unease 40 years ago. Just as 'Red' China's atomic test in 1964 prompted the Pentagon to consider undertaking a preventive strike against her,[1] so too did the Sino-Soviet rift of 1969 set the Kremlin thinking along the same lines. As their hopes of controlling China's nuclear ambitions through the Test Ban Treaty and American pressure faded, the Soviets were reduced to contemplating the obliteration of her research complex at Lop Nor.[2] Having turned down their last opportunity to preserve the strategic balance in Asia without incurring unacceptable costs themselves, they could only watch as Beijing gradually expanded its atomic armoury. Meanwhile, Mao's rapprochement with Washington exacerbated Soviet fears. Certainly, Brezhnev became openly concerned about the possibility that China might seek Western aerospace technology to enhance her military capabilities still further.[3]

As others have aspired to join the nuclear club, the Non-Proliferation Treaty of 1968 notwithstanding, and rocket systems have found their way into the armed forces of numerous states, similar misgivings have become more widespread.[4] Today, Cyprus – where Britain has sovereign bases – and the whole of NATO's southern flank lie within range of 'theatre' missiles based in Africa and the Middle East. Indeed, in the light of the growing sophistication and continuing proliferation of rockets, it seems probable that in no aspect of aerospace power will millennial technology have a greater part to play than in missile attack and defence.

The very success of her aerial campaigns in the 1990s was bound to stimulate some putative adversaries to search for ways to counter or negate the USA's military might in general and her aerospace power in particular. Ballistic rockets bearing WMD have frequently been cited as the most likely armaments of choice, fuelling American interest in active countermeasures. Certainly, weaker polities have come to see missiles as relatively inexpensive and reasonably flexible instruments with which they might offset the West's present dominance of the skies. Consequently, ever since the Gulf War of 1991, in which Iraq made significant use of Scud ballistic missiles, the Pentagon has devoted ever-increasing resources to the perfection and procurement of armaments that might grant the territory and deployed forces of both her and her allies some active defence against weapons of this genre. However, as NATO has expanded eastwards in the aftermath of the Cold War, and more states have acquired either WMD or steadily improving delivery systems, or both, this quest has become ever harder. In fact, the transatlantic alliance's worst-case scenario is that, by 2010, most, if not all, of its territory will lie within reach of ballistic missiles, many of which might be armed with unconventional payloads.

Recognizing that achieving air superiority in future conflicts would demand a capacity to ward off not just crewed aircraft but also UAVS and ballistic and aerodynamic missiles, NATO as a whole began intensifying its countermeasures as long ago as 1994. Its aim was to assemble an extended, integrated air defence (EIAD) from four distinct components: deterrence, counterforce operations, and active and passive defences. The last of these included arms control and disarmament programmes – such as the Missile Technology Control Regime and the ABM and Non-Proliferation Treaties – which, together with deterrence, were accorded the most significance. Recently, however, there has been a loss of faith, most notably on the USA's part, in legalistic, multilateral solutions to the problems posed by certain types of weaponry and in the reliability of deterrence, particularly against those putative adversaries who might be prepared to engage in suicidal attacks.

Whenever armed force is employed, be it by governments or non-state actors such as terrorists, its ultimate goal can be only either coercion or denial. Whereas both of these are political objectives, in the case of the former there is an implicit bargain between the party meting out the violence and its victim, while, in the latter, conditioning the target's conduct is not the intention; brute force is employed to deprive somebody of something, or to prevent a particular pattern of behaviour, or both. Subtle though the distinction between coercion and denial might appear, it is of paramount importance: if the aims behind the employment of violence are identified, we have criteria by which we can gauge its success or failure.

The terrorist movement Al-Qaida and its appendages, for instance, are pursuing a strategy of denial, not coercion. It is difficult to negotiate a peace with such adversaries, for their violent activities are more an attempt to put the clock back – something that cannot be done – than the pursuit of a viable political agenda. It is not inconceivable that they and 'rogue' states might seek to threaten or assail the West with ballistic missiles, but the practical problems in doing so would be formidable enough. For most states and probably all terrorists, unorthodox, 'asymmetric' stratagems are more promising.

Certainly, the use to date of ballistic missiles by 'rogue' states such as North Korea and Iraq has, tellingly, been of more political significance than operational importance. The former has pointedly engaged in intermittent 'test' launches over the Yellow Sea and Sea of Japan, while the latter's bombardment of Israeli cities with Scuds during the Gulf War of 1991 sought to split the polyglot coalition arrayed against her. If only because he was deterred from employing chemical or biological agents by the implicit threat of nuclear retaliation,[5] Saddam contented himself with the unleashing of missiles armed with high-explosive warheads. Although dismissive of the military threat posed by these rockets,[6] Norman Schwarzkopf, the Allies' commanding general, soon received orders to make every effort to neutralize them.

Indeed, the very scale of the 'Great Scud Hunt' is revealing. Among the many resources committed to it were Patriot air defence missiles, which had to be rushed from testing into emergency production.[7] Although the deployment of Patriots reassured the Israelis sufficiently to stop them taking unilateral action and thereby jeopardizing the coalition's fragile cohesion, their operational effectiveness was bitterly disputed. An anti-missile missile had never been used under combat conditions before. Having claimed a uniform 96 per cent interception rate, the Pentagon subsequently reduced this figure to 70 and 40 per cent for the Saudi Arabian and Israeli theatres respectively, while one analyst went on to maintain that, overall, it was just 20 per cent. Subsequent assessments even cast doubt on this modest claim.[8] By contrast, numerous patrols by Allied planes and special forces appear to have constrained the Iraqis' scope for using their Scuds efficaciously. Although, contrary to what was claimed at the time,[9] no transporter-erector-launchers were actually destroyed,[10] the Scud units were not only driven from their optimum launch sites in southern and western Iraq but also reduced to firing missiles singly, rather than in salvoes, in rather haphazard 'shoot and scoot' attacks.

Nevertheless, if the Allies' counterforce operations against the Scud enjoyed some success, active defence had proved ineffectual. Neither had arms control offered a comprehensive solution, not least because, in today's porous, increasingly globalized economy, the diffusion of technology and know-how can at best be retarded. Although the improved Patriots used in the Gulf War of 2003 seem to have managed to shoot down a few Iraqi rockets, if only because of their association with nuclear weapons and the perennial difficulties in actively defending against them, ballistic missiles still appear to many to be the most potent instruments of aerospace power. Some states are in the process of acquiring them by fair means or foul, to which others – notably the USA, Israel and Taiwan – are responding with attempts to perfect active BMD.

Most of the countries that are developing or otherwise acquiring missile technology are doing so with very circumscribed ambitions in mind, some of which have little to do with operational military considerations; a craving for political or scientific prestige, or economic aspirations – such as the desire to participate in a lucrative export trade or to nurture certain technical or industrial capabilities – can partly or wholly account for their behaviour. China's decision to try to manufacture ICBMs with atomic warheads offers a prime, early illustration of this. Having been threatened with nuclear attack on several occasions, she was anxious to acquire a deterrent, however modest. Indeed, Beijing has since given repeated, if unverifiable, assurances that its atomic arsenal is purely for defensive purposes and that it would never initiate the use of nuclear weaponry. Moreover, China seems to have been attracted to these armaments as much by other considerations as by military ones: by her desire to break the nuclear monopoly enjoyed by the superpowers; because of the association of such weapons with great power status; and because they were perceived to be attributes of a modern state at the forefront of economic and scientific development.[11]

Certainly, if military strategy is the art of applying force in pursuit of political objectives, then it can prove very difficult to incorporate the active use of WMD especially into this process, precisely because of their exceptionally destructive nature. Yet the political influence that accrues from the possession of any type of armaments is ultimately founded on that weaponry's utility. Although deterring aggression is palpably preferable to having to defeat it, conventional deterrence is inherently contestable. Identifying and achieving the appropriate blend of EIAD elements in a dynamic, scenario-dependent environment is virtually impossible, however. Military capabilities take years to develop or regenerate once lost, yet political intentions can alter overnight. Moreover, not only do force-balance issues affect each pillar of the defensive triad, complicating research and procurement decisions as well as operational matters, but also the elements of EIAD are as mutually competitive as they are complementary. This exacerbates force design and strategic planning difficulties.[12]

If, for instance, arms control or efficacious counterforce capabilities might reduce if not obviate the need for active defence preparations, then powerful counterforce or active defence capabilities could diminish the requirement for passive defences. However, providing an appropriate level of passive and active protection for anything but deployed forces would be dauntingly expensive. Just as unalloyed defence could not offer complete protection because furnishing passive defences for entire countries is largely impracticable and would offer only sparse protection against WMD, so too could active defences be circumvented by unconventional delivery means, including acts of terrorism. That radiological bombs and chemical and biological agents are, if used optimally, mass casualty weapons with differing characteristics from instruments of mass destruction – notably nuclear warheads and some 'conventional' devices such as fuel-air explosives – only deepens the defender's quandary.

Whereas the debate in the USA has tended to concentrate on the opportunity costs and technical feasibility of missile defence, within Europe, where threat perceptions vary, the subject poses overlapping financial, technological, political, moral, legal, doctrinal and commercial dilemmas, many of which can be resolved only through international consensus. Consequently, the issue is often viewed very differently from the two sides of the Atlantic. The Military Operational Requirement endorsed by the alliance's Supreme Headquarters in 1997 envisaged acquiring the wherewithal to deal with land-based missile threats emanating from within 2,200 miles (3,540 km) of NATO's frontiers. Yet, whereas the Americans already possess some point defences to help safeguard crucial allies and expeditionary forces and are now developing a national umbrella to protect their homeland, Europe's active missile-defence capabilities are embryonic and seem likely to remain flimsy for some years to come. Moreover, the incorporation of new states has shifted the transatlantic alliance's 'front line' towards powers with rocket inventories.

Although NATO's passive-defence safety net is gradually being strengthened, there are in any case lingering fears within the organization that no active defence could be made utterly impermeable to orthodox threats and that excessive interest in such a shield might prove counterproductive; potential aggressors might be tempted to believe that, if tested, the alliance would lack the moral courage to retaliate, not least with its nuclear firepower. For NATO's existing deterrence and counterforce capabilities confront any state bent on coercion, particularly one with rather limited means, with a dilemma. Any pre-emptive missile attack it dared to unleash, be it one involving conventional warheads or WMD, would almost ineluctably be too circumscribed to prove decisive and yet would be all but guaranteed to provoke reprisals that would be immensely damaging. This outcome is particularly probable in the event of any WMD attack on Western Europe. Whereas, during the Cold War, the British and French nuclear forces might occasionally have appeared superfluous, in today's geostrategic environment such independent deterrents have greater significance.[13] Alas, neither they nor any other armaments will necessarily ward off foes who are pursuing a denial strategy, particularly non-state actors, who do not present a viable target against which to retaliate.

To date, arms control accords with a bearing on missile defence have concentrated almost exclusively on ballistic models, leaving the proliferation of cruise missiles and their brethren, UAVs, largely unchecked. Yet it is probable that, in future, the weapons of influence preferred by those states that either cannot afford or do not want to invest in advanced, crewed aircraft and other sophisticated aerospace platforms[14] will be cruise missiles and UAVs, not ballistic rockets. This is primarily because of technical and financial considerations, but aerodynamic platforms also have much to recommend them from an operational perspective. Although the trajectory of the more modern ballistic rockets can be finely adjusted by means of inertial or satellite navigation systems and the missile fins,[15] most older models are rather inaccurate, with a circular error probable (CEP) measured in hundreds of feet.[16] Adequate for the delivery of nuclear warheads though this might be, advanced aerodynamic missiles are accurate to within a few feet. This makes them much more suitable for 'surgical', conventional strikes, while their precision, variable flight paths and comparatively low velocity make them perfect for the dispersal of biological or chemical agents. Although state of the art precision-guidance mechanisms – such as Terrain Contour-Matching and Digital Scene-Matching Area Correlation – remain the preserve of the world's most advanced aerospace forces, devices that can be purchased on open markets can serve as reasonably adequate substitutes. Similarly, target information can be gleaned from maps and commercial satellite images.[17] Lastly, not least because they are prone to be bulky and need to be stabilized before launch, ballistic rockets are that much more vulnerable to counterforce measures. Relatively compact cruise missiles, by contrast, require less logistical support, can be transported in protective canisters and can be unleashed from a variety of surface and airborne platforms; even commercial ships, aircraft and trucks could be adapted for this purpose.

Cruise and ballistic missiles present a defender with contrasting difficulties. In the latter's case, their sheer speed is the fundamental problem. A missile with a range of 300 miles (483 km), for example, will be in its boost phase for some 40 seconds. It will achieve a velocity in excess of a mile per second (1.6 km/sec.), with a total flight time of about 6.0 minutes. Longer-range rockets have commensurably longer boost phases and overall flight times, but also have still greater terminal velocities. A missile with a reach of 2,000 miles (3,200 km) can attain speeds of 11,000 mph (17,700 kmh).

Clearly, the interception of such rapidly moving and relatively small targets demands the utmost accuracy in time and space; the difference between success and failure could lie in a fraction of a second or an angle of a couple of degrees. Moreover, since the missile's flight is ephemeral and early interception is desirable so as to minimize the scope for collateral damage, exceptionally swift intelligence gathering, processing and dissemination capabilities are called for, as well as interceptors that can be launched immediately, can home in on their quarry within moments, and have sufficient range, power and accuracy to reach and destroy their targets. In any event, if an opportunity for more than one shot at an incoming missile is to be practicable, then a tiered defence is essential, with shorter-range endo-atmospheric interceptors seeking to eradicate any missiles that permeate the upper, exo-atmospheric layer. A defence of some extent is also desirable so that space can be traded for time.

The period available for active defence measures to be implemented is, however, predicated upon the reach of the interceptor and the quality of the supporting surveillance system, in so far that this effectively determines the maximum range at which an approaching missile can first be engaged. The faster the interceptor, the lower its minimum effective altitude; the sooner it can be unleashed, or the slower the target, the larger the defensive 'envelope' will be. Only once the defence's controlling headquarters is alerted to an incipient attack can other sensors be 'cued', the missile tracked, an interception vector plotted and weapon systems activated.

The first difficulty in all of this is that no single type of sensor is universally dependable; a variety of surveillance systems have to be integrated into a network. Further problems beset the design of a suitable interceptor. The USAF is currently exploring the possibility of using a gigantic laser mounted in an airliner as a means of shooting down missiles from perhaps 200 miles (320 km) away. Such directed energy weaponry has the potential to strike targets almost instantaneously and across a 360 degree radius. However, the projection of a suitably destructive laser beam over long distances is immensely difficult. If it can be made to work at all, the airborne laser will not come into service before the end of the decade. In the meantime, armaments that push existing technology to new limits will have to be relied upon, namely 'conventional' missiles that are capable of exceptionally high speeds, that have extraordinarily large engagement 'envelopes' and ranges, and that are supported by sensors that can 'see' far and well enough to discern fleeting targets.

The type of warhead to be fitted to interceptors is also a cardinal consideration. Normally, air defence missiles carry a high-explosive fragmentation device; a proximity or impact fuse detonates an inner core of explosive, peppering the target with metal shards. While such weapons are efficacious against aircraft – which are comparatively large, soft-skinned, slow-moving targets – their employment in a BMD role presents appreciably greater challenges. Again, the sheer speed of ballistic missiles is a fundamental problem. Proximity fuses and their supporting information processors need to be extremely sophisticated in order to cope with the closing velocities encountered in missile interceptions. A split-second delay in detonation can mean that the target escapes unscathed. (Indeed, early BMD systems, such as Sentinel, were fitted with small atomic warheads, just to be sure.) The alternative solution is still more taxing, however. If a collision between an incoming missile and an interceptor can be contrived, the very speed of the former can be exploited to bring about its destruction, making the fitting of an explosive warhead to the latter unnecessary. All that is required is a pseudo-warhead of sufficient robustness to guarantee that, on impact, the interceptor does not disintegrate without transferring its energy to the target. But accomplishing such a 'kinetic kill' is easier said than done, for it demands extraordinary exactitude, which is dependent upon the interceptor's organic sensors and nimbleness. Whereas the cool of the upper atmosphere can be exploited as a backdrop for IR (infrared) detectors, at lower altitudes radars can bring the missile close to its quarry. Thereafter, terminal-phase thrusters enable it to change course abruptly if necessary, ramming itself into the target.

Integrating several systems like this is technically very demanding. Furthermore, alluring though it is, the combination of contrasting types of sensor can prove counterproductive, since an opponent might only need to mislead one effectively to neutralize the others. Indeed, missile interception is essentially a sequential process: if a solitary link in the chain fails, then so does it all. Getting each component of this intricate technology to function sufficiently well is difficult enough; successfully combining it all into an EIAD network is still harder. Indeed, maintaining the entire system at a sufficiently high state of readiness to respond to an attack (should one ever come) that might only last a few minutes is a major problem in itself – and the larger the defensive web, the more complex that problem becomes.

Moreover, most states at all capable of using ballistic missiles for military purposes would probably have little difficulty in adding to the defender's difficulties through, for instance, the use of decoys. Obliged to engage each and every target that presented itself, the interceptor batteries would be susceptible to rapid exhaustion. The minimum altitude and guidance requirements of anti-missile missiles compound this danger, as do potential havens between the layers of defence, for the altitude at which any interception occurs remains an important factor in determining the degree of damage limitation that the defender can achieve. There is no way of discerning from a missile in flight the nature of its payload. When countering rockets with nuclear or radiological warheads, for example, even a successful interception could well lead to irradiated material falling on the territory of the defending state or on that of its neighbours, while the neutralization of chemical and biological warheads demands the creation of circumstances too adverse for the agent to survive under. Thus, simply scoring a hit on an incoming missile will not always prove sufficient. In any event, unless wreckage from the target is burnt up as it plunges through the atmosphere, such debris might still be capable of inflicting considerable damage.

The design of many of the established nuclear powers' existing strategic missiles already anticipates some refinements to the defences of putative adversaries. The British, for example, selected Trident primarily because its sophistication would, it was believed, continue to meet an essential requirement for deterrence, dependability. Particularly where WMD are concerned, even an interception rate of 99 per cent might prove insufficient; and Trident, with its numerous rockets, each topped with multiple decoys and warheads, offered a virtual guarantee that at least a handful of weapons would penetrate any defensive shield that was likely to materialize in the foreseeable future.

However, primarily acquired to counter a Soviet threat that has since receded, Trident also encapsulates some of the procurement conundrums that lurk within the concept of EIAD. Unlike the USA, no single European country could afford the financial costs involved in the construction of a comprehensive shield, even if the necessary technology were available. Britain's government, for instance, completed some BMD feasibility studies some time ago, but is incapable of acting in isolation, if only because force balance issues within each element of the defensive triad and the sheer variety of potential threats bedevil procurement decisions.

Certainly, premature or excessive investment in one capability could all too easily leave others lacking. For example, as far as active defence is concerned, since crewed platforms, UAVs and ballistic and aerodynamic missiles might be used simultaneously by an attacker, there is a need to counterpoise AA defence, theatre BMD and cruise missile defence while simultaneously achieving an appropriate blend of systems within each of these categories. Theatre BMD, for instance, raises questions of balance between, among other components, upper- and lower-tier interceptors and between area and point defence. On the other hand, the systems needed to deal with, say, aerodynamic missiles have contrasting performance characteristics from those required to parry ballistic models. Whereas the latter have a high, parabolic flight path that makes them relatively easy to discern, they represent very difficult targets to hit. Conversely, the former, once detected, are comparatively easy to destroy. Yet modern cruise missiles are very hard to find. Masked by terrain features and radar 'clutter', they pose obvious problems for ground-based line-of-sight sensors, which might also struggle to maintain a 'fix' on a target capable of abrupt manoeuvre. The move towards low-observable, 'stealthy' designs will make discerning aerodynamic missiles that much more difficult, accentuating the need for both layered defences and the detection of incoming missiles as close as possible to their launch point so as to maximize the time and opportunities available for their interception.

Indeed, given the difficulties involved in shooting down a missile once it is in flight, it is tempting to obviate this through a pre-emptive attack. Not only do such blows call for an intelligence gathering and dissemination mechanism that is almost infallible, however, they also constitute a questionable policy, from both a legal and moral standpoint. At a time when international law moulds aerial strategy more than ever before, such considerations merit as much attention as technological factors in any discussion of EIAD.

For many governments, the doctrine enunciated as long ago as 1906 by the US State Department with regard to the *Caroline* case has enduring importance. This stipulated that the use of force in self-defence should be confined to instances in which the 'necessity of that self-defence' is immediate, overwhelming and leaves neither choice of means nor time for deliberation.[18] Yet Article 51 of the UN Charter does not clarify whether or not a state can pre-empt an armed attack and still claim that it is acting in self-defence.

This controversial issue divides both polities and legal opinion, with a 'permissive' school of thought maintaining that there are acts of self-defence that are directed against neither the 'political independence' nor the 'territorial integrity' of other states.[19] Certainly, the prerogative of anticipatory self-defence embodied in the *Caroline* criteria has been invoked by several states since the UNO's establishment, implying that they see Article 51 of its charter as neither the ultimate source of that right nor as something that qualifies or curtails it. Many less developed states, however, have consistently interpreted the right of self-defence much more stringently. The lawyers and polities of the 'restrictive' school argue that the UN Charter superseded existing customary laws, such as the *Caroline* criteria, and that, if taken together, Articles 51 and 2/4 rule out any entitlement to anticipatory self-defence; an attack must first occur *before* the right to self-defence can be invoked.[20] In any case, its exercise remains subject to the principles of necessity and proportionality. As one legal authority stresses, it 'permits only the use of force to put an end to an armed attack and to any occupation of territory or other forcible violation of rights which may have been committed'.[21]

The permissive school, by contrast, would argue that if, for example, a state were to attempt to intercept a ballistic missile that had been unleashed against it, this would constitute a lawful use of force as an act of self-defence; even if the ballistic missile were still in its boost phase and had yet to cross the frontier of the target state, an armed attack could be deemed to have begun. Whether, on the other hand, a pre-emptive strike against missiles that have yet to be fired could be legally justified is very doubtful, however imminent their launch might appear.

Similarly, if only partly because of their doubtful legality, preventive attacks intended to stop a state acquiring a given military capability have been rejected by the great powers on several occasions prior to Britain and America's invasion of Iraq in 2003. Following in the wake of Israel's raid on the reactor at Osirak in 1981 and Operation 'Desert Fox' in 1998, this was the culmination of protracted attempts to stop Baghdad developing, let alone using, WMD. The US and UK maintained, however, that the numerous resolutions passed by the UN Security Council with regard to Iraq's WMD programmes furnished an 'arguable case' in law – a claim that, predictably, was disputed by the 'restrictive' school and, to the irritation of London and Washington, by several members of the Security Council, among others.

The Iraqi campaign also witnessed numerous 'blue-on-blue' incidents, including the destruction – in skies that were all but free of Iraqi aircraft – of a British Tornado by an American Patriot. This tragedy furnishes a small insight into the thorny command and control problems to which a fully fledged EIAD would give rise. In the event of a crisis, there might be little – if any – time either to delegate responsibility or to seek political endorsement for the use of force. Certainly, the empowerment of military personnel through enhanced aerospace technology raises significant questions regarding rules of engagement. Congested as it is with civil air traffic, the West's airspace is hardly an ideal environment in which to initiate an aerial defence, particularly if any attack involved both ballistic and aerodynamic missiles, for distinguishing the latter from friendly aircraft could prove very difficult. In any case, the interception of missiles, which might be carrying WMD, is not a matter that any responsible government would contemplate with equanimity. Unlike the USA, which is flanked by immense oceans, most European states would face the prospect of 'collateral damage' afflicting either their own territory or that of adjacent countries.

The Europeans are in a quandary over missile defence. If early interception is essential for their security, it also demands, not just suitable aerospace hardware, but also a common security policy and strategic doctrine. Whereas the USA is at liberty to develop a national shield that, controlled by her own political and military institutions, will be both operationally autonomous and technologically autarkic, this solution is not available to the Europeans. On the one hand, their differing geostrategic situations and threat perceptions might tempt individual countries to seek their own solutions to the challenge of active missile defence. On the other, their very propinquity and the need to trade space for time in which military operations can be executed, the pooling of sovereignty through international organizations such as the EU and NATO, and financial and technical resource constraints against a backcloth of declining defence expenditure all make a multi-national approach unavoidable. Alas, even if there were some all-embracing political institution that could impose such an approach, the patchy interoperability of so many of the Continent's armed services would compromise the military effectiveness of any EIAD.

It remains to be seen whether the Europeans will muster the necessary political will and martial capabilities to contribute significantly to an Occidental EIAD. In any case, missile defence and its wider implications are likely to prove as controversial for at least some European states as was the stationing of Soviet and American nuclear weaponry on their soil during the Cold War.

Abbreviations

AA	Anti-Aircraft
ABM	Anti-Ballistic Missile
ASV	Air-to-Surface
AWACS	Airborne Warning and Control System
BEF	British Expeditionary Force
BMD	Ballistic Missile Defence
CAS	Chief of the Air Staff
CEP	Circular Error Probable
EDI	European Defence Initiative
EIAD	Extended Integrated Air Defence
EU	European Union
EURAC	European Air Chiefs' Conference
FOFA	Follow-on Force Attack
FRY	Federal Republic of Yugoslavia
GNP	Gross National Product
GPS	Global Positioning System
IAF	Israeli Air Force
ICBM	Intercontinental Ballistic Missile
ISR	Italian Social Republic
JSTARS	Joint Surveillance and Target Attack Radar System
KLA	Kosovo Liberation Army
MAD	Mutual Assured Destruction
MOAB	Massive Ordnance Air-Blast
NATO	North Atlantic Treaty Organization
PGMS	Precision-Guided Munition
RAF	Royal Air Force
SAC	Strategic Air Command
SALT	Strategic Arms Limitation Talks/Treaty
SAM	Surface-to-Air Missile

SAP	Strategic Air Plan
SDI	Strategic Defence Initiative
SOE	Special Operations Executive
STOL	Short Take-Off and Landing
UAV	Uninhabited Aerial Vehicle
UK	United Kingdom
UN	United Nations
UNO	United Nations Organization
US	United States
USA	United States of America
USAAF	United States Army Air Force
USAF	United States Air Force
USSR	Union of Socialist Soviet Republics
VTOL	Vertical Take-Off and Landing
WMD	Weapons of Mass Destruction

References

Chapter 1: War in and from the Skies, 1903–1943

1 See D. Gates, *Warfare in the Nineteenth Century* (Basingstoke and New York, 2001), pp. 19–20, 142, 166.

2 See R. Wohl, *A Passion for Wings: Aviation and Western Imagination, 1908–18* (New Haven, CT, 1994), pp. 115–22.

3 See P. Morgan, *Italian Fascism* (Basingstoke, 2003 edn).

4 See C. Coker, *War and the Illiberal Conscience* (Oxford, 1998); A. Gat, *Fascist and Liberal Visions of War* (Oxford, 1998).

5 See R. Mallett, *Mussolini and the Origins of the Second World War* (Basingstoke, 2003).

6 E. V. Rickenbacker, *Fighting the Flying Circus*, ed. A. Whitehouse (New York, 1973), pp. 6, ix.

7 'Casualties and Medical Statistics', *History of the Second World War: Medical Series*, ed. W. Franklin Mellor (London, 1972), pp. 829 ff.

8 See D. R. Philpott and R. H. Barnard, *Aircraft Flight* (London, 1989).

9 See P. W. Gray and S. Cox, eds, *Air Power Leadership* (London, 2002).

10 See A. Stokes and K. Kite, *Flight Stress* (Aldershot, 1994).

11 H. Penrose, *British Aviation: The Pioneer Years* (London, 1967), pp. 112–15, 122–7, 135, 140–45.

12 See ibid., *passim*.

13 *The Parliamentary Debates (Hansard): House of Commons Official Report*, 5th series, LXXXII, col. 1589.

14 Quoted in W. Raleigh and H. A. Jones, *The War in the Air*, 7 vols (London, 1932–7), vol. VII, pp. 8–14.

15 See G. Po, ed., *D'Annunzio: scritti messagi, discorsi e rapporti militari* (Rome, 1939), pp. 75–88.

16 G. Douhet, *Diario critico di guerra*, 2 vols (Rome, 1921–2), vol. II, pp. 14, 17.

17 Ibid., vol. II, pp. 21–2, and vol. I, pp. 65–9.

18 *Ibid.*, vol. II, pp. 21–2, and G. Douhet, *Scritti inediti*, ed. A. Monti (Genoa, 1951), pp. 14 ff.
19 Douhet, *Diario*, vol. II, pp. 16, 19–21.
20 See Douhet, *Scritti enediti*, pp. 114–31.
21 See R. Barker, *The Royal Flying Corps in France* (London, 1995).
22 See W. Mitchell, *Memoirs of World War I* (New York, 1960), pp. 268–9.
23 R. Chesneau, *Aircraft Carriers of the World* (London, 1992 edn), pp. 94–5, 157, 198–201.
24 See D. J. Dean, 'Air Power in Small Wars: The British Air Control Experience', *Air University Review*, XXXIV/5 (1983), pp. 24–31.
25 W. Mitchell, *Winged Defense: The Development and Possibilities of Modern Air Power, Economic and Military* (New York, 1925).
26 See A. F. Hurley, *Billy Mitchell* (New York, 1964), pp. 90–108.
27 Mitchell, *Winged Defense*, notably pp. xvi, 5–6, 99–138. Also see Hurley, *Billy Mitchell*, pp. 122–3.
28 Chesneau, *Aircraft Carriers*, p. 153.
29 See U. Bialer, *The Shadow of the Bomber* (London, 1980).
30 See A. Horne, *To Lose a Battle: France, 1940* (London, 1969; repr. 1979), p. 112.
31 See D. Loza, *Attack of the Airacobras*, trans. and ed. G. F. Gebhardt (Lawrence, KA, 2002).
32 Horne, *To Lose a Battle*, pp. 113–16.
33 *Ibid.*, p. 220.
34 G. Douhet, *Command of the Air*, trans. D. Ferrari (New York, 1942), p. 50.
35 See A. Price, *Aircraft Versus Submarines, 1912–80* (London, 1980).
36 See B. D. Powers, *Strategy without a Slide-Rule: British Air Strategy, 1914–39* (London, 1976); M. Smith, *British Air Strategy between the Wars* (Oxford, 1984).
37 C. Webster and N. Frankland, *The Strategic Air Offensive against Germany* (London, 1961), vol. IV, Appendix 13, pp. 205–13.
38 See M. S. Sherry, *The Rise of American Air Power* (New Haven, CT, 1987), p. 58; R. Schaffer, *Wings of Judgement: American Bombing in World War II* (New York, 1985), pp. 20–34.
39 H. H. Arnold and I. C. Eaker, *Winged Warfare* (New York, 1941).
40 A. P. de Seversky, *Victory through Air Power* (New York, 1942), pp. 146–7.
41 See T. Coffey, *Decision over Schweinfurt* (New York, 1978).
42 See M. Middlebrook, *The Battle of Hamburg* (London, 1980).
43 It is estimated that there were some 1,100,000 civilian casualties in Germany as a result of American strategic bombing. *United States Strategic Bombing Survey* [hereafter USSBS], 'The Effects of Bombing on German Morale' (Washington, DC, 1947), p. 1.
44 See J. Sweetman, *The Dam Raid* (London, 1982).
45 See A. Harris, *Bomber Offensive* (London, 1947), p. 15.
46 Webster and Frankland, *Strategic Offensive*, vol. IV, Appendix 49, pp. 494–5.
47 R. Beaumont, 'The Bomber Offensive as a Second Front', *Journal of Contemporary History*, XXII (1987), pp. 14–15; Air Ministry, *Rise and Fall of the German Air Force, 1919–1945* (London, 1947), pp. 283–6.

48 Air Ministry, *Rise and Fall*, p. 298.
49 See M. Middlebrook, *The Nuremberg Raid* (London, 1973).

Chapter 2: The Aerospace Era, 1943–2003

1 *Hansard*, CCCLXII, cols 51–61.
2 *Ibid.*, CCCLX, col. 1,502.
3 *Ibid.*, CCCLXI, cols 787–96.
4 Quoted in J.R.M. Butler, *Grand Strategy: United Kingdom History of the Second World War* (London, 1957), vol. II, p. 239.
5 H. D. Hall, *North American Supply* (London, 1955), p. 140.
6 V. Hardesty, *Red Phoenix: The Rise of Soviet Air Power* (London, 1982), pp. 97–104; R. Wagner, ed., *The Soviet Airforce in World War II* (London, 1974), pp. 114–34.
7 A. Beevor, *Stalingrad* (London, 1998); J. Förster, ed., *Stalingrad* (Munich, 1992); D. M. Glantz and J. House, *When Titans Clashed: How the Red Army Stopped Hitler* (Lawrence, KA, 1995).
8 E. Bradford, *Siege: Malta, 1940–43* (London, 1985).
9 See S. Harvey, 'The Italian War Effort and the Strategic Bombing of Italy', *History*, LXX (1985), pp. 32–45.
10 N. Kokonas, *The Cretan Resistance, 1941–45* (London, 1993); C. Macdonald, *The Lost Battle: Crete, 1941* (London, 1993).
11 C. D'Este, *Bitter Victory* (London, 1988); A. Wood, *History of the World's Glider Forces* (Wellingborough, 1990), pp. 61–71.
12 See Schaffer, *Wings of Judgement*, pp. 35–59; R. Neillands, *The Bomber War* (London, 2001), pp. 382–406.
13 W. F. Craven and J. L. Cate, *The Army Air Forces in World War II*, 6 vols (Washington, DC, 1948–55), vol. III, p. 8.
14 W. Murray, *Luftwaffe: Strategy for Defeat* (London, 1985), pp. 211–15.
15 See M. Middlebrook, *The Berlin Raids* (London, 1988).
16 See A. McKee, *Dresden, 1945: The Devil's Tinderbox* (London, 1982).
17 A. Price, *Instruments of Darkness* (London, 1967), pp. 201–9.
18 F. Ruge, *Rommel und die Invasion* (Stuttgart, 1959), pp. 169–70; Air Ministry, *Rise and Fall*, pp. 323–35, 327–32.
19 E. Rommel, *The Rommel Papers*, ed. B. H. Liddell Hart (London, 1953), pp. 455, 485.
20 See T. Powers, *The Secret History of the Atomic Bomb* (London, 1993).
21 B. Collier, *The Defence of the United Kingdom* (London, 1957), pp. 398, 523; N. Longmate, *The Doodlebugs* (London, 1981).
22 See N. Longmate, *Hitler's Rockets* (London, 1985).
23 Collier, *Defence*, p. x.
24 See B. Ford, *German Secret Weapons* (London, 1970), pp. 104–11; Collier, *Defence*, pp. 527–8.
25 R. V. Jones, *Most Secret War* (London, 1978), pp. 523–75.
26 See M. Middlebrook, *Arnhem, 1944: The Airborne Battle* (London, 1994).
27 See C. Ryan, *A Bridge Too Far* (London, 1974).

28 See D. S. Parker, *To Win the Winter Sky* (London, 1994).

29 Quoted by R. Pineau in *The War Lords*, ed. M. Carver (London, 1976), pp. 396–7.

30 See M. Fuchida and M. Okumiya, *Midway*, trans. M. Chihaya (London, 1955); G. V. Prange, *Miracle at Midway* (New York, 1982).

31 See J. Thompson, *Imperial War Museum Book of the War in Burma, 1942–45* (London, 2002), *passim* and pp. 354–77.

32 Air Ministry, *Wings of the Phoenix: The Official Story of the Air War in Burma* (London, 1949), pp. 52–5.

33 *Ibid.*, pp. 66–7.

34 *Ibid.*, pp. 69–93; D. Rooney, *Burma Victory: Imphal and Kohima* (London, 1992), *passim* and pp. 59–70; Air Command, Southeast Asia, *A Review of Air Transport Operations on the Burma Front* (Delhi, 1944), *passim*.

35 See Air Ministry, *Wings of the Phoenix*, pp. 98–105.

36 See D. Rooney, *Wingate and the Chindits* (London, 1994).

37 See A. Probert, *The Forgotten Air Force* (London, 1995).

38 See S. Eadon, ed., *Kamikaze: The Story of the British Pacific Fleet* (Worcester, 1991), pp. 105–17 and *passim*.

39 See A. Axel and H. Kase, *Kamikaze: Japan's Suicide Gods* (London, 2002), pp. 33–45, 147–52.

40 See Schaffer, *Wings of Judgement*, pp. 107–8.

41 *Ibid.*, pp. 128–33. It was estimated that, altogether, some 2,200,000 civilians were slain or hurt in the offensive. See: *USSBS* (Pacific Theatre), 'The Effects of Strategic Bombing on Japanese Morale' (Washington, DC, 1947), p. 1; and *ibid.*, 'Summary Reports' (Washington, DC, 1946), pp. 16–18, 20.

42 Quoted in L. C. Gardner, *Spheres of Influence* (Chicago, 1993), p. 103.

43 *Public Papers of the Presidents: Harry S. Truman, 1947* (Washington, DC, 1963), pp. 178–9.

44 US State Department, *Foreign Relations of the United States* (Washington, DC, 1861–) [hereafter *FRUS*] (1948) , vol. I, pt 2, p. 667.

45 B. Brodie, ed., *The Absolute Weapon* (New York, 1946), p. 76.

46 *FRUS* (1955–7), vol. XX, p. 297.

47 See *FRUS* (1958–60), vol. VII, pp. 941–2, and vol. X, pp. 269–81.

48 C. von Clausewitz, *On War*, ed. M. Howard and P. Paret (Princeton, NJ, 1976), p. 605.

49 See V. Zubok and C. Pleshakov, *Inside the Kremlin's Cold War* (Cambridge, MA, 1996), p. 66.

50 *FRUS* (1948), vol. I, pt 2, pp. 624–8.

51 See N. Khrushchev, *Khrushchev Remembers: The Last Testament*, trans. and ed. S. Talbott (Boston, MA, 1974), p. 444; D. A. Brugioni, *Eyeball to Eyeball: The Inside Story of the Cuban Missile Crisis* (New York, 1991), p. 302; R. M. Bissell *et al.*, *Reflections of a Cold War Warrior* (New Haven, CT, 1996), pp. 112–13

52 Quoted in Bialer, *Shadow of the Bomber*, p. 21.

53 Quoted in J. G. Blight and D. A. Welch, *On the Brink* (New York, 1989), pp. 198–200, 254.

54 See S. J. Zaloga, *Target America: The Soviet Union and the Strategic Arms Race,*

1945–64 (Novato, CA, 1993), pp. 150–54, 191; A. I. Gribkov and W. Y. Smith, *Operation Anadyr* (Chicago, 1994), pp. 10–11; and Khrushchev, *Last Testament*, pp. 46–8.

55 Reproduced in J. Baylis, *Anglo-American Defence Relations, 1939–84* (2nd edn, London, 1984), pp. 109–10.

56 *FRUS* (1961–3), vol. XVI, pp. 702–4.

57 Gribkov and Smith, *Operation Anadyr*, pp. 25–7, 45–6; Zubok and Pleshakov, *Kremlin's Cold War*, p. 265.

58 See, for instance, J. L. Gaddis, *We Now Know: Rethinking Cold War History* (Oxford, 1997; repr.), pp. 269–72.

59 Clausewitz, *On War*, pp. 75–7.

60 See Harris, *Bomber Offensive*, p. 80.

61 A. Hitler, *Mein Kampf* (London, 1939 edn), pp. 124, 137, 250.

62 See P. Stahl, *KG 200: The True Story* (London, 1981).

63 C. E. LeMay and M. Kantor, *Mission With LeMay* (Garden City, NY, 1965), p. 564.

64 See R. A. Pape, *Bombing to Win: Air Power and Coercion in War* (Ithaca, NY, and London, 1996), p. 190.

65 See G. Porter, *A Peace Denied: The United States, Vietnam and the Paris Agreement* (Bloomington, IN, 1976); A. E. Goodman, *The Lost Peace* (Stanford, CA, 1975).

66 See Pape, *Bombing to Win*, pp. 202–5.

67 See *ibid.*, footnote 111, p. 202.

68 H. A. Kissinger, *White House Years* (Boston, MA, 1979), p. 1,161.

69 See *ibid.*, pp. 226, 271–3, 292, 304–5, 309–11, 433–41, 475, 1,102–6, 1,114–23, 1,144–54, 1,161, 1,174, 1,186–8, 1,201–27, 1,253, 1,301–4.

70 For details of the air war here, see M. Clodfelter, *The Limits of Air Power: The Bombing of North Vietnam* (New York, 1989); G. Lewy, *America in Vietnam* (New York, 1978).

71 Pape, *Bombing to Win*, pp. 9, 202, 176.

72 Quoted in H. S. Commager, S. E. Morison and W. E. Leuchtenburg, *A Concise History of the American Republic* (New York and Oxford, 1977), p. 737.

73 The speed of supersonic aircraft is frequently expressed as a multiple of the speed of sound at the Earth's surface, a measure that bears the name of the Austrian physicist Ernst Mach. Mach 1.0 is thus approximately 760 mph (1,220 kmh). Since the speed of sound varies with altitude, knots are also used to measure aircraft velocities. A knot equals one nautical mile (a latitudinal second) per hour. Most fixed-wing planes do between 500 and 2,000 knots (925–3,700 kmh).

74 See W. W. Momyer, *Air Power in Three Wars* (Washington, DC, 1978), pp. 254–5.

75 D. Gates. 'Light Divisions in Europe', *Occasional Paper*, XXXIX, Institute for European Defence and Strategic Studies [hereafter IEDSS] (London, 1989).

76 J. McCausland, 'The Gulf Conflict', *Adelphi Paper*, CCLXXXII, International Institute for Strategic Studies [hereafter IISS] (London, 1993), p. 24.

77 S. W. Lytle, 'British Army Aviation in the 1990s', *RUSI Journal*, CXXXIX/2 (London, 1994), p. 28.

78 These can be steered by either built-in navigational systems fed with coordi-

nates by satellites, or laser-guidance systems. In the latter case, adjusting its trajectory with fins, the bomb follows a laser beam that is focused on the target by an aircraft. Unlike those steered by lasers, satellite-guided missiles and bombs can overcome adverse atmospheric conditions, such as smoke or dense cloud.

79 P. S. Meilinger, *Ten Propositions Regarding Air Power* (Washington, DC, 1995), pp. 4–5.

80 See R. E. Venkus, *Raid on Qaddafi* (New York, 1992).

81 C. Weinberger, *Fighting for Peace* (New York, 1990), p. 197.

82 See: I. J. Bickerton and M. N. Pearson, *The Arab–Israeli Conflict* (London, 1993); A. H. Cordesman and A. R. Wagner, *Lessons of Modern War: The Arab–Israeli Conflict, 1973–89* (New York, 1991); T. G. Fraser, *The Arab–Israeli Conflict* (London, 1995); and C. Herzog, *The Arab–Israeli Wars* (London, 1984).

83 See *FRUS* (1964–8), XI, pp. 282–4, 286–8, 407–17, 421–3, 426–9, 499–502, 512–15, 653–7, 659–61, 669–72, 674–80, 704–13, 744–7.

84 M. Rühle, 'Preserving the Deterrent', *Occasional Paper*, XXI (IEDSS, London, 1986), p. 7.

85 See C. Bluth, *Soviet Strategic Arms Policy before SALT* (Cambridge, 1992), pp. 199–218.

86 See M. J. Sheehan, *Arms Control* (Oxford, 1988), pp. 46–8, 57–60, 106; M. Mandelbaum, *The Nuclear Question: The United States and Nuclear Weapons, 1946–1976* (Cambridge, 1980), pp. 192–4; J. Voas, 'Soviet Attitudes towards Ballistic Missile Defence and the ABM Treaty', *Adelphi Paper*, CCLV (IISS, London, 1990), pp. 10–11 and *passim*; Bluth, *Soviet Strategic Arms Policy*, pp. 199–218.

87 See P. Podvig, ed., *Russian Strategic Nuclear Weapons* (Moscow, 1998).

88 *Hansard*, DXXXVII, col. 1,899.

89 See M. Wörner, 'A Missile Defence for Europe', *Strategic Review*, XIV/1 (1986), pp. 13–20; D. S. Sorenson, 'Ballistic Missile Defence for Europe', *Comparative Strategy*, V/2 (1985), pp. 159–78; D. L. Hafner and J. Roper, eds, *ATBMs and Western Security* (Cambridge, MA, 1988).

90 'Interview with Marshal N. V. Ogarkov', *Krasnaya Zvesda*, reproduced in *Strategic Review*, XII/3 (1984), pp. 85–6.

91 K. E. Greer, 'Corona', in *Corona: America's First Satellite Program*, ed. K. C. Ruffner (Washington, DC, 1995), pp. 21–2, 120.

92 Quoted in D. Gates, *Non-Offensive Defence* (New York and London, 1991), p. 175.

93 *Ibid.*

94 Department of Defense, *Conduct of the Persian Gulf War* (Washington, DC, 1992), p. 43 [hereafter *Persian Gulf War*].

95 Ministry of Defence, *A Short History of the Royal Air Force* (London, 1994), p. 104.

96 See N. Cigar, 'Iraq's Strategic Mindset and the Gulf War', *Journal of Strategic Studies*, XV/1 (1992), pp. 1–29.

97 See S. Biddle and R. Zirkle, 'Technology, Civil–Military Relations, and Warfare in the Developing World', *Journal of Strategic Studies*, XIX/2 (1996), pp. 171–212.

98 *Persian Gulf War*, pp. 109–14.

99 See *Short History of the Royal Air Force*, pp. 103–9.

100 *Persian Gulf War*, p. 190; and J. Pimlott and S. Badsey, *The Gulf War Assessed*

(London, 1992), p. 122.

101 See: H. S. Hansell, *The Air Plan that Defeated Hitler* (Washington, DC, 1972), pp. 15–18, 195–210, 251–3, 279, 291–5; and RAF, *Air Power Doctrine (AP3000)* (2nd edn, London, 1993), p. 71.

102 See R. A. Mason, *Air Power: A Centennial Appraisal* (London, 1994), pp. 234–78.

103 See, for instance, J. A. Warden, 'Employing Air Power in the Twentyfirst Century', in *The Future of Air Power in the Aftermath of the Gulf War*, ed. R. Schultz and R. Pfaltzgraff (Maxwell, AL, 1992).

104 See Ministry of Defence, *Kosovo: An Account of the Crisis* (London, 1999).

Chapter 3: Aerospace Power's Evident Nature and its Impact on War and Peace

1 J. C. Cooper, *The Right to Fly* (New York, 1947), pp. 1, 4, 7, 11, 13.

2 RAF, *Air Power Doctrine*, p. 13.

3 EURAC, *Air Power Paper: A European Perspective on Air Power* (Paris, 2001), p. 6.

4 D. MacIsaac, 'Voices from the Central Blue: The Air Power Theorists', *Makers of Modern Strategy*, ed. P. Paret (Oxford, 1986), p. 624.

5 EURAC, *Air Power Paper*, p. 2.

6 Quoted in Hurley, *Mitchell*, p. 93.

7 See, for instance, C. Coker, *Waging War without Warriors: The Changing Culture of Military Conflict* (London, 2002).

8 Cooper, *Right to Fly*, p. 1.

9 See Mitchell, *Winged Defense*, pp. 6, 64–5, 205.

10 Quoted in Thompson, *War in Burma*, p. 14.

11 See Gates, *Warfare in the Nineteenth Century*, pp. 66 ff.

12 See P. W. Gray, ed., *British Air Power* (London, 2003), pp. 21–48.

13 See A. Aldis, ed., *The Second Chechen War* (Strategic and Combat Studies Institute [herafter SCSI], Shrivenham, 2000).

14 Quoted in W. C. Westmoreland, *A Soldier Reports* (New York, 1980), p. 119.

15 Quoted by D. Gates in *Perspectives on Air Power*, ed. S. W. Peach (London, 1998), p. 39.

16 *The Military Balance, 2001–2002* (IISS, London, 2001), p. 158.

17 See Ministry of Defence, *Kosovo: Lessons from the Crisis* (London, 2000), pp. 34–43.

18 See H. Hagman, 'European Crisis Management and Defence', *Adelphi Paper*, CCCLIII (IISS, London, 2002), pp. 31–3 and *passim*.

19 Commager, Morison and Leuchtenburg, *American Republic*, p. 721.

20 Mitchell, *Winged Defense*, p. 77.

21 See W. G. Sebald, *On The Natural History of Destruction*, trans. A. Bell (London, 2003).

22 Cooper, *Right to Fly*, p. 7.

Chapter 4: Bases Ashore and Afloat

1 J. Blackwell *et al.*, *The Gulf War: Military Lessons Learned* (Washington, DC, 1991), pp. 20–21.

2 *Short History of the Royal Air Force*, pp. 81–2.

3 See *Documents on British Policy Overseas: Britain and America*, ed. R. Bullen and M. E. Pellen (London, 1986), Series I, pp. 3–33, 159–60.

4 *Ibid.*, p. 317. Also see pp. 161–3, 194–5, 280–3, 316–20, 379–83, 399–401.

5 See K. Harris, *Attlee* (London, 1982), p. 464.

6 See M. Gowing, *Independence and Deterrence: Britain and Atomic Energy, 1945–52* (London, 1974), vol. I, p. 312.

7 See: *FRUS* (1951), vol. I, p. 803.

8 Quoted in Gowing, *Independence*, vol. I, p. 312.

9 See S. Duke, *US Defence Bases in the United Kingdom* (London, 1987), p. 59.

10 *FRUS* (1950), vol. VII, p. 1,462.

11 Harris, *Attlee*, p. 464.

12 D. Acheson, *Present at the Creation* (New York, 1969), p. 484.

13 See 'Dean Acheson Talks to Kenneth Harrison', *The Listener*, 8 April 1971; *FRUS* (1950), vol. III, p. 1,464 5; *FRUS* (1951), vol. I, pp. 875 6.

14 *FRUS* (1948), vol. I, pt 2, p. 689. Also see *FRUS* (1951), vol. I, p. 815.

15 See *FRUS* (1948), vol. I, pt 2, pp. 688–9.

16 See Gowing, *Independence*, vol. I, p. 253; and Lord Sherfield, 'Britain's Nuclear Story', *Round Table*, CCLVIII (April 1975), p. 195.

17 See *FRUS* (1947), vol. I, p. 805.

18 See *FRUS* (1951), vol. I, pp. 814 and 822.

19 *FRUS* (1950), vol. VII, pp. 1,463–4.

20 *Ibid.*

21 *FRUS* (1951), vol. I, p. 810.

22 Gowing, *Independence*, vol. I, p. 316.

23 *Ibid.*, p. 317.

24 *FRUS* (1951), vol. I, p. 890. Also see Gowing, *Independence*, vol. I, p. 317.

25 *FRUS* (1951), vol. I, pp. 886–7, 889.

26 Gowing, *Independence*, vol. I, p. 318.

27 *FRUS* (1951), vol. I, pp. 893–4.

28 *Ibid.*, footnote, p. 892.

29 *Hansard*, CDLXXXXVI, col. 280.

30 US State Department, *Bulletin*, XXVI (N656) (21 January 1952), p. 83.

31 See p. 107 above.

32 H. Macmillan, *Riding the Storm* (London, 1971), p. 494.

33 H. Macmillan, *Pointing the Way* (London, 1972), p. 238.

34 Foreign Affairs and National Defense Division, Congressional Research Service, *US Military Installations in NATO's Southern Region* (Washington, DC, 1986), p. 8.

35 Quoted in *The Guardian*, 28 April 1983, p. 1.

36 *Hansard*, 6th Series, XXXXVII, col. 300

37 Foreign Affairs and National Defense Division, Congressional Research Service,

US Military Installations and Objectives in the Mediterranean (Washington, DC, 1977), p. 49.

Chapter 5: Missile-Defence Dilemmas

1 R. Foot, *The Practice of Power: US Relations with China since 1949* (Oxford, 1997 edn), pp. 178–81, 188–93.
2 *Ibid.*, pp. 128–9, 133, 176, 189.
3 *Ibid.*, pp. 138–9.
4 See, for instance, *The Strategic Defence Review: Supporting Essays* (London, 1998) [hereafter *SDRSE*], Essay Five, pp. 13–15.
5 See *Report of the Canberra Commission on the Elimination of Nuclear Weapons* (Canberra, 1996), p. 37; Secretary of Defense, *Public Statements* (Washington, DC, 1990), vol. IV, p. 2,547.
6 See R. Atkinson, *Crusade: The Untold Story of the Persian Gulf War* (London, 1994), pp. 173–4.
7 K. S. McMahon, *Pursuit of the Shield* (Lanham, MD, 1997), pp. 55–92, 297–306.
8 See House Committee on Government Operations, 'Performance of the Patriot', *Congressional Record*, House of Representatives, 102nd Congress, 1st and 2nd Sessions, 1991–2 (Washington, DC, 1992), pp. 179–85; T. Postol, 'Lessons of the Gulf War Experience with Patriot', *International Security*, XVI/3 (1991), pp. 119–71; T. Postol and R. Stein, 'Patriot Experience in the Gulf War', *International Security*, XVII/1 (1992), pp. 199–240.
9 See C. L. Powell, *A Soldier's Way* (London, 1995), pp. 510–11.
10 W. C. Story, *Third World Traps and Pitfalls* (Maxwell, AL, 1995), p. 25.
11 See Foot, *Practice of Power*, pp. 167–72, 177–8.
12 For a British perspective, see *SDRSE*, Essay Five, pp. 1–17.
13 See *The Strategic Defence Review* (London, 1998), pp. 16–20; and *SDRSE*, Essay Five, pp. 1–4, 11, 13–15.
14 See J. R. Harvey, 'Regional Ballistic Missiles and Advanced Strike Aircraft', *International Security*, XVII/2 (1992), pp. 41–83.
15 See: I. Lachow, 'The GPS Dilemma', *International Security*, XX/1 (1995), pp. 126–48.
16 The CEP is the radius of a circle around the target within which the warhead has a 50 per cent chance of landing.
17 See S. Berner, 'Proliferation of Satellite Imaging Capabilities', in *Fighting Proliferation*, ed. H. Sokolski (Maxwell, AL, 1996), pp. 95–129.
18 See L. Henkin *et al.*, *International Law Cases and Materials* (2nd edn, St Paul, MN, 1987), pp. 662–3.
19 See Y. Dinstein, *War, Aggression and Self-Defence* (2nd edn, Cambridge, 1994), p. 228.
20 See I. Brownlie, *International Law and the Use of Force by States* (Oxford, 1963), pp. 275–8.
21 C. Greenwood, 'Command and the Laws of Armed Conflict', *Occasional Paper*, IV (SCSI, Camberley, 1993), p. 7.

Selected Further Reading

Air Ministry, *Rise and Fall of the German Air Force, 1919–1945* (London, 1947)

Armitage, M., and R. A. Mason, *Air Power in the Nuclear Age* (London, 1985)

Bergquist, R. E., *The Roles of Air Power in the Iran–Iraq War* (Maxwell, AL, 1988)

Bialer, U., *The Shadow of the Bomber* (London, 1980)

Boog, H., ed., *The Conduct of the Air War in World War II* (New York, 1992)

Brookes, A., *V-Force: The History of Britain's Airborne Deterrent* (London, 1982)

Chapman, K., *Military Air Transport Operations* (London, 1989)

Chesneau, R., *Aircraft Carriers of the World* (London, 1984)

Clodfelter, M., *The Limits of Air Power: The Bombing of North Vietnam* (New York, 1989)

Cooper, M., *The Birth of Independent Air Power* (London, 1986)

Craven, W. F., and J. L. Cate, *The Army Air Forces in World War II*, 6 vols (Washington, DC, 1948–55)

Department of Defense, *Conduct of the Persian Gulf War* (Washington, DC, 1992)

Douhet, G., *Command of the Air*, trans. D. Ferrari (New York, 1942)

Dutton, L., *et al.*, *Military Space* (London, 1990)

Elsam, M. B., *Air Defence* (London, 1989)

Ethel, J., and A. Price, *Air War South Atlantic* (London, 1983)

Futrell, F., *Ideas, Concepts, Doctrine: Basic Thinking in the US Air Force, 1907–60* (Maxwell, AL, 1989)

Gray, P. W., and S. Cox, eds, *Air Power Leadership* (London, 2002)

Hallion, R. P., *Air Power Confronts an Unstable World* (London, 1997).

Hardesty, V., *Red Phoenix: The Rise of Soviet Air Power* (London, 1982)

Hayward, K., *British Military Space Programmes* (London, 1996)

Kennett, L., *The First Air War, 1914–18* (New York, 1991)

Kirby, S., and G. Robson, *The Militarisation of Space* (Brighton, 1987)

Kreis, J. F., *Air Warfare and Air Base Defense* (Washington, DC, 1988)

Lewy, G., *America in Vietnam* (New York, 1978)

Longmate, N., *Hitler's Rockets* (London, 1985)

Mason, R. A., *Air Power: A Centennial Appraisal* (London, 1994)

Meilinger, P. S., *The Paths of Heaven: The Evolution of Air Power Theory* (Maxwell, AL, 1997)

Middlebrook, M., and C. Everitt, *The Bomber Command War Diaries* (London, 1985)

Mitchell, W., *Winged Defense: The Development and Possibilities of Modern Air Power, Economic and Military* (New York, 1925)

Momyer, W. W., *Air Power in Three Wars* (Washington, DC, 1978).

Morrow, J. H., *The Great War in the Air: Military Aviation, 1909–21* (Washington, 1993)

Mrozek, D. J., *Air Power in the Ground War in Vietnam* (Maxwell, AL, 1988)

Murray, W., *Luftwaffe: Strategy for Defeat* (London, 1985)

Neillands, R., *The Bomber War* (London, 2001)

Omissi, D. E., *Air Power and Colonial Control, 1919–39* (Manchester, 1990)

Overy, R. J., *The Air War, 1939–45* (London, 1980)

Pape, R. A., *Bombing to Win: Air Power and Coercion in War* (Ithaca, NY, and London, 1996)

Paris, M., *Winged Warfare: The Literature and Theory of Aerial Warfare in Britain, 1859–1917* (Manchester, 1991)

Penrose, H., *British Aviation: The Pioneer Years* (London, 1967)

Philpott, D. R., and R. H. Barnard, *Aircraft Flight* (London, 1989)

Podvig, P., ed., *Russian Strategic Nuclear Weapons* (Moscow, 1998).

Powers, B. D., *Strategy without a Slide-Rule: British Air Strategy, 1914–39* (London, 1976)

Price, A., *Aircraft Versus Submarines, 1912–80* (London, 1973)

——, *Instruments of Darkness* (London, 1967)

Probert, A., *The Forgotten Air Force* (London, 1995)

Raleigh, W., and H. A. Jones, *The War in the Air*, 7 vols (London, 1932–7)

Saward, D., *Bomber Harris* (London, 1984)

Schaffer, R., *Wings of Judgement: American Bombing in World War II* (New York, 1985)

Schultz, R., and R. Pfaltzgraff, eds, *The Future of Air Power in the Aftermath of the Gulf War* (Maxwell, AL, 1992)

Seversky, A. P. de, *Victory through Air Power* (New York, 1942)

Sherry, M. S., *The Rise of American Air Power* (New Haven, CT, 1987)

Smith, M., *British Air Strategy between the Wars* (Oxford, 1984)

Smithies, E., *Aces, Erks and Backroom Boys* (London, 1990)

Stares, P. B., *Space and National Security* (Washington, DC, 1987)

Stokesbury, J. L., *A Short History of Air Power* (New York, 1984)

Towle, P. A., *Pilots and Rebels: The Use of Aircraft in Unconventional Warfare, 1918–88* (London, 1989)

Vallance, A., *Doctrines of Air Power Strategy* (London, 1996)

Venkus, R. E., *Raid on Qaddafi* (New York, 1992)

Wagner, R., ed., *The Soviet Airforce in World War II* (London, 1974)

Walker, J. R., *Air Superiority Operations* (London, 1989)

Webster, C., and N. Frankland, *The Strategic Air Offensive against Germany*, 4 vols (London, 1961)

Wohl, R., *A Passion for Wings: Aviation and Western Imagination, 1908–18* (New Haven, CT, 1994)

Zaloga, S. J., *Target America: The Soviet Union and the Strategic Arms Race, 1945–64* (Novato, CA, 1993)

Index